The Devil Sat on My Bed

The Devil Sat on My Bed

Encounters with the Spirit World in Mormon Utah

ERIN E. STILES

OXFORD
UNIVERSITY PRESS

Oxford University Press is a department of the University of Oxford. It furthers
the University's objective of excellence in research, scholarship, and education
by publishing worldwide. Oxford is a registered trade mark of Oxford University
Press in the UK and certain other countries.

Published in the United States of America by Oxford University Press
198 Madison Avenue, New York, NY 10016, United States of America.

© Oxford University Press 2024

All rights reserved. No part of this publication may be reproduced, stored in
a retrieval system, or transmitted, in any form or by any means, without the
prior permission in writing of Oxford University Press, or as expressly permitted
by law, by license, or under terms agreed with the appropriate reproduction
rights organization. Inquiries concerning reproduction outside the scope of the
above should be sent to the Rights Department, Oxford University Press, at the
address above.

You must not circulate this work in any other form
and you must impose this same condition on any acquirer.

Library of Congress Control Number: 2023952446

ISBN 978–0–19–776375–9 (pbk.)
ISBN 978–0–19–763963–4 (hbk.)

DOI: 10.1093/oso/9780197639634.001.0001

Paperback printed by Marquis Book Printing, Canada
Hardback printed by Bridgeport National Bindery, Inc., United States of America

Contents

Acknowledgments   vii

1. Introduction   1
2. The Realm of the Spirits   17
3. Spirits, the Eternal Family, and Collective Ethical Responsibility   51
4. Where the Veil Is Thin: Temple Work, Posthumous Baptism, and the Gratitude of Spirits   85
5. The Devil Sat on My Bed: The Slippery Edge of Righteousness   118
6. The Power of the Priesthood, Gender, and Evil Spirits   149
7. Conclusion   189

Bibliography   193
Index   207

Acknowledgments

In many ways, this book is a homecoming. I grew up in beautiful Cache Valley, and although my family is not Mormon, I was immersed in the culture and lore of the region throughout my idyllic childhood, adolescence, and young adulthood, and I consider the valley my true home. I cannot imagine having a happier childhood or a more wonderful group of friends and neighbors. And so, this book is gratefully dedicated to the people of Cache Valley.

I would like to thank a number of people in particular for their help with this project. First and most importantly, I would like to thank all of those who agreed to interviews about their experiences of and knowledge about the spirit realm. Because I have kept the identities of interviewees concealed to protect their privacy and the special nature of these experiences, I will not thank them by name here. Howeverplease know how grateful I am that you shared such incredible experiences with me. I hope I have done you justice in the writing of this book.

I would also like to thank those who agreed to read and provide feedback on drafts of the manuscript and related works. In alphabetical order, thanks go to Katryn Davis, Adam Dunstan, Jennifer Hammond, Haug, Brian Howell, Rebecca Johnson, David Knowlton, Tawnee Madsen, Shannon Montez, Liam Murphy, Kimberly Nalder, and Eric Olsen. Thanks are also due to the helpful anonymous reviewers of the draft manuscript who provided such thoughtful suggestions for improving this book.

A number of students at the University of Nevada have helped me with collecting archival materials and coding interviews and narratives. Thank you to Sierra Meszaros, Alexandra Wolfgram, Samantha Vanillo, and especially Katryn Davis, who accompanied me to Utah for fieldwork and archival research more than once.

I would also like to thank my colleagues at the University of Nevada. Thanks to Carolyn White, who first encouraged me to write this book, and thanks also to, Debbie Boehm, Sarah Cowie, Chris Morgan, Sandhya Narayanan, Daniel Enrique Perez, and Mikaela Rogozen-Soltar for their ongoing support.

A special thanks goes to Kathleen Kelly of Gray Bevins Editorial for her constant encouragement and her insightful feedback on drafting a book proposal for this project.

I would also like to thank the Charles Redd Center for Western Studies at Brigham Young University for two grants supporting the field and archival research for this project. At the University of Nevada, I would like to thank the College of Liberal Arts and the Vice President's Office for Research and Innovation for the financial support of this project. Thanks also go to my Utah family members, and especially my mother and late father for caring for the kids while I was in the archives and jaunting about the valley.

At Utah State University, I would like to thank the staff of Special Collections, especially Terri Jordan, for help with the archival research.

Some material in this book, such as some interview excerpts and folklore narratives, has been previously published elsewhere, and it is used here with the generous permission of the publishers. Material in Chapters 3 and 4 origially appeared in *JRAI: Journal of the Royal Anthropological Insitute*, Wiley-Blackwell (2023), and material in Chapter 5 appeared in the *Journal of the American Academy of Religion*, Oxford University Press (2022). Thanks also to the artist Clark Kelly Price for permitting a reproduction of his painting, "When the Angels Come." Finally, I would like to thank my husband and children for their enthusiasm, love, and support, and for spending so much time with me in Utah.

1
Introduction

When I was growing up in a small town in beautiful, bucolic Cache Valley in far northern Utah I remember a few occasions on which a friend interrupted our games to announce, simply, "The Devil sat on my bed last night." My childhood memories of play always involve a core group of kids, mostly girls, from my neighborhood. My siblings and I were the only non-Mormons in our group of friends, although there were a couple of "Jack Mormon" families in the neighborhood.[1] We were all imaginative, and our play was almost always "pretending." Our childhood world was inhabited by witches and fairies, unicorns and elves, and orphans with spectacular powers. We had the most wonderful adventures. Given this rich world of imagination, I do not remember being at all concerned about the Devil's visits to my friends (I was raised Episcopalian, and devils were never mentioned in my family's church), and I think I must have understood them as part of our fantastic play. I remember that my friends did not seem particularly concerned either. The Devil visiting was just something that happened sometimes. We would listen politely to the teller of the tale, and then resume our activities. The stories were never very elaborate, and I do not remember the Devil doing anything other than just sitting at the end of the bed, often with glowing red eyes.

In their well-known book on Mormon folklore, *Saints of Sage and Saddle* (1956), the folklorists Austin and Alta Fife, often considered the founding figures in Utah folklore studies, report a very similar tale from their own childhoods in the same valley. They write that Grandmother, "a Mormon steeped in its lore and legend, if not in its theology," walked three miles to report to Mother that the "old devil" came into her bedroom the previous night to tell her, "Old woman, you're all in!" Grandmother, they write, retorted, "Why you old son of a bitch, git right out of here! I'm not all in!" (1956, 232).

These devil narratives were a distant memory for me until just a few years ago, when I was conducting research on folklore surrounding marriage and

---

[1] The term "Jack Mormon" refers to non-active, non-practicing Mormons.

The Devil Sat on My Bed. Erin E. Stiles, Oxford University Press. © Oxford University Press 2024.
DOI: 10.1093/oso/9780197639634.003.0001

2 THE DEVIL SAT ON MY BED

gender in the excellent Fife Folklore Collection at Utah State University, named after the aforementioned duo. Around this time, a colleague at another university had asked me about Latter-day Saint conceptions of evil. His question sparked my memory of the devil stories. At first, I wondered if those stories were just part of the lush realm of childhood imagination we inhabited. However, while working in the Fife collection, I happened across files filled with student narratives accounting for tales of experience that were similar to—but so much richer than—my childhood memories. I realized that what I remember as "devil stories" were not just spur of the moment tales told among friends to augment our imaginative play, but rather part of the incredibly rich lore about and experiences of the spirit world that are aspects of everyday Mormonism in northern Utah. Latter-day Saint scripture and prophetic teachings describe a robust spirit realm, and for many Mormons[2] in northern Utah, these teachings become manifest in encounters with spirits. Reports of spirit encounters are common in the community, and people describe visits from benevolent spirits offering aid and from malevolent spirits tempting and harassing believers. This book is the result of my desire to explore the lived experiences of the spirit realm more fully.

A rich body of work in anthropology shows us that spirit experiences are common in many parts of the world. The main argument of this book is that we must understand spirit experiences in northern Utah as particularly Latter-day Saint phenomena. By that, I mean that spirit stories and experiences are interpreted, explained, and remembered with reference to Latter-day Saint cosmology and particular conceptions of the nature of the person, the spirit, and the family in the Latter-day Saint tradition. Those who have experienced visits from spirits do not understand them as a random one-offs, but rather interpret them within a larger cultural and religious framework of the important relationships between the living and non-living beings, or what some scholars have recently started referring to as "metapersons" (Sahlins 2013; Pina-Cabral 2019).

Many scholars have documented Utah and wider Mormon country's extensive folklore tradition, much of which focuses on encounters with mysterious beings. There are well-known folktales about encounters with religious figures like the biblical Cain (Bowman 2011) or the legendary Three Nephites (Fife 1940; Lee 1949), Book of Mormon figures regarded as immortal

---

[2] In 2018, The Church of Jesus Christ of Latter-day Saints officially discouraged the use of the term "Mormon" or "Mormonism"; however, because the term is still in wide usage by scholars and by Latter-day Saints themselves, I use it here interchangeably with "Latter-day Saints."

disciples of Christ who appear to aid those in need. There are also numerous tales of the nefarious Gadianton Robbers, also from the Book of Mormon (Reeve 2011; see also Fife and Fife 1956). There are even stories about a mysterious aquatic creature, known as the Bear Lake Monster, in the lake bearing that name northeast of Cache Valley. In addition to this rich tradition of folklore, many Latter-day Saints report powerful spiritual experiences in which they feel the presence of the Holy Spirit; this is referred to as "inspiration," "personal revelation," "prompting," or sometimes, "spiritual experience." The anthropologist and folklorist Tom Mould has studied such experiences extensively through ethnographic research in North Carolina and archival research in Utah (Mould 2011; see also Brady 1987).

However, in northern Utah, people also experience other kinds of spirit visitations, and these experiences are the subject of this book. These are visits from helpful benevolent spirits who are either pre- or post-mortal, and encounters with harassing malevolent spirits who never had a mortal existence. Most commonly, people receive visitors from the first category, benevolent *individual spirits*. These spirits are entirely distinct from the Holy Spirit and are not well-known figures like the Three Nephites. Rather, they are of *individual* significance to the recipient of the visit, usually the spirit of kin. Benevolent spirits always appear in human form, and they are always identifiable as particular individuals. The recipient may recognize the spirit, or the spirit may identify itself by name. It is not unusual to be visited by a deceased relative, a more distant ancestor, or even the spirits of future children. One may also be visited by a grateful recipient of posthumous baptism. These benevolent spirits frequently offer comfort or help. The spirits of deceased relatives intervene with spiritual guidance or even physical protection. The spirits of future children are often prescient, providing reassurance about fecundity or implicitly guiding their future parents along a moral path. Thankful recipients of baptism may save living children from harm, preserve the earthly family, or offer gratitude.

Encounters with the Devil or malevolent spirits are less common, and they typically appear in order to harass and tempt. Unlike benevolent spirits, evil spirits are never identifiable as individuals and are not considered to have ever been among the living. Rather, they are followers of Satan. Those who are harassed by evil spirits describe them as shadowy figures, an oppressive presence, or a hostile feeling taking over a room. We might understand encounters with evil spirits as attacks on righteous activity or spiritual progress, or the consequence of not living righteously. Anyone might be visited by a spirit, and it is always clear to the recipient of the visit whether the spirit is benevolent or malevolent.

Despite the title, the book is not really about the Devil. Indeed, Satan himself is a very rare visitor, and visitation from his minions—evil spirits (also sometimes known as "devils" or, less often, "demons")—are only the smaller part of the rich spiritual world that interacts with the living in northern Utah. Encounters with benevolent spirits are far more common. This book is thus about spirit experiences of all kinds, and how the richness of these encounters—whether benevolent or malevolent—must be understood with reference to local conceptions of righteousness, spiritual worth, right living, and the mutual journey of the living and their spirit kin toward spiritual achievement and eternal life.

The "Cultural Kindling" of Northern Utah

Most of the spirit encounters I discuss in this book happened to Latter-day Saints in northern Utah, mostly in the region known as Cache Valley, which is nestled between the Bear River and Wasatch ranges on the border of Utah and Idaho. The valley is roughly coterminous with Cache County, one of Utah's northernmost counties. The largest city in the valley is Logan, with a population of just over fifty thousand in 2020. Many small farming towns and bedroom communities bring the county population up to about 130,000. In 2010, the county was between eighty and eighty-five percent Mormon (accessed Association of Religion Data Archives). In 2020, about eighty-five percent of the population of Cache County identified as white.

Historically, the valley was Northwestern Shoshone territory and it was a seasonal settlement for the Fish Eater branch of the Shoshone (Heaton 1993). Early white traders, fur trappers (known locally as Mountain Men), and explorers, like Jim Bridger and Charles Fremont, reported to Brigham Young that the beautiful fertile valley would be ideal for settlement, and so followed the first Mormons, in part inspired to move north from the Salt Lake Valley because of the terrible drought in 1855 (Ricks 1953). The first Mormon settlers arrived in the 1850s, nearly all of them of European descent (primarily British, Irish, and Danish), and most of those I worked with on this project are descendants of these settlers. When reading older histories of the valley like that of Joel Edward Ricks (1953) and Hyrum Campbell (1948), one notices that the surnames of the original settlers are still common in the valley today. One of the first families to settle in the valley were the Maughans, who founded Maughan's Fort in the southwestern part of the valley, which later became the town of Wellsville. The town liesnear the mouth of Sardine Canyon, which cuts through the steep and narrow mountain range that eventually became known by the settlers as the Wellsville Mountains. By 1859, Wellsville was one of six small Mormon settlements in the valley (Ricks 1953, 17). Other early settlements were Logan, Mendon, Providence (the town I grew up in)[3], and Smithfield. The relationship between the Shoshone and the settlers was fraught. John W. Heaton's MA thesis, which considers the relationships between the Shoshone population and the Mormon settlers until 1870, shows that it was an extremely difficult time for the Shoshone who, Heaton argues, after many attempts at resistance, "submitted" to living under the authority of the white settlers (1993). Indeed, the northern end of the valley was the site of the horrific Bear River Massacre of 1863, when over three hundred Shoshone people—including women and children—were killed by the United States Army (Fleisher 2004).

Since 2017, I have been collecting narratives of spirit visitations in this part of Utah, sometimes with the help of a graduate student, Katryn J. Davis. I began with reading narratives about spirit visits, usually written as first-, second-, or third-hand accounts, from the archived student folklore collections in the library of Utah State University. The collection contains submissions from university folklore classes from the late 1960s to the present, and I have focused primarily on accounts from 1980 until the present. Following this, I began to gather first-hand accounts of spirit experiences and the spirit realm through ethnographic interviews and informal conversations. All told, I have read about two hundred accounts of spirit experiences, and have conducted about thirty interviews.

Spirit experiences are very common. Indeed, everyone I approached about this project in Cache Valley—and I mean that literally, *everyone*—either had had spirit experiences of their own or knew about the spirit experiences of people in their close family and friendship circles. No one thought the topic was strange or surprising, and most greeted my interest with enthusiasm. It is important to note that this book focuses particularly on Latter-day Saint experience in this region of northern Utah, and I do not claim to represent the religious lives or spiritual experiences of all Latter-day Saints nor the

---

[3] The folklorists Austin and Alta Fife even dedicate a chapter to Providence in their well-known *Saints of Sage and Saddle* (Fife and Fife 1956, 1980).

global body of the church. To be sure, in informal conversation I have had with Latter-day Saints from outside of Utah, it seems that the experiences and interpretations I describe in this book are not as common elsewhere.

So, what is special about Cache Valley? Why do experiences with spirits of various kinds seem so common here? Stories of uncanny encounters are part of the rich tradition of folklore in many parts of Utah, and there is a widespread cultural acceptance that such encounters can happen. To explain the preponderance of spirit encounters in this region, I have found the idea of "cultural kindling" used by anthropologists Julia Cassaniti and Tanya Luhrmann (2014) to be particularly helpful. "Cultural kindling" refers simply to the ways in which particular aspects of certain cultural environments may give rise to particular interpretations of experiences. Cassaniti and Luhrmann use this idea to understand different kinds of spiritual experiences across cultures: "We suggest here that the local culture of a particular religion serves a similar function in shaping the way people pay attention to what they sense and feel in search of evidence of the spiritual and lowering the threshold of its identification through the body" (2014, S341). They find that, for example, the existence of a cultural term for uncanny experience, such as "Holy Spirit Experience" leads people to interpret unusual emotional or physical states in that cultural framework. Cassaniti and Luhrmann focus particularly on the phenomenology, or the sensory aspect, of spirit experience, and suggest that "phenomenological experience is always the result of the interaction between expectation, cultural invitation, spiritual practice, and bodily responsiveness" (2014, S341).

As I will discuss throughout this book, there is ample "kindling" in northern Utah for understanding uncanny experiences with reference to the spirit realm. Of course, northern Utah Mormons draw on the same scriptural sources that all Mormons do, but I propose that the region's rich and saturated history of folklore and storytelling is one of the reasons that spirit experiences are so common. To understand this, what is perhaps most useful from Cassaniti and Luhrmann's article is their discussion of the *cultural invitation* to experience—"the implicit and explicit ways in which a local social world gives significance and meaning to sensation, whether mental or bodily, and the behavioral practices (such as meditation) that may affect sensation" (2014, S342). This, in turn, leads to an increased likelihood that particular individuals will have such experiences of the supernatural. Although this book looks at spirit experiences broadly, not all of which have a distinct sensory aspect, the idea of cultural invitation is compelling—there is ample cultural kindling in the community to allow people to be particularly attuned to encounters with spirits. And the environment is *saturated*—Latter-day Saints are the overwhelming majority in the valley, and tales and stories are widely known and shared in the community. Certain types of spirit encounters might thus be easily "kindled."[4] When I discussed this theory of cultural kindling with the people I worked with on this project, the idea usually resonated. For example, in the first of a series of conversations with Brad Miller,[5] a high school seminary teacher, I referenced the idea of "cultural kindling," and he nodded and explained that in his view, these stories from folklore legitimize personal experience and it "gives people the freedom to say, 'I think I had that, too.'"

The Latter-day Saint folklore tradition, including that of northern Utah, has been well documented from the mid-twentieth century to the present. Notable contributors to this body of scholarship include Austin and Alta Fife (Fife 1940; Fife and Fife 1956), from whom the Utah State University folklore collection gets its name; Hector Lee (1949); Richard Dorson (1964); David Hufford (1982); Wayland Hand (1983); Margaret Brady (1987); William A. Wilson (1989, 1995); and Richley Crapo (1987). More recently, W. Paul Reeve and Michael Scott van Wagenen edited an excellent collection on the supernatural in Mormon folklore and history (Reeve and van Wagenen 2011), and Tom Mould (2011), as noted, has explored personal revelation from the Holy Spirit. The folklorist Eric Eliason (2014) has considered the nature of "folk magic" and early Mormon use of "seer stones," and also folklore surrounding what he terms "angelic future children," which I address in Chapter 4.

There is clearly a long history of Mormon folklore describing uncanny encounters, and the tales are circulated widely, thus preparing the ground or, perhaps, providing a framework for interpreting certain kinds of unusual experiences with reference to this body of narrative. In *The Angel and the Beehive*, the renowned sociologist of Mormonism Armand Mauss (1994) wrote about the interplay between a this-worldly orientation (using the metaphor of the beehive) and an otherworldly dimension (represented by the angel) in Mormonism. And more recently, Reeve and van Wagenen (2011),

---

[4] During my research, I was asked more than once if I had had spirit encounters of my own. I always replied that I was not aware of any such experiences, but I added that perhaps that was because I do not have exactly the same "kindling," and thus I would not be able to recognize spirit encounters for what they were. Even though I grew up in this community, my family has never been Mormon, and stories of spirits were not shared in my family or in our small Episcopal church.

[5] All names and some other identifying details have been changed to protect participant privacy.

in the introduction to their edited collection on history and folklore, describe the "demon haunted world" that Mormons inhabit.

Today, personal experiences of spirits take place in this environment, rich with discursive tradition of didactic, moralizing tales that are shared in social circles, church events, and community events. Drawing a parallel to work in the anthropology of Islam, my primary area of research before I embarked upon this project, I find inspiration in the anthropologist John R. Bowen's early work on religion among the Gayo in Aceh, Indonesia. In his book, *Muslims through Discourse* (1993), Bowen responded to Talal Asad's call for "discursive" approach to Islam (Asad [1986]2009) by considering Gayo Muslim life through various kinds of speech events and local interpretations of scripture. Similarly, this book attempts what we might call a "Mormons through discourse" approach by drawing on not only on scripture, but the rich heritage of lore and talk about spirits.

In a review of research on Latter-day Saint folklore, William A. Wilson (1995) proposed that most of the best-known twentieth-century researchers in this area, such as Hector Lee, Austin and Alta Fife, and Richard Dorson, studied the subject to understand Mormon history and the Mormon past, thus paying scant attention to the role of folklore in contemporary Mormon lives. Wilson himself, on the other hand, explores late twentieth-century Mormon folklore in an attempt to understand something about contemporary Mormon life. He argues that "Among few people has the telling of stories played a more important role than it has among the Mormons. Indeed, the preeminent event in the Mormon experience—the starting point for all subsequent events in Mormon history—has been made known to generations of Mormon youth and to numerous converts to the Mormon faith by the telling and re-telling of the 'Joseph Smith Story'" (Wilson 1995, 305).

Wilson describes how this and other "faith-promoting" stories are told in daily life, in church meetings and church socials, and in casual gatherings among friends and family. The dominant genre are narratives that both the teller and the listeners believe to be actual events, either third-hand legends or first-person memorates, most of which intend to promote faith (hence "faith-promoting") and proper action: "Most of them are solemn tales designed to validate faith and promote accepted behavior" (1995, 306). Elsewhere, Wilson similarly characterizes evil spirit narratives as "cautionary tales" that "show what happens when one surrenders to the alluring powers of evil" (1989, 101). Based on his research in the folklore collection at Brigham Young University, which now bears his name, Wilson divides narratives into two broad categories: those of historical nature that relate events of the early church, and those that account for the active presence of God in modern life. He concludes his survey by arguing against Hector Lee's (1949) view from the mid-twentieth century that Mormon life would eventually become more rational and science-based and less focused on the miraculous (or what many contemporary anthropologists of religion call the "enchanted," following sociologist Max Weber's [1946] discussion of the process of "disenchantment"). By contrast, Wilson argues that:

> Mormons are no strangers to rational and scientific thought. They have always valued education and have continued over the years to send large numbers of their youth to secular institutions to earn baccalaureate and graduate degrees. At the same time, the foundation of their faith has remained a belief in the possibility of personal revelation and in a loving God who hears and answers prayers and comes to the aid of the faithful in times of need. Far from simply opening a window to the past, the narratives resulting from and validating this belief serve vital, on-going roles in the lives of contemporary Mormons. (1989, 324)

This book heeds Wilson's call to study folklore in daily life. In doing so, we will see that spirit encounters are not limited to legend and folklore, but are common among the living today. Indeed, we will see that life in northern Utah is very much enchanted. The chapters that follow will show how the rich tradition of folk narratives of otherworldly encounters contributes to a fertile environment in which teachings about the spirit world come to life in the lived experience of contemporary Latter-day Saints. The folklorist David Hufford, in his book *The Terror that Comes in the Night* (1982), makes a brief but similar argument. Hufford does not offer extensive analysis, but in his short section on Cache Valley, he argues that "Mormon culture" provides a tidy framework for understanding night terrors (what he calls "Old Hag" attacks) as evil spirit attacks: "The combination of a strong belief in the supernatural . . . and a tradition of telling 'faith-promoting' accounts of personal experience practically guarantees that Old Hag attacks will be discussed and readily accommodated" (1982, 223).

In the chapters that follow, we will explore how Latter-day Saints in northern Utah experience unseen worlds. As we will see, righteous spirits may communicate with, support, and guide the living. Evil spirits harass the righteous and tempt the vulnerable. Stories about the uncanny and the supernatural abound in Cache Valley, although there is little published work on these narratives as most work in folklore looks at other regions of Utah. Exceptions are Hufford's brief documentation of few evil spirit stories from Logan (1982), and Wayland Hand's notes about a few folk narratives and practices that originated in Cache Valley, such as practices of using peepstones to find treasure and stories about driving away witches from Providence (Hand 1983).[6] Today, many people are familiar with a tale about Satan attacking the Logan Temple in its early years, which we will discuss in Chapter 5. Another well-known narrative in Cache Valley (and elsewhere in Mormon contexts), which we discuss in Chapter 4, tells of a benevolent spirit rescuing a child who had fallen into a canal while her parents baptized for the dead in the temple. In most versions of the narrative, the heroic spirit had just been posthumously baptized by the child's parents.

A key proposition of this book, then, is that the widespread circulation of narratives about experiences of the unseen world creates an environment in which people understand that the spirit world is close, and that consequently experiences of spirits—both benevolent and malevolent—are possible. The exchange of such narratives is common, and thus makes it possible for people in the community to understand and, sometimes, share their own experiences. As we will see, spirit visitations happen anywhere—at home, while performing temple work, when driving on a highway, or while serving a mission. Although the recipients of visits may be awake or asleep, I do not make much of the difference between dream visits or waking visits because most of my research participants do not. For most, a spirit visit is a spirit visit whether it happens when one is awake or asleep.

Different Registers of Understanding Mormonism

Throughout the book, I consider how Latter-day Saints n northern Utah use conversations about spirits to differentiate between registers of Mormonism. There are about two million Mormons in Utah, making up nearly sixty percent of the population. However, with a global population of around sixteen million, far more members of the church live outside of Utah than in

---

[6] I have come across only a few stories of witches in northern Utah. Austin and Alta Fife note in *Saints of Sage and Saddle* that Jack Mormons were sometimes thought to be witches, and they share several accounts of witches—and methods of warding off witches—from Cache Valley (1956, 261–262; see also Hand 1983).

Utah, and Latter-day Saints sometimes draw a distinction between the church and "Utah." Indeed, many people I worked with on this project differentiate between what they understand as the "real" teachings of the church and Utah or Mormon "culture." I have identified three general registers of understanding Mormonism.[7] One is the institutional body of The Church of Jesus Christ of Latter-day Saints; another is "Mormon culture" or, sometimes, "Utah Mormon culture"; and third is the "true" religion or what are perceived to be the actual teachings of the church or the original way the religion was practiced. As we will see in several instances throughout the book, the distinctions are usually noted by people who are critical of aspects of the instituoinal church and its hierarchical leadership *or* are critical of aspects of Utah Mormon culture. In such criticisms, actions of the church or Utah culture are contrasted with what are regarded as the true teachings of the religion.

Some participants parse this more as a two-way opposition: doctrine (meaning teachings) vs. culture (meaning how things are done in Utah). A man named Darren, for example, differentiated between what he called "doctrinal beliefs/doctrinal Mormonism" vs. "cultural beliefs/cultural Mormonism." He began by explaining that, in his view, although there is a distinction between "doctrine" and "culture," in Utah the two often get intertwined: in that what is actually Utah *culture* is often interpreted as *doctrine*. Darren explained like this:

> So, you're probably aware of this having grown up in Utah, but there are very fine delineations between what Mormons would call "doctrine" and there's these other things that're just "culture." It's Mormon culture, but it blends right? And so Mormon culture becomes so intertwined that members of the church perceive it as doctrine, but when they go back to try to confirm what their belief or experiences are they find that they're not actual over-the-pulpit documented doctrines. They're just things that people are living by, or believing, or assuming are true, or whatever.

---

[7] Church members, especially those who are not originally from Utah but move to Utah, frequently differentiate between "Utah Mormonism" and Mormon life elsewhere, and newcomers to Utah are often quick to note that the way the religion is practiced in Utah is quite different from their experiences in, say, California. This is not the focus of this book but would make an excellent future project.

We will return to Darren's comments in the next chapter. I find these sorts of differentiations between registers significant because, as we will see in later chapters, people I interviewed used these distinctions to account for what they viewed as potentially problematic beliefs and practices. A key example comes in Chapter 6, which focuses on how members of the Latter-day Saint priesthood use priesthood power to combat evil spirits. Some interviews differentiated between the institutional body of the church, Utah culture, and the "real" religion to critique gender inequity in the church. Women cannot be ordained to the formal priesthood and thus cannot access formal priesthood powers, but several people referenced early Mormon women's spiritual ministrations as reflecting the "true" spiritual capacity of women.

Outline of Chapters and Key Contributions

Overall, this book examines the extent to which interpretations of spirit encounters in northern Utah reflect local conceptions of righteous action and spiritual progress that are tied to broader ideas in Mormon cosmology. Most research on spirit experiences in anthropology and related fields focuses on places outside of the wealthy, industrialized North, and so this book makes an important contribution to understanding the lived experience of spirit worlds in a part of the world that is so often represented as "disenchanted." In addition to an important ethnographic case study in an understudied part of the world, I see this book as making two additional broad contributions to the interdisciplinary field of Mormon Studies and to anthropological research on religion, particularly work on Christianity and the small but growing field of the anthropology of Mormonism.

In Chapter 2, I consider how Mormons in northern Utah connect spirit experiences to broad ideas in Latter-day Saint cosmology and teachings. The chapter explores the differences between benevolent and malevolent spirits, and how both types are connected to happenings in what is known as the pre-existence and the Plan of Salvation. These experiences are inherently Mormon in that they are always understood with reference to Latter-day Saint teachings and ideas about cosmology, salvation, and the nature of righteous personhood. Indeed, at several points throughout the project, upon hearing that I was studying spirit visitations, non-Mormon acquaintances would offer to share their own experiences with me. While I was grateful for their enthusiasm for and interest in the project, I always politely declined because I am particularly interested in understanding what is characteristic of Mormon experience.

The Eternal Family, Ethical Kinship, and the Person

Chapters 3 and 4 discuss encounters with benevolent spirits. Such visitations are often interpreted by the recipients of the visits—and the wider community—with reference to critical teachings on the nature of salvation and the eternal family. And, as part of this, spirit visits emphasize the necessity of right action as framed by teachings of the church, known in local parlance as "righteousness." Spirit visits are tied to goals of salvation and eternal life, which is dependent on proper action, and spirits and the living exist in relationships of mutual aid and responsibility. In this community, an understanding of the righteous person is tied to a sense of communal, mutual ethical action. Benevolent spirits always visit the living for a reason, offering their living kin aid, succor, and support. These sorts of visits indicate that the Latter-day Saint cosmological notion of the possibility and reality of a bonded (or *sealed*) eternal family, which is perhaps the essential central teaching of the church, is not simply an abstraction to long for in the afterlife. Rather, as we will see, all members of the family—the living, the spirits of the dead, and spirit children yet to be born—work together toward a particularly Latter-day Saint understanding of salvation and eternal life. Both living and spirit kin are connected through mutual ethical responsibility aimed at helping each one another with spiritual progress and the path to eternal life.

The encounters described in Chapter 3 are the most common type: visits from the spirits of close kinfolk, such as deceased grandparents or future children. These may be spirits of the deceased, but they may also be "spirit children," which are spirits of those not yet born. The chapter shows that most Latter-day Saints who experience such visits understand them as confirming the key teachings of The Church of Jesus Christ of Latter-day Saints that propose the eternality of the family. Benevolent kin spirits visit to comfort, aid, and advise, and what emerges from accounts is that these visits show that the path to salvation is, for Latter-day Saints, essentially a collective ethical responsibility.

Chapter 4 continues with the theme of collective ethical responsibility for salvation by exploring encounters with benevolent spirits of more distant kin and ancestors that occur during "temple work." Active Mormons in good standing frequently engage in temple-based ritual activities that aim to further the cause of salvation for the deceased. Frequently, rituals such as proxy baptism are performed for deceased kin of living Mormons, and spirits may appear to encourage or commend such ritual activities. Such encounters emphasize the interdependence of members of the spirit world and the living, who share responsibility of salvation. These interactions illustrate a particular Latter-day Saint understanding of the nature of the righteous person as something that is inherently perfectible, but that is only perfectible vis-à-vis one's relationships to others—both the living and non-living.

The mutual responsibility that the living and their spirit kin have for one another shows a kinship network based on ethical relationships, as the anthropologist Marshall Sahlins has recently articulated in his book *What Kinship Is . . . And Is Not* (2013). The encounters discussed in this book show that we should consider that these relationships exist not just between the living, but also between the living and spirit members of the family. As we will see, spirits show a concern and care for living members of their family by offering aid, wisdom, and knowledge. Deceased relatives appear to reassure the living and offer protection and support. The "spirit children" of God that are awaiting mortal existence visit to implore or foretell their future birth and joining of a mortal family. In turn, the living have a responsibility to their spirit kin. The living give birth to spirit children and thus provide the mortal body that Latter-day Saint teachings stress is necessary for salvation. Furthermore, much of the ritual work that is performed in temples by church members is good standing is focused on performing ritual activities to assist the deceased on their path to eternal life.

Like members of the church themselves, I understand Mormonism as a branch of Christianity. Like other Christians, Latter-day Saints recognize Jesus Christ as the son of God and believe in the salvational nature of his crucifixion. The Old and New Testaments are key components of scripture, but Latter-day Saints recognize other sources of scripture, most notably the Book of Mormon, which tells of Israelites migrating to the the Americas and Jesus Christ's visit to them. As I will explain in the following chapters, this network of ethical relationships between the living and the non-living contributes to contemporary understandings of the person as necessarily being defined and understood in relationship to others. Accordingly, this bolsters important arguments from scholars of Mormonism, notably in the work of anthropologist Fenella Cannell (2017), who ask us to expand our understanding of Christianity beyond a too-narrow focus on individualism.

Evil as a Cosmological Force

Righteous action and making the right choices—and helping one another do so—are key to understanding how Latter-day Saints in Utah understand encounters with benevolent spirits. Malevolent spirits, on the other hand, usually appear in an attempt to thwart righteous action or to encourage unrighteous action. These encounters are discussed in Chapters 5 and 6, and a second major contribution of this book is that it shows a contemporary understanding of evil centered on Satan as an active cosmological force in the world. Although encounters with benevolent spirits are far more common, many Latter-day Saints—particularly young people—report harassment by evil spirits. Chapter 5 shows that such visits are understood as the active, real presence of Satan or his minions, who are attracted to various types of unrighteous actions and also seek to thwart the exceptionally righteous. These encounters are thus an exceptionally good illustration of the slippery edge of righteousness in northern Utah and show a local Latter-day Saint conception of evil that regards Satan and his minions as aggressive, active agents in the lives of the living.

In northern Utah, most negative spirit visits are attributed to non-individuated evil spirits, minions of Satan rather than Satan himself. For Latter-day Saints, negative experiences always seem to happen at the edge of righteousness, or at the moral boundary, as I have argued elsewhere (Stiles 2022). Evil minions are attracted to unrighteous behaviors like drinking, smoking, and illicit sexual activity, but they are also attracted to the exceptionally righteous. Indeed, as we will see, missionaries are frequent targets of evil spirits. However, rather than considering evil as a gloss for vice or a means for coping with rapid social change, Latter-day Saints in this community foreground evil as Satan, an actual and relentless cosmological reality bent on tempting the living from the path of righteousness or thwarting their righteous endeavors.

The living are not powerless against evil. Latter-day Saints emphasize the importance of agency—choice—in every mortal life, and the spiritual power associated with the Latter-day Saint priesthood can combat evil influence.

Chapter 6 explores gender, masculinity, and the power of the priesthood through the practice of "casting out" evil spirits. The formal, institutionalized body of the priesthood is held only by men. and Chapter 6 shows that the spiritual authority used to cast out spirits is a point of "gender distress" (Thornton 2016), and both women and men contest assumptions about the masculine nature of priesthood power. The chapter revisits the theme of local distinctions between the formal institution of the church, a cultural Mormonism particular to Utah, and the true essence of the religion.

2
The Realm of the Spirits

One morning in June 2018, I met an old friend for breakfast at a popular café in Cache Valley. I had reached out to Jake after running across one of his college essays in the wonderful student folklore collection at Utah State University. Jake is married and the father of several children. He is a college graduate, a professional, and a former missionary who is active in The Church of Jesus Christ of Latter-day Saints. When someone is described as "active," it means that they attend church regularly and participate in the religious life of the community. Jake's college essay, which he had submitted for a folklore class in the 1990s, caught my attention because he described his grandfather's experience with a benevolent spirit. After reading the paper, I got in touch with Jake to tell him about my project and to ask if he might tell me more about what happened to his grandfather. He was enthusiastic about the project and told me that he had had a number of spirit experiences himself. "We believe the spirit world is right around us," he said. "Basically . . . there's a veil that's been drawn over our eyes. If we could lift it up, we'd see it, you know, we'd be able to see 'em . . . we all kinda interact . . . .They're here, but they have other things to do. They've got their concerns, and we've got ours. And, you know, very occasionally we'll get a gift, maybe, of a visit."

The following autumn, I met a graduate student named Shauna for tea at her home in Reno, Nevada, where I live. Shauna is originally from northern Utah, but she and her husband, Darren, left Utah after college and eventually settled in Nevada. Shauna and Darren were no longer active in the church, but they had been for most of their lives, and they were both interested in talking to me about the project. As we sipped our tea, Shauna told me that as a youngster, she was "super afraid of the evil spirits, but really wanted to meet a good spirit and just feel like . . . you know, like I was a *good enough person* to have a personal witness . . . . Like if you were spiritual enough that things could [happen]."

This chapter explores how Latter-day Saints in northern Utah understand and talk about the spirit realm with reference to key ideas in Mormon cosmology. For many in this community, the spirit world is alive, present, and manifest in everyday encounters, and discourse about spirits and the unseen world is very much a part of life. As I have written elsewhere, Latter-day Saint cosmology describes a dynamic spirit realm that is always co-present as an everyday reality (Stiles 2022). Well-known tales of benevolent encounters or demonic interference are widely shared in church meetings, at social events, and at family gatherings. Personal experiences of spirits might be shared in one-on-one conversations with friends or within the bosom of the family. Students in college folklore classes, like Jake, write papers about the time an ancestral spirit helped Aunt Violet with her genealogy research or when the spirit of a future younger brother visited the family to let them know he would soon be born.

Although I recognize the importance of scriptures and formal teachings about the spirit realm, throughout this book I prioritize how everyday people think about and talk about their experiences with the unseen world. Therefore, rather than beginning this chapter with a summary of church teachings and scriptural sources on spirits, I bring these sources into the discussion when the people I worked with on the project do, and I attend to the ways in which people interpret, understand, and debate scriptural verses and teachings about the spirit realm. This book thus considers what John R. Bowen has referred to as "the social life of scriptures" in his work with Gayo Muslims in Indonesia (Bowen 1992, 1993); James Bielo is another anthropologist who takes a similar approach, addressing the social life of scriptures in an edited collection by that name, which considers how Christians engage with the Bible (Bielo 2009).

I have found that when talking to people about spirit experiences—either their own experiences or those of others—Latter-day Saints in northern Utah frequently reference cosmological ideas about the pre-existence, the post-existence, and the path to eternal life to understand the meaning of such encounters. The encounters are nearly always interpreted within a distinctly Latter-day Saint cultural and theological framework. Spirits are not simply in the world going about their business in haphazard fashion. Rather, there is a *reason* that spirits, both benevolent and malevolent, are in the world, and the explanation is found in this cosmology.

On Spirit Encounters as the "Heart of What Latter-day Saints Embrace"

During the COVID-19 pandemic lockdown in 2020 and 2021, I scheduled a series of Zoom conversations with Brad Miller, a seminary teacher at a high school in Cache Valley.[1] I have known Brad since we were adolescents, although we had not kept in touch. Brad holds a Bachelor's degree in Philosophy and Master's degree in Education, and he is a born scholar and educator. Our many conversations were a fascinating mix of theological and scholarly reflections and personal experience. The first time we talked I told him about research I was doing, and he expressed unreserved enthusiasm and seemed to grasp exactly what I was getting at in the project. He told me that he thought this ever-present possibility of spirit encounters—as experiences distinctly *different* from the inspiration of the Holy Ghost—was at "the heart of what Latter-day Saints embrace."

Indeed, everything seems to come back to the spirit world. I began our first recorded interview simply by asking Brad why he decided to become a seminary teacher. He responded by describing an intriguing experience he had as a teenager. He was recently reminded of it when he visited our old high school for a football game. Before the game, he said, he had spent some time walking around the campus, which sparked the following memory:

> If you remember where the seminary building is? I'm walking from the ... high school to the seminary. I remember on the lawn ... I received this feeling that came over me and even some kind of feeling or voice.... I'm not even quite sure of this ... it said, "You will one day teach in that building." And ... I was a senior in high school. I'm like, "What? I'm not teaching here." I mean, I had no idea what I was gonna do for a career! And I was just walking over to the seminary just like hundreds of students do every day. I was a little late, so I was alone. I remember walking on the grass, and I felt this impression come over me, "You will teach right there in

---

[1] Most middle and high schools in Utah have seminary buildings that are just off campus. The church runs the seminaries, and Mormon students who so choose are granted "released time" from the high school classes to take seminary classes; in effect, seminary was a high school class period just like any other, although of course all legal requirements for public high school was met by the off-campus seminary and the time "released" from regular coursework. In my memory, students just walked across the lawn of the main building of the high school to the matching seminary building. Those of us who did not take seminary classes took an extra class in our schedules, although as I recall from an article I wrote for our school paper, non-Mormons could have asked for "released time" to study other religions.

that class in that building." Wow! And I shook it off thinking it was weird. Because . . . I had no desire to be a teacher.

After serving a mission, graduating from college, and earning a graduate degree, Brad did indeed become a seminary teacher, and he taught for a few years in the very building outside of which he had the mysterious communication. He remains somewhat baffled by the experience. Unlike most of the accounts in this book, Brad was unable to attribute the message to a particular spirit being. He was not sure who brought the message, as it was not clearly evident to him if it was an ancestor or inspiration from the Holy Ghost. What I find so telling about Brad's account is that in response to my simple query about a rather prosaic matter—his decision to become a high school seminary teacher—he answered with reference to a spiritual experience very much in keeping with other people's experiences: an otherworldly intervention offering guidance and prescience.

Brad's account of the mysterious communication launched a series of illuminating discussions. When I asked how he interpreted the experience in light of Latter-day Saint teachings, he replied that, with my question, I was really getting at the core of my entire project: the reality of spiritual intervention in our lives *beyond* the inspiration of the Holy Ghost. Brad emphasized this by saying that, in addition to the Holy Ghost, "We have this whole other layer of ministering angels, of angels coming down and talking to people, which we also believe, [and] which the Book of Mormon declares."

Reflecting on his own experience walking to seminary that afternoon long ago, he queried rhetorically, "Was that Grandpa telling me? Was it the Holy Ghost telling me? Does it matter? I don't know. But somewhere, in the unseen world, I was told 'this is what you'll do.'"

Benevolent Spirits, Angelic Ministration, and the Plan of Salvation

The historian Benjamin Park has written about the nineteenth-century development of Mormon angelology, and he proposes that studying changing views on angels is a fruitful way to study Latter-day Saint thought of that period (Park 2010, 4). Considering angel beliefs vis-à-vis broader ideas about the spirit world is also a productive way to understand twenty-first-century religious thought and practice. Throughout our conversations, Brad used the evocative phrase *angelic ministration*. He was not correcting me by saying that the beings I was referring to as "spirits" were actually "angels." Rather, he was using what I regard as, perhaps, a more formal term for this specific type of spiritual communication. When I asked how he teaches his high school seminary students about spiritual experience, he unequivocally differentiated between Holy Ghost inspiration and angelic ministration, emphasizing again that the latter are a key and core part of what it means to be a Latter-day Saint. "Generally speaking," he said:

> We teach that communication from God will come through the Holy Ghost. I think scripturally that's established, I think the curriculum is established through scripture, and that the Holy Ghost is the revealer of truth, the testifier, that's what received this, what we call *revelation, inspiration*. But . . . you have this other thing we'll call *angelic ministration*. And how to blend those two is really hard. And so I don't stand up in front of my classroom and tell my students that if they'll pray and, and seek answers, that Grandpa will come and tell them things or angels will come and tell them. That's not coming out of my mouth. I'm not directing and trying to influence them to think that way. However, it's a possibility. Yeah, it's something that happens . . . . We pray to Heavenly Father; the Holy Ghost is the Revealer of Truth. But through all of that process, there are hundreds and thousands of examples where God sends, as a messenger from heaven, an angel, here comes an angel to deliver a message. And so we open up scripture every day. And we read about these stories. And so the idea is, why not transfer it to their everyday life? It can happen here, it can happen now, it can happen with you. And certainly it does happen.

When I asked Brad directly if spirits and angels were the same, he replied that this was another key question of my project: "Who *are* these beings that are coming with messages?" First, he explained, there are "resurrected beings," who have bodies, such as the angel Moroni from the Book of Mormon, and Peter, James, and John from the New Testament, all of whom Mormons believe were resurrected. However, Brad said, visits from these beings are unlikely. And in my research, it is true that I have not come across any recent encounters with these resurrected beings. More typical, Brad said, are visitors from spiritual beings *without* bodies, which he referred to as "unembodied angels." These are usually either the spirits of unborn children or the spirits of deceased relatives and ancestors.

To explain, Brad referenced the Doctrine and Covenants (D&C), which is one of the major works of Latter-day Saint scripture, along with the Bible, the Book of Mormon, and *The Pearl of Great Price*.[2] The Doctrine and Covenants records God's revelations to Joseph Smith, the first prophet of the church, and, to a lesser extent, revelations to the prophets who succeeded Smith as leaders of the church. Brad opened a Latter-day Saints scripture app on his phone and advised me to download it, which I did and which I found to be extremely useful. Remarking on how interesting section 129 of the Doctrine and Covenants is, Brad explained that "angels ... don't always come as embodied ministers, they can come as unembodied, but they still have a spirit. They still look like a person." Finding the relevant verses on the scripture app, he read aloud:

> There are two kinds of beings in heaven, namely angels who are resurrected personages and having bodies of flesh and bone—
> For instance, Jesus said, '*handle me and see for a spirit hath not flesh and bones, as you see we have.*'"
> Secondly, the spirits of just men made perfect, they who are not resurrected, but inherit the same glory. (D&C 129:1–3)

Brad summarized these verses in his own words, "So that's a long way of saying the spirits of those who have not been resurrected yet."

I asked, "Okay, like that could be Grandpa?"
"Exactly."

When I commented on how frequently the spirits of kin seem to interact with the living, Brad had a practical explanation for why visits from these "unembodied angels" are more common than visits from other spirit beings, like the "angels" referenced in the verse above. He told me that it has to do with God's pragmatism and the importance of the *eternal family*.

"So let's just say God wanted to communicate something to you, right? Is he gonna just choose some random person up in heaven? Or doesn't it sound

---

[2] *The Pearl of Great Price* is a collection of Joseph Smith's writings and translations of writings from other prophets.

more reasonable that Grandpa Stiles would come down? Because there's a connection. There's a love, there's a concern, there's an interest."

I also discussed spirits and angels with two nineteen-year-old missionaries in Cache Valley, whom I call Elder Neilson and Elder Collins. Like Brad, the missionaries first explained resurrected beings and emphasized that the reason for these resurrections—when all other mortals must wait until judgment—was so they could return to earth to teach and "bring to pass the restoration of the Gospel." Moreover, like Brad, they emphasized that most angels, however, would *not* have a body—these angels are the spirits of the deceased or those not yet born. Elder Collins said, "If they've died they had a body, but they don't any more. And if they haven't come to earth yet, then they don't have a body."

In late 2020, when Christmas was fast approaching, Brad taught me about the prevalence of angelic ministration with reference to stories of Christ's birth from the New Testament, which he observed is full of ministering angels. He noted, in particular, the annunciation and the angel visiting the shepherds. He also referenced Charles Dickens's *The Christmas Carol* as a literary example of spirit visitations. Brad directed me to an influential talk called "The Ministry of Angels" given by Elder Jeffrey Holland, a member of the Quorum of the Twelve Apostles[3] and a former president of Brigham Young University. Brad shared one of his favorite excerpts from this talk with me: "Usually such beings are not seen. Sometimes they are. But seen or unseen they are always near" (Holland 2008). We discussed this, and Brad said that he interpreted Holland's talk as a call for the church to place more emphasis on the ministry of angels. He said that, in his own opinion, seminary teachers were not currently emphasizing this idea to the extent that they could.

Later that day, after our Zoom call, I read a complete transcript of the talk. Elder Holland (2008) describes a very broad understanding of angelic ministration, and he includes the kindness and generosity of the living as akin to angelic ministrations. I understood Holland's broader point the same way that Brad did—the talk notes recent emphasis in church teachings on a greater embrace of the reality of angelic or spirit intervention in daily life. Holland proposes that angelic ministration happens continually and that the living should embrace such experiences, writing, "Sometimes their [the

---

[3] The Quorum of the Twelve is the second highest governing body of the church, which ranks just below the office of the President, who is also regarded as the Prophet.

angels'] assignments are very grand and have significance for the whole world. Sometimes the messages are more private. Occasionally the angelic purpose is to warn. But most often it is to comfort, to provide some form of merciful attention, guidance in difficult times" (Holland 2008).

I have noticed that most Latter-day Saints in northern Utah do not make a stark distinction between spirits and angels. Like Brad's explanation of "unembodied angels," many others used the terms interchangeably. For example, when I asked Lyne, a friend who has had numerous spirit encounters, if she used the term "angels" and "spirits" interchangeably, she replied, "Yeah, it is the same thing. So the angels—or what we refer to as the angel—could be the spirit of someone who lived or hasn't become [mortal] yet."

The Plan of Salvation and the Eternal Family

A key argument of this book is that Mormons in northern Utah experience the spirit world in a particularly Latter-day Saint way. This is evident in the way that people reference key cosmological ideas in Mormonism when discussing or interpreting their own spirit encounters and those of others. For example, as we saw earlier in this chapter, Brad stressed the importance of family connections beyond the world of the living as the basis for understanding the spirit realm. In the *economy of heaven*, he explained, referencing Elder Holland again, God is more likely to send the spirit of a family member, like Grandpa, than an unknown angel or spirit; we will revisit the idea of the economy of heaven in the next chapter. Indeed, I have found that nearly all experiences with benevolent spirits are engagements with otherworldly members of the family—the spirits of the deceased and those not yet born. Spirit experiences thus provide witness to the reality of the *eternal family*, which is a key teaching—perhaps *the* key teaching—of the church. Spirits and the eternal family are the subject matter of the next two chapters. Here, it will suffice to note that the church teaches that a family that is "sealed" in a temple will be together forever. Temple marriages seal husband and wife together for eternity, and children who are "born in the covenant" of such a marriage are sealed to their parents. Children who are not born in the covenant, such as adopted children, may be later sealed to their parents.[4]

---

[4] The anthropologist Fenella Cannell has written about Latter-day Saints adoptions in her broader work on "forever families" (Cannell 2017).

Jake connected his belief in spirits (which he here refers to as "ghosts") directly to his belief in the afterlife. He explained, "The spirit world is kind of all around us. But, just like here [in the mortal world], there's good and bad on that side. And so I've always—as a kid I was raised that way—and so I believe in ghosts. Now, what ghosts are, I don't know. But I believe that they're there, because I believe in an afterlife; I believe that there are quote unquote what we call 'ghosts.'"

Jake refers to the afterlife as the basis for his belief in "the spirit world."[5] Many of my interviews and conversations about the spirit realm began like this, with a discussion of premortality and postmortality. Latter-day Saints often understand spirit experiences, both negative and positive, with reference to the path toward redemption known as the Plan of Salvation, which begins before mortality in the pre-existence and continues after death. Jake references the Plan in the following:

> Because we believe that, before the world, we all were in a spiritual form .... We'd reached a certain point, you know, and Heavenly Father[6] had a plan. We all want our kids to progress like we do, and He wants us to progress. OK, here's the plan: We're going to make this world here, we're going to go down on the world, you do your thing. Now because you're kids, you're going to do stupid bad stuff, and you know stupid bad can't come live on a heavenly level, so we've gotta have a *plan*.

He paused, and I asked, "Is this the Plan of Salvation?" Jake confirmed that it was.

Shauna also explicitly connected the spirit world to the Plan of Salvation. Like Jake, she equates the two in a way that suggests that spirits and the living are intertwined in the quest for salvation. When I asked how she learned about the spirit world as a child, she explained:

> That's something you're taught from . . . infancy. It's called the "Plan of Salvation" . . . there's a diagram they'll draw out . . . . there's the pre-earth life,

---

[5] Jake's use of the term "ghost" is unusual. Although he is clearly referring to spirits, most people do not use the term ghost, but rather spirit or angel. Indeed, this is relevant to Heonik Kwon's recent essay weighing in on the long debate among anthropologists about ancestor versus ghost. Drawing on his research in Vietnam, Kwon argues against Pascal Boyer's (2002) assertion that an inherent fear of corpses is responsible for fear of ghosts; Kwon argues that "the distinction between ghost and ancestors can actually be less clear than is usually assumed" (Kwon 2016, 191).

[6] Latter-day Saints commonly refer to God as "Heavenly Father."

where there was a war in heaven. Some of the people went with Satan, and some of the people went with Jesus . . . . the good people are the only people that get a chance to have a body, and all of Satan's minions are jealous of bodies. They were cast out, and then the rest of us who want to follow God's plan were allowed to be born, and have a body, and to be tested.

Jake and Shauna both mention God's plan, and the Plan of Salvation is a key teaching of the church. It is also sometimes referred to as the "quest for glory" or the "path to godhood." Each individual is on a path to redemption called the Plan of Salvation, the path toward the ultimate reward in the afterlife. However, as we will see in the next two chapters, the journey of spiritual progress is not solitary. Rather, in popular understanding, the entire family—both living and spirit members—works together toward the goal of eternal life.

As Jake observed, the journey begins in the pre-existence, when all spirits co-exist with the divine. (In official church writings, this is also referred to as "premortality," although nearly everyone I spoke with for this project referred to it as the "pre-existence.") Numerous sources of scripture reference the premortal existence. In *The Pearl of Great Price*, which contains revelations to Joseph Smith, Moses 3:5 reads, "And I, the Lord God, had created all the children of men; and not yet a man to till the ground; for in heaven created I them; and there was not yet flesh upon the earth, neither in the water, neither in the air." Latter-day Saints also cite parts of the Old and New Testaments and other Mormon scripture as the basis of teachings about the pre-existence. To progress along the path to salvation, the mortal birth of the spirit is necessary. Yet people recognize the continuity of the spirit from the pre-existence to postmortality and, as we will see in the next chapters, it is these pre- and postmortal spirits who visit to aid and comfort the living. In Latter-day Saint teachings, belief in the eternal family and the Plan of Salvation go hand in hand: a key promise is the continuity and everlasting inseparability of the sealed earthly family. For many Latter-day Saints, visits from the benevolent spirits of kin provide evidence of the eternality of the family.

When I spoke with Darren, Shauna's husband, he also emphasized pre- and postmortal existence as the basis for spirit experiences. Darren is a father, college graduate, and professional. He is also a former missionary, and he has had intriguing spirit encounters in his life—one as a child and one a missionary, which I will describe in a later chapter. Although he did not grow up in Utah, he moved to southern Idaho for college, where he met Shauna.

They married, and then moved to Salt Lake City to finish their studies at the University of Utah.[7] We met for the first time in his spacious office, where he volunteered to spend his lunch break talking with me. Throughout our conversation, he referenced the extensive training in Latter-day Saint scripture that he had had as a missionary, and he focused on elucidating the scriptural basis for his understandings of the spirit world. As noted in Chapter 1, Darren explained that although there is a distinction between "doctrine" and "culture," he thought that, in Utah, the two often get intertwined. In his view, what is actually "Utah culture" is often interpreted by Mormons in Utah as "doctrine."

Darren explained that spirit experiences originate from the belief that, in the premortal existence, spirits lived together with God. In his view, most interactions between the living and spirits take place at times of transition from the world of spirits to the world of the living, such as at birth and death. He used stillbirth, the tragic merger of birth and death, as an example:

> So there's a belief that this exists, but the interaction with those spirits, the only time that you'll hear stories—I've not had personal experience with this, but I've heard umpteen stories—[is when] somebody who had a stillbirth-born baby or whatever, right? And so where those kind of transitions are, or what they perceive as pre-life to post-life, then they'll say they felt something or they saw something.

Darren remarked that the church's teachings on spirit beings are complicated. We talked a bit about the teachings from the Doctrine and Covenants, and he focused on the relation between one's mortal life and the promise of eternal life.

"In the Doctrine and Covenants," he explained, "they speak about life after death. And this life after death is based ... on how you've lived your life and what commitments you've made or not made. You've got some kind of reward out there. And there's these varying levels of reward, and in those rewards you can live in perpetuity in that spiritual state of whatever it is you're doing."

Latter-day Saints in northern Utah frequently explain the origins of benevolent spirits with reference to the Plan of Salvation, the pre- and postmortal

---

[7] Darren reflected several times on the particularities of what he viewed as "Utah Mormonism" versus what he experienced growing up as a Mormon in California.

existence of spirits, and the attendant necessity of mortality. And, as we will see in the next chapters, spirits are always connected in some fashion to the necessity of mortal life on earth for spiritual progress toward salvation: benevolent spirits who interact with the living are always either premortal or postmortal. Malevolent spirits, however, are quite different.

Malevolent Spirits, the War in Heaven, and the Importance of Choice

In the pre-existence, one-third of spirits rejected the chance to have a mortal body, and they became followers of Lucifer during what is known as the War in Heaven. These are the evil spirits that harass and torment the living. Evil spirits aim to destroy the work of God, under the direction of Satan, whom Latter-day Saints understand as a fallen angel, Lucifer. Most Latter-day Saints understand the War in Heaven as a cosmic battle between good and evil, between Jesus Christ and Lucifer, both spirit children of God.[8] Scriptural sources for the War in Heaven are many, and Latter-day Saints cite sections from the Book of Mormon, the Doctrine and Covenants, *The Pearl of Great Price*, and the Old and New Testaments when referencing the War in Heaven. In short, because God chose Jesus to be the savior, Lucifer rebelled. In *Saints of Sage and Saddle*, Austin and Alta Fife begin a chapter titled "The Spirit World" with a fascinating excerpt from the journal of the fourth president of the church, Wilford Woodruff (1807–1888). In this passage, Woodruff attempts to account for how many fallen spirits were sent to earth, and he concludes ominously that there must be one hundred evil spirits for every person on earth, and thus everyone must take care and be wary (1956, 213):

> We will suppose that there were 100,000,000,000 of fallen spirits sent down from heaven to earth, and that there are 1,000,000,000 of inhabitants upon the face of the earth today, that would make one hundred evil spirits to every man, woman and child living on the earth; and the whole mission and labor of these spirits is to lead all the children of men to do evil and to effect their destruction.

---

[8] In his book, *Joseph Smith, Jesus, and Satanic Opposition: Atonement, Evil, and the Mormon Vision* (2010), the anthropologist and theologian Douglas Davies argues that Jesus, Satan, and Joseph Smith make up a trinity of sorts: Jesus is the antagonist of Satan, and Joseph Smith inherited Jesus's priestly authority. We will take up this idea again in Chapter 5.

Now, I want all our boys and girls to reflect upon this, and to see what danger they are in, and the warfare they have to pass through. (Cited in Fife and Fife 1956, 213)

Nearly a century-and-a-half after Woodruff penned these words, these spirits are still a threat. When Jake told me about a frightening encounter he had with a menacing spirit, which I will recount in detail in Chapter 5, he explained it by referencing the War in Heaven. Jake explained that most spirits joined with God and Jesus Christ, also a spirit child of God, and were therefore granted the opportunity to be born on earth into the mortal body that is necessary for embarking on the journey toward eternal life. The rebellious spirits who followed Lucifer were denied mortality, but they are present among the living today. He observed that these nefarious spirits are the agents of malevolent harassment. In the excerpt below, note Jake's emphasis on choice and free will: Jesus Christ stressed that spirits should *choose* to follow him, while Lucifer advocated *compulsion*:

So two people come forward, and Christ says, "Well, I'll go teach 'em, and it'll be up to them to decide." . . . You know, the mainstream Christians say, "Oh the Mormons believe that Christ and Lucifer are brothers!" Well, yeah, in a spiritual sense, we do. And we believe all of us are. And Lucifer says, "Well, I'll go down, and I'll make sure every one of them do exactly what they're supposed to do, and then every one of them is gonna get back here." And so [for Lucifer] there was really no choice in it. Well, you know, there's this quote unquote "War in Heaven." You know how that went down . . . . But a third of 'em followed Lucifer and they never got a body.

Like Jake, many others emphasized the importance of choice and agency in the pre-existence and in the mortal coil. Lyne and I talked about the War in Heaven for quite some time. She also stressed that spirits *chose* to follow Jesus Christ or to follow Lucifer. Spirits were not compelled to follow Christ. She explained, "Everybody that's here on this earth *chose* to be here. Because when we were in heaven those that have bodies . . . chose Christ to be the Redeemer instead of having Satan saying, you know, 'I'll force you to be good but then I want all the glory.'" Lyne frequently revisited the importance of choice and free will in mortal life. Life, she explained, is a series of tests requiring us to make the right choice.

Darren also stressed choice and agency. "In the pre-life," he said, "there's also a belief that we all had some choice to come here and experience life in some form or another." He clarified that in the pre-existence, spirits did not choose to become Mormon, but rather chose a mortal life, in which they would be faced by numerous other choices:

> And that wasn't, "Hey, I'm coming to this life as a Mormon!" That's not their belief, it's [rather] "I'm coming to this life to experience life." And you're going to have a lot of choices, of which one may be to become a Mormon or not. And in that pre-existence state, there were several that rebelled, and those who rebelled didn't get a chance to come to this earth, and didn't get to get a body and participate in this life.

Darren focused on the consequences of being denied a mortal body. He surmised the spirits without a body would be eternally envious of humanity, which was one of the reasons they harassed the living. He said, "Mormons believe that that third [the spirits who followed Satan] are distraught, and um, unhappy, that they didn't get to come experiences this [life] and that they perturb us or cause us grief. [They] potentially cause us grief in this life in some way or another."

I confirmed that this "third" were what people referred to as evil spirits, and he agreed: "Most [Mormons] would believe that any and all negative experiences with any spiritual beings or, you know, 'postmortal,' would be from those third."

This is an important point: evil spirits are those that never had and never will have a mortal body. Darren stressed that ancestral spirits—former mortals—never cause problems for the living. "It's not, you know, that my grandfather died and is creating a negative experience for me." Certainly, in the hundreds of spirit encounter accounts I have collected through ethnographic and folklore research, the spirits of kin are almost never implicated in negative encounters. Indeed, Jake was the only person who even suggested the possibility that a malevolent spirit could be postmortal:

> What we believe about the spirit world is [that] the same general type of person we are here goes over there with us. So just because you died, doesn't suddenly mean you're gettin' your wings and you're all great and wonderful. And there's a lot of the thought that goes into that is that some of these experiences with what we would call the "evil spirits" may be the spirits

of . . . bad people. And they've maybe got bad intentions or maybe there's hauntings because they're not pullin' themselves away from that place.

Although Jake explained that it was possible that the spirits of "bad people" could result in harassments or hauntings of the living, his view on this matter is unusual. Spirit harassment is nearly always attributed to those spirits who followed Lucifer in the War in Heaven.

Indeed, I have come across only two narratives that might be construed as a postmortal spirit causing trouble for their living relatives and in both cases the trouble was caused indirectly and could be attributed to loneliness rather than wickedness. Both narratives are archived in the student folklore collection at Utah State University. The first, which the collector describes as legend from the town of Benson in the northern part of Cache Valley, tells of a man who died as soon as he was "sealed" to two deceased women in the Logan Temple in 1922, meaning that they would be his wives in eternity.[9] The man, called Christian Rindlisbacher, had been asking his wife for permission to be sealed to the women and when she finally reluctantly agreed, they rode in a horse-drawn wagon to the temple. After the sealing, they emerged from the temple, and the man died as he was pulling up the horses and wagon to the gate. His wife said: "I knew just as soon as I agreed to this that she would take him from me" (Gereaux 1982). Clearly, the living wife meant that as soon as he was sealed to a deceased woman, she would "take" her new husband. The other tale is also from the north end of the valley and relates a dream about a deceased grandmother taking the spirit of an infant so she would not be lonely (Thompson 1996). These accounts are quite different from the other malevolent spirit encounters that we will explore in Chapters 5 and 6. In both, the explanation is that the deceased member of the family somehow causes the death of a living family member to have them for companionship in the afterlife. The seemingly nefarious action then can be explained by lonesomeness, not evil.

The Discernment of Spirits

As we have discussed, the Doctrine and Covenants (section 129) differentiates between spirits and angels. In practice, I have noticed that differentiating

---

[9] Although a man can be married to only one living woman, he can be sealed to additional women.

between angels and benevolent spirits is not particularly important, and most people use the terms interchangeably. However, the ability to distinguish benevolent from malevolent spirits *is* important, at least theoretically. In several interviews, people described a well-known method of differentiating between good and bad spirits with a handshake, which also has its basis in the Doctrine and Covenants (129:4–8).[10] Shauna described it to me as follows, saying that she learned it as a child:

> Sometimes you'll see a spirit and you don't know if it's evil or good. And the way you can tell is if you try to shake hands with it. And if it tries to shake your hand you won't be able to feel it and [you will] know it's an evil spirit. And if it won't try to shake your hand, it's a good spirit 'cause it's not going to try to deceive you.... That was the test. If you see a spirit, ask them to shake their hand, and if it's a bad one then, you know, command them to leave. But if it's a good one, then you can talk to them.

Shauna's husband Darren talked about the handshake method with reference to doctrine. "So," he said, "the doctrinal part of that little nuance [the handshake] is in the Doctrine and Covenants. Joseph Smith had claimed to have some experiences.... You have these spiritual visitations, and if you want to find out [if] it is a God-send, an angel-send, [another] positive other experience, that you offer them a handshake. This is actually in the Doctrine and Covenants."

Darren paused. When he continued, he said, "So, you handshake them. And if they're a good person, they won't try to deceive you and offer a handshake because they don't have a body to actually complete that handshake. However, if they handshake you, then it's a deception, and that's one of these other negative spirits, right?"

Darren was referring to a portion of the Doctrine and Covenants in which Joseph Smith teaches what are known as the "three keys" to discerning spirits. If one offers a handshake, angels as "resurrected beings" have bodies of flesh and bone, and thus the hand they offer in return will be solid. Spirits of "just men made perfect" will not offer a hand, as they do not have bodies. The devil, by contrast, will offer a hand but the receiver will feel nothing:

---

[10] The handshake method is not particular to Utah. The anthropologist Hildi Mitchell has referenced the handshake with her work with Mormons in the United Kingdom, writing that "even Mormon children know how to tell the difference between them [good and bad spirits]" (2001, 164)

When a messenger comes saying he has a message from God, offer
him your hand and request him to shake hands with you.
If he be an angel he will do so, and you will feel his hand.
If he be the spirit of a just man made perfect he will come in his
glory; for that is the only way he can appear—
Ask him to shake hands with you, but he will not move, because it
is contrary to the order of heaven for a just man to deceive; but he
will still deliver his message.
If it be the devil as an angel of light, when you ask him to shake
hands he will offer you his hand, and you will not feel anything;
you may therefore detect him.
These are three grand keys whereby you may know whether any
administration is from God. (D&C 129:4–9)

When the young missionaries, Elder Nielson and Elder Collins, discussed the importance of the handshake test, Elder Collins said, "So, the good spirit would be like, I cannot. I'm just here to deliver my message." He pondered the remote possibility that you would actually get a physical handshake, which would indicate a resurrected being. "And if the spirit does shake your hand, you're talking to a resurrected being, which is one in a million chance." The majority of mysterious visitors are not resurrected beings, but just ordinary spirits.

Jake's view on the handshake differed somewhat. He de-emphasized the scriptural aspect of it, and he referred to the practice as "cultural Mormonism":

So you get "cultural" Mormonism.... I remember one of the stories I heard when I was a kid was, "Well, you can tell the difference between a good spirit because somewhere in the scripture it says that Satan can appear as [a/the] spirit of light, because he's a deceiver and he can deceive you." And you can tell the difference by offering to shake their [the spirits'] hand. Because if it's a good spirit, they're somebody that's had a body, and they won't shake your hand.... But if it's a bad spirit, they wanna deceive you and say, "okay" and they'll stick their hand out and you won't be able to feel anything because they've never had the [body].

When I asked if he had ever tried the handshake method, knowing how many uncanny encounters he had, he replied, "No. I look at that as . . . you know . . . one of those Mormon folklore things." Although Jake touched on the scriptural basis for the handshake, he dismissed it as relatively insignificant by calling it "Mormon folklore." Like many others, Jake frequently differentiated between "religion" and "cultural Mormonism." In his view, "Mormon culture" sometimes lacked the true spirit of the religion. We will return to this in a later chapter.

When Brad and I discussed the discernment of spirits, he told me he had never heard of anyone actually using the handshake, but he asserted that the essential teachings in the Doctrine and Covenant were clear: "Some angels have bodies, some angels don't . . . and some angels are from the dark side." However, he contextualized the teachings as more pertinent to the concerns of members of the early church in Joseph Smith's time, and he thought that the handshake was unlikely to be used in the present.

Brad said, "I guess you *could* do the handshake. But, again, I personally have not heard any stories since that revelation where that's actually even transpired. I think you probably wouldn't even remember to do that! No, it would be so shocking! It'd be like an angel would tell you something, and how do you know if it's right or wrong?"

To Brad, it was critical to consider the historical context of this section of the Doctrine and Covenants, and he thought it much more relevant to the early days of the church. He explained that in the those times, there was a lot of confusion about such communications, and so the revelation clarified certain matters of relevance to that early community:

> And so this idea of discernment of spirits in the early part of the church, people were coming up to Joseph Smith saying, "An angel came to me, and this is what he told me," and Joseph Smith said, "Well, don't do it. That's not right. That's not right. That's not right. Where are you getting this? That's not right. It's the wrong spirit. It was a spirit from the wrong side." And so there was so much confusion. That's where this revelation came out, you know?[11]

Park (2010) has made a similar point about the early church. He considers this aspect of early Mormon history in the wider context of antebellum

---

[11] Like Brad, in our conversations Darren also emphasized the temporal importance of the Doctrine and Covenants, suggesting that certain teachings should be considered in the timeframe in which they were revealed. He described it as teachings for the "contemporary timeframe with Joseph Smith," and explained that the revelations to Smith were teachings that "he should be giving to the people there [at that time]."

America, a time in which there was much religious preoccupation with discerning spirit types. Park proposes that the emphasis on the handshake was an attempt to ground ideas about angels and otherworldly beings in a rationalistic mode of thought, where the identity of a mysterious visitor could be confirmed empirically (2010, 4).

Although the handshake method regularly came up in conversation, like Brad, I have never encountered anyone who has used (or needed to use) the method in a spirit encounter. To be sure, all those who have encountered spirits were very clear on whether their visitor was benevolent or malevolent. I never talked to anyone who had any question about whether a spirit visitor was friend or foe.

Whom Do the Spirits Visit? Righteousness and Need

Among northern Utah's Latter-day Saints, spirit visits can happen to anyone: women and men, young and old, the devout and the uncertain, the righteous and those who are struggling. I have found that Mormons in this community use two general registers to describe the likelihood of spirit encounters. One register focuses on *righteousness*, or the lack thereof. In this register, people interpret benevolent visitation as confirming the righteousness of certain individuals. Malevolent spirits are attracted to unrighteous actions or seek to thwart the exceptionally righteous. In the other register, benevolent spirits of kin visit those in need of guidance, reassurance, comfort, or even physical aid. The two registers overlap in spirit encounters that are interpreted as steering the recipient toward a path of righteousness. Although spirits may certainly visit Latter-day Saints of high spiritual standing who are active in the church, they visit those who are less active and less devout just as frequently. Brad emphasized this when he explained that benevolent spirit experiences can happen to *anyone*—one does not need to be spiritually advanced and of high rank in the church. Rather, he said, spirits come to those in need.

Righteousness

In northern Utah, Latter-day Saints frequently emphasize *righteousness* when discussing spirit encounters. Righteousness is an important cultural framework in this community and it is key to understanding how people interpret spirit encounters: benevolent spirits visit to condone or encourage righteous action, and evil spirits are attracted to both unrighteous behavior and exceptional righteousness.

But what does it mean to be "righteous"? In his now classic mid-century book, *The Mormons*, the sociologist Thomas O'Dea characterized the Book of Mormon as essentially about good and evil, and the cycle of righteousness and destruction (O'Dea 1957, 26–27). O'Dea wrote that "action" is central to "Mormon conceptions" and to the key elements of Mormon theology (1957, 151, 154) and he drew a parallel between the continual progression of God to that of the required progression of humanity, with a profound emphasis on mastery over the material world (1957, 152). And, as O'Dea demonstrates, this resonates profoundly with the Mormon emphasis on the necessity of choice and free will. He writes that "Mormonism conceives of man [sic] as free and sees him as advancing to Godhood through proper exercise of that freedom" (1957, 153).

I draw on O'Dea's framing from the 1950s because of the connection to the present-day Latter-day Saint emphasis on righteousness as "right action." In the cultural context of northern Utah, "righteousness" refers to choosing to live in accordance with the teachings of the church. Essentially, righteousness is correct action. And, from making righteous choices, spiritual advantage might flow. When I spoke with Jake, much of our initial conversation focused on the possible spiritual benefits of making the right choices. Jake explained that in his family:

> Things that would happen—good or bad—were attributed to how somebody was living their life . . . . It was understood that, okay, there's not a puppet master pulling all the strings. But, if we're living a righteous life, it's more likely that maybe, you know, more good things will happen, or conversely, some of the bad things might pass by your door . . . If you pay your tithing as an LDS person it doesn't mean money's gonna fall out of the sky, but maybe it means [that if] some sort of bad thing could happen it will help warrant some protection from it.

He offered numerous examples of the benefits of "right living." One was a story about his great-grandparents in Denmark, who were mysteriously guided to the church because they were "living the right way."

They were seeking and living a certain way, so they get this visitation from this strange man that points them in the right way [to a Mormon church], because the other street down this way is where a different religion was meeting. And they're good and wonderful, but . . . . they were trying to find the right thing and so they were given that [visitation]. If they hadn't been living the right way they still probably would have ended up over here at this one, which would have taken 'em down a good path, but they didn't get . . . the best and full path.

Jake paused, and then explained to me that in his family, this story was used to teach that spiritual guidance (like his grandparents' mysterious guide to the Mormon church) comes to those who are "living right." He said, "If you're not living right, there's no guarantee that you'll get that help. And, just because you're living right doesn't mean that nothing bad is ever going to happen. So it was framed in that way, too."

Jake explained that because he was raised to always consider the benefits of "living right," he and his wife endeavor to communicate the same to their children. However, he emphasized that right living was not some kind of foolproof plan because, ultimately, everyone will be tested. It is through this testing that people grow spiritually:

That's actually what we teach our kids. Right? You can't walk around thinking, "Well, I'm doing this and so everything good is going to fall out of the sky." . . . We're here to be tested and to grow, and to become better people. And we're trying to live up to certain ways and expectations. And if we're doing those things, then . . . we do have the right to some help if it's needed. But if the man upstairs is pulling all the strings, what growth is there? It's like a helicopter parent. Your child doesn't have growth if you're a helicopter parent, right? Or the growth is maybe not sufficient. So we are put here [on earth] and we will have experiences and we may miss out on some experiences if we're not prepared for them spiritually.

Several months after this conversation, I reached out to Jake again, asking him to elaborate on the relationship between righteousness and morality. He explained by echoing the themes from our first conversation about the importance of right living: "Morals are a belief, but righteousness is more of a verb. Morality is more a descriptor. Righteousness is a way of living, of acting on your morals."

Although this book focuses on how Latter-day Saints in northern Utah understand righteousness, it is important to emphasize the commonalities across Mormon communities in the understanding that right action leads to reward. For example, in her research in a Latter-day Saint community in the United Kingdom, the anthropologist Hildi Mitchell comments on the necessity of right action. She connects action to the notion of spiritual progress that is key to Mormon ideas of salvation, writing "spiritual salvation depends on earthly action" (2001, 162). She proposes that "Mormon theology and ancient history combine, since the Book of Mormon is officially held to be an historical document. Together, they *set up a moral code grounded in worldly action*, which mirrors and supports the importance of earthly activity—both ritual and economic—in the process of eternal progression" (2001, 175, emphasis added). Although Mitchell does not explore spirit experiences, she connects this right action in a broad sense to interactions with the spirit realm, and she explains that Mormons are participating in "a moral economy in which spirits, mortals, and gods all play their part" (2001a, 162). To illustrate, Mitchell focuses on proper economic life as essential to the Plan of Salvation:

> Mormon economics is at a basic level a moral economy . . . Any debates about the correct use of economic means share the basic assumption that humanity may progress towards Godhood through righteous living in a material world. Debates about what constitutes righteous living in terms of this material world are debates about morality, which are informed by the cultural template offered by Mormon cosmology. (2001a, 182)

Here, Mitchell equates debates about righteous living with debates about "morality." However, as I will explore in Chapter 5, Latter-day Saints in northern Utah differentiate between what is "righteous" and what is "moral." "Righteous" is the broader term, encompassing all kinds of proper action; the term "worthy" is also often used to refer to a righteous person or righteous behavior. What is "moral," on the other hand, is understood more narrowly, and typically refers to sexual chastity and sexual propriety. A person described as immoral or having "moral problems" is usually understood as someone who is engaging in illicit sexual activity.

Spiritual progress thus depends on making the right choices. The first choice was in the pre-existence, when spirits chose to follow either Christ or Lucifer. For those who followed Christ, numerous choices follow in the realm of the living, and these are frequently framed as "tests." And, as we will see in the next two chapters, spirit beings may visit to guide the living to make the right choices. Like Jake, many others I spoke with consistently emphasized choice and individual determination in living righteously. Jake noted that God is not a "puppet master" pulling the strings. Rather, people have agency, and must choose how they are going to live. One of the benefits that might result from righteous living is a greater chance of having a meaningful spiritual experience.

Elder Neilson and Elder Collins, the young missionaries, similarly emphasized the importance of right action when I asked if there was anything a person could do to encourage the visit of benevolent spirits. Elder Neilson explained, "With good spirits, you can't control that [their appearance]. You can put yourself in a lifestyle that makes it more likely to happen and that is [by] living righteously. But other than that, you can't control it."

Similarly, Shauna said that as a child she associated spirit visitations with righteousness. "I was super afraid of the evil spirits, but really wanted to meet a good spirit and just feel like.... you know, like I was a *good enough person* to have a personal witness.... Like if you were *spiritual* enough that things could [happen]."

Shauna explained that her older brothers were "bad dudes" who drank and smoked: "And so I kind of went the other way and kind of became extra righteous."

When I asked her to elaborate, she said: "I would try to do everything right. You know, if they said, 'You can't be alone with a boy,' I would make sure I was never, ever, *ever* alone with a boy.... I just did everything I could. You know, praying and reading my scriptures and, um, I just was pretty devout. Or, I tried to be.... and I think I was very obedient almost out of... um... superstition."

Shauna's use of the term "spiritual"—"if you were spiritual enough things could happen"—is indicative of the way many Utah Mormons use the term. The term "spiritual" generally refers to piety and religiosity, and it is often is used as a way to talk about these qualities in other Mormons, particularly in terms of their outward actions. The term "spiritual" commonly describes someone with qualities of piety, devotion, and a strong "testimony," which is the term used for public statements of belief in the teachings of the church.

Jeannette, a married mother who holds a graduate degree, connected righteousness, right action, and obedience. She explained that in the cultural framework of the church, the blessings that come from righteousness are "predicated on obedience." One of our first conversations about this project was in 2018. Like Shauna, she explained that, when she was young, she "wanted to have something happen to confirm her righteousness," but never had such a spiritual experience.

A few years later, in 2021, Jeannette and I discussed righteousness again. At this point, she and her husband had formally left the church and moved away from Utah. Her comments reflected her dissatisfaction with the church. She explained that now she had a different understanding of what it means to be righteous. However, she also talked about what she thought it meant in her life in the church. As in our previous interview, she emphasized that righteousness is about action, but this time she described it more negatively, as "marking off all of the boxes."

In this conversation, Jeannette tied the necessity of right action directly to ideas of salvation and to anxiety about salvation. Her comments reflected some of the reasons she had left the church. "It's not about who you really are. It is what you do. Absolutely. You have to earn your value in the Mormon church. And it's by checking off all the boxes, and they keep you needing them. Because you never can do enough . . . . You're earning your way back to heaven."

As an example, Jeannette shared memories of her baptism. Like most Mormons, she was baptized through full immersion when she was eight years old. Latter-day Saints consider eight years to be "age of accountability," when children are able to determine right from wrong. She questioned whether a child of eight can actually think critically about wanting the baptism. She recalled that her own baptism had been a difficult day for her. She remembered that right after her baptism, she and her sister had an argument in the car, someone's hair was pulled, and Jeannette screamed at her sister. She recalled her parents telling her she was no longer perfect, and she remember thinking that the baptism washed her sins away only for a few minutes! She remembered thinking that just a few minutes after the baptism, she was again in jeopardy of not going to heaven. Jeannette used this to emphasize the necessity of righteous action: "And that's why there's a lot of working and working and working. Trying to save yourself."

The anthropologist and theologian Douglas Davies has remarked on the theological difference between Mormons and other Christians in ideas of salvation: in Mormon understanding, the notion of grace is different in that it is, ultimately, dependent on correct action. In the following, Davies refers to *exaltation*, which is the ultimate goal of Latter-day Saints and might be understood as the culmination of salvation—in which the spirit becomes perfected, like God, and through which humans can essentially *become* like gods (this will be discussed further in Chapter 4):

> Exaltation, as the foundational Mormon process of salvation, operates on a grammar of theological discourse that differs from that of most mainstream Christian groups. For historical and textual reasons Mormonism still possesses a language of grace, but it operates in a ritual system that largely supports a different kind of rationale of human experience, expectation, and behaviour. (Davies 2000, 65)

Davies does not use the term righteousness, but he describes *holiness* in a way that is very similar to the way northern Utah Mormons use righteousness, as "the ethically active side of the philosophical notion of truth" (2001, 33). Similarly, O'Dea wrote many years ago that "Mormonism has elaborated an American theology of self-deification through effort, an active transcendentalism of achievement" (1957, 154).

Those in Need

Profound spiritual experience is not simply the reward of the righteous, and there is another common register for understanding spirit experiences. In this register, benevolent spirits come to those in need—regardless of their righteous worth. At the beginning of my first conversation with Brad, I asked him about the prevalence of visits from the spirits of ancestors. He nodded eagerly, chuckled knowingly, and then reflected on just how common such visitations are. He told me that he did not think spirits were just dropping in to say, "Hi, how's it going?" Rather, he said, benevolent spirits visit to *provide aid when it is needed*. In this register, spirits do not attend to the most obedient, the most pious, or the most spiritual. Rather, they appear to offer succor to the distressed and guide the imprudent back to the path of righteousness.

An excellent example of benevolent ministration to the needy comes from a well-known story about angels assisting nineteenth-century Mormon pioneers with their handcarts on their long trek to the Salt Lake Valley.[12]

---

[12] The story is very popular, and it was dramatized in a 2011 movie produced by the church called *17 Miracles*.

There are many familiar versions of the tale in Cache Valley, and narratives re-telling the event abound in the student folklore collection at Utah State University. In one account, a student writes that her father told the story when their family was on the Martin-Willie handcart trek—an event in which families and groups can recreate the experience of the pioneers. The student writes:

> Jane was pregnant and it was starting to get colder every day. Each day brought new struggles and freezing temperatures. Jane's husband was stricken with illness as they were reaching the hardest part of their journey. They were almost to Rocky Ridge and she didn't know how she could carry on. Her husband wasn't able to pull the cart any further, so she put him in the cart and started to pull. She carried on as best she could and then she reached Rocky Ridge. As she started up the rugged terrain she felt her burden become lighter as if people were helping her push the cart along. When she reached the top of the ridge she looked back to see that no one was there. (Bevan 2011)

Like many contributors to the student folklore collection, Bevan adds a section to submission called "texture," in which she gives context for the narrative. She writes:

> As my father told this story, he got choked up about the thought of this woman having to go through what she did. In each story my father's admiration for these pioneers grew, as he continued to tell this particular story, he made it clear that he knew she wasn't really alone. But that the angels were watching from above and helping when they could. (Bevan 2011)

One summer afternoon in 2018, my graduate student Katryn Davis and I were chatting with Mrs. Williams, the great-aunt of an old friend. The charming and gregarious lady lived in an attractive neighborhood in a small town in the southern end of the valley. Katryn and I remarked upon a large, framed print displayed in her tidy, cheerful living room. The original painting, called "When the Angels Come" is by the artist Clark Kelley Price, and depicts the handcart story (see Figure 2.1). I asked Mrs. Williams about the painting, and she talked about the angels helping the pioneers. She said, "I was always taught—and I remember primary lessons teaching this—I was always taught that angels didn't have wings."

THE REALM OF THE SPIRITS 43

Figure 2.1 When the Angels Come. Painting by Clark Kelly Price, used with permission.

I asked her what she meant, and she said, "No they don't have wings, they're people."

"Does that mean angels and spirits are the same?" I asked.

Mrs. Williams answer, "Yes!" She laughed as she told us, "When I see a Christmas pageant and they have angels out there, they're winged! You know, that's not right, they don't have wings!"

Reflecting on the possibility of spirits visiting with aid and assistance, I once asked Lyne, who has had a number of benevolent spirit experiences, if there was anything one could do to encourage such a visit. Lyne replied that perhaps this was possible, but that it would certainly depend on what you *needed*. She explained:

> I would think you could always pray and say, you know, "Hey, could you give me an experience here or there? I would like one." I don't know when they'll come, but the other night I prayed, "Heavenly Father, oh my gosh, please give me something, because I'm just feeling, there's so much going on!" What He gave me was not what I wanted.

Lyne told me that this prayer was at a time of transition for her. A lot was going on in her life. She was contemplating a move, and one of her children had been struggling with the challenges of adolescence. She told me that God answered her prayer, but in a way she did not expect. Instead of a visit from her deceased mother, which she had hoped for, she received divine communication about her teenager:

> I wanted my mom to come sit on my bed and say "everything is fine," but what He just told me was—what I got was just to warn that while [my teen] teeters, say, he has more availability to influence so just to really watch out for it. So, I told him [about this message]. And my kids are always really open to what I say because they know I don't make it up. Then I thought, well, [Heavenly Father] did give me something and it wasn't what I expected or wanted but something did come.

I thought about this for a bit, then asked Lyne if she understood this communication as a case of praying for one kind guidance but receiving another.

She affirmed, saying, "I wanted something that would make me feel better about moving, but God for some reason decided that's not what I needed, but He was willing to tell me that [my teenager] needed to kind of be careful right now. So, He still answered me, but answered me in a way that *He* knew was most beneficial, not in the way that *I* wanted or thought was beneficial to me."

In this case, Lyne prayed to God hoping for the reassurance of a spirit messenger—her mother—but got a message directly from God about her teen. When I asked if it would be possible to pray to an intermediary like a spirit or angel, she replied, "Well, no, we are told to pray to God, our Father in Heaven. However, there's no reason not to ask Him that your mom would come and be with you for the day or that you can ask for inspiration from them."

Thus, while it may not be appropriate to pray directly to a spirit or any being other than God, one could certainly ask God—like Lyne did—to send a spirit. However, God may not answer one's prayer in the expected way. In reflecting on her many spiritual experiences, Lyne said that, ultimately, they were the reason she decided to stay active in the church, even when faced with frustrations with her ward[13] and the broader institutional body.

---

[13] A "ward" is a geographic unit that attends church together, something like a congregation or a parish; it is usually based on location, community, and neighborhood, and it is presided over by a "bishop," an important calling for men in the community. Mormons in northern Utah nearly always

Andrea, a primary school teacher, expressed a similar sentiment about spirits responding to those in need. However, she told me that when she was younger, she had had a different view, and she had suspected that sharing spirit experiences was something of a competition.

She explained, "Well... like people who have those things happen to them. It almost felt like they in some way were more spiritual or were more worthy to receive those kinds of things and those kinds of experiences."

She continued, explaining that her views had changed:

> But as I've gotten older, I realize maybe they [spirits] just come to people who need them and I'm good.... I don't know why they happen to some people and why they don't to others. Yeah, but I don't think that Heavenly Father picks someone and says, "You're my chosen one and so I'm going to give you this experience." You know, I don't think that happens. Honestly, sometimes people are way more in tune than others and since my mom died I have wished to feel her.... I know that she's there I know that she can see me, she can hear me. She's right here you know with us when we need her, and I don't think that I need to see her or hear her to know that she's here.

Spiritual Progress and Spirit Prison

A person's righteous worth during their mortal life impacts what happens after death, and the road to salvation necessarily passes through the spirit realm. Latter-day Saint teachings on the afterlife are complex, and there are different types and levels, which we will explore in the next few chapters. Here, it will suffice to note that the spirit realm after death is an active place. Not only do spirits interact at times with the living, but spirits of the postmortal also engage with and assist each other with spiritual progress. An excellent example of this is in understandings of *spirit prison*, where the spirits of the righteous may be engaged in teaching the unrighteous and leading them toward the goal of eternal life.

When Katryn and I talked with Mrs. Williams, she reflected on her late husband's activities in the spirit realm. She told us what a good man he had

---

attend church in their "ward"—meaning where they live—unless they are attending a special ward for single, unmarried adults, known as a "singles ward."

been, and she reflected on the time they spent as missionaries in the United Kingdom. She was certain he was busy teaching spirits in the spirit world.

"My husband was a missionary," she said, "I see him up there with my brother-in-law. They're teaching the spirits in the spirit world right now. The scriptures tell us that."

Mrs. Williams explained that a righteous person would be likely to have such duties in the spirit world. "If they're righteous—and he *was*—he's teaching people in the spirit world right now to help prepare them."

I asked her if the righteous spirits were preparing others for the resurrection. She answered, "Yes, the resurrection, millennium, all that!"

I remarked on how interesting it was that someone who did not live a good life in this world could improve spiritually in the next, and I asked Mrs. Williams to tell me more about what happens to the spirit after death. Mrs. Williams explained, "Well, we go to paradise. The righteous go to paradise and then the unrighteous go to —." She cut herself off and laughed. When she continued, she said that the unrighteous also go to the spirit world. "But they're taught," she said. "The scriptures tell us that they are taught the Gospel." She continued:

> There are good righteous people on the earth today that have never been taught about our Father in Heaven Jesus Christ. It's hard to believe that but it really is. My husband and I were teaching a gentleman in England, he was a fine man. You thought he was a president or a bishop. You know just dressed clean and neat. And as I told him [about the spirit world] he looked at me and says, "You really believe this, don't you?" Yes, it's true. And he says, "Why isn't my pastor teaching me things like this?" He says, "He never tells me any stuff like this." We were teaching him about the apostasy and how when the Gospel was restored to the earth, you know, and now we do have a prophet here on the earth, just like the apostles [did], just like it used to be. And then I think he got really interested. He said, "You know what? I could never join the Mormon church." I said, "Why?" And he says, "Because it's only six of us in my church and I play the organ." And I thought, "Well, I guess you're not quite converted yet!"

I also discussed spirit prison with Elder Neilson and Elder Collins. Like Mrs. Williams, they were patient and responsive, and took the time to make sure I understood. Elder Neilson explained, "We believe that after we die there is the spirit world and the spirit world has two states. That is, spiritual paradise and spiritual prison. Spiritual paradise is for those who have faith in Jesus Christ, have repented and have been baptized by proper priests of authority. And they have to continue to endure and obey the commandments of God."

Elder Collins noted that spirit prison is addressed in the Doctrine and Covenants (138), and then explained in his own words:

> I'll just give you an overview. He [Joseph Smith] says that he saw Jesus Christ talking to, basically, like messengers, because Jesus Christ could not go and visit the people in spirit prison because they were filthy. They had, you know, sinned. And Jesus Christ was perfect. So, and there's people in the spirit world that he could go and visit, not saying that they were perfect, but that they were righteous and followed the Gospel. And he told those people to go and teach the people in the spirit prison.

The two young men told me that the teachers in spirit prison could be the prophets of the Old Testament, the apostles from the New Testament, or even the spirits of regular people.

I asked, "Like Grandpa?"

"Yeah," Elder Neilson said. "And, like, these people—these spirits—they go into spirit prison and they teach the Gospel to those who either rebelled against God or never knew about Jesus Christ and his life."

The missionaries explained that teaching in spirit prison is intimately connected with salvation. If a spirit accepts the teachings in spirit prison, then they are open to accepting posthumous proxy baptism and the other necessary *ordinances*—the Latter-day Saint term for mandatory or preferred ritual actions—that are performed by the living in the temple. These ritual activities on behalf of the dead make up the body of what is commonly referred to as "temple work," and is the subject of Chapter 4.

I asked the missionaries about how this worked. "So, then you're baptizing," I asked. "I mean, you're being baptized by proxy for somebody who never received the scripture or the Gospels in this life. And so they would be technically in the spirit prison. Is that correct?"

Elder Collins assured me that this was correct, and that if the spirit in prison accepted baptism after the teachings, they would move to paradise. Elder Neilson agreed with Elder Collins's explanation, and he referred me to a section of the New Testament, 1 Peter 3:19, noting that Latter-day Saints take it quite literally. Elder Neilson read the verse aloud, "By which also he went and preached unto the spirits in prison." He then read from the

Doctrine and Covenants, which explains that Joseph F. Smith, the nephew of the prophet Joseph Smith, had a vision of Jesus Christ's visit to the place between crucifixion and resurrection (D&C 138:16) and his appointment of messengers to teach these spirits. He noted that the following verses this section also reference the vicarious baptism of the dead. Elder Neilson read the following verses aloud:

> Thus, was the gospel preached to those who had died of their sins without knowledge of the truth or in transgression having rejected the prophets. These were taught faith in God, repentance from sin, vicarious Baptism for the remission of sins, the gift of the Holy Ghost by the laying on of hands. And all other principles of the gospel that were necessary for them to know, in order to qualify themselves that they might be judged according to men of the flash and according to God in the spirit. (D&C 138:32–34)

Elder Neilson paused after reading, so we could reflect on the words. When he continued, he explained that these verses show that, "In this life, it is required for us to have ordinances and ordinances are promises or covenants that we make with our Heavenly Father. It's a physical action to show that we want to follow Christ."

We talked a bit more about spirit prison. Elder Collins told me that, "We believe that sprit prison is a place for two kinds of people. People who have rebelled against our Heavenly Father and choose not to follow him. And people who do not yet know about God and about Jesus Christ. Such as people in Africa or China who were never taught about the Gospel. Who never knew about Jesus Christ."

When Lyne and I talked about spirit prison, she took care to differentiate her views on religious teachings from what some other Mormons thought. She said, "Well, some people think if you haven't joined the Gospel then you're going to spirit prison. That's not true. I think people that haven't proven themselves very worthy, I guess [go to spirit prison]. Spirit prison is a place where you're taught."

As usual, Lyne had an intellectual take on matters of the spirit realm. She explained that the term "prison" was metaphorical, and simply referred to the bounded nature of the spirits' existence—it was not that the imprisoned spirits were inherently bad, just that they did not enjoy the freedom of other spirits to be able to go on what she called "God's errands." She said, "I don't think that it says it is because they are bad and that's why they're there [in prison]. It's that they are bound to the spot they're at because they're *learning*, but they're not free for the errands. That doesn't mean they won't be [eventually free for errands]."

With this comment about the future availability for God's errands, Lyne strongly emphasized the possibility of spiritual progress. Her view of a spirit prison is as a way station, of sorts, where some spirits must pause for a period of growth that enables them to progress spiritually.

Like Lyne, Andrea connected spirit prison with spiritual progress. She said that she sometimes felt the presence of her deceased mother, and she reflected that her mother could visit her as a spirit because she had been a good person.

However, she explained, if someone had lived a bad life, their spirit would not be able to visit the living, "So, when the body dies the spirit still exists and it's still there and then they go to the spirit world or spirit prison. In spirit prison they have a chance to repent and make up for what they've done; people can go from the spirit world to the spirit prison to teach and they help the people in spirit prison."

Andrea's comments illustrate a spirit world full of interaction and activity. Those who lived unrighteous lives might be doomed to spirit prison, where they will, hopefully, make progress as they are taught the gospel. Those who lived righteous lives might have the responsibility of teaching and guiding those in spirit prison. As per teachings in the Doctrine and Covenants, spirit prison is temporary, and repentance is possible: "And so it was made known among the dead, both small and great, the unrighteous as well as the faithful, that redemption had been wrought through the sacrifice of the Son of God upon the cross" (138:35).

Conclusion

As noted at the beginning of this chapter, the first time I talked with Brad, he told me that, in his view, spirit encounters are the *heart of religion* for contemporary Latter-day Saints. This chapter has aimed to set the stage for an intimate examination of both positive and negative spirit encounters in the chapters that follow. Throughout this book, we will see that spirit visitations are not interpreted as random or arbitrary for Latter-day Saints in this community. Rather, encounters are loaded with meaning, and the visits of both benevolent and malevolent spirits are understood in the broader context of Latter-day Saint cosmology. For the recipients of such visits, spirit encounters of all kinds confirm the essential teachings of the church. In all my conversations, it is clear that people understand benevolent spirits with reference to essential teachings about the eternal family and spiritual progression toward this goal. Malevolent spirits are understood vis-à-vis church teachings about the War in Heaven in the pre-existence, and the decision some spirits made to follow Lucifer. As Brad posited, these encounters are truly at the heart of the religion.

3
Spirits, the Eternal Family, and Collective Ethical Responsibility

I interviewed the two young missionaries, Elder Collins and Elder Neilson, one afternoon in early summer 2018. We met at a church building, sometimes called a ward house or a meetinghouse, in a small town nestled against the Bear River Range on the eastern side of the valley. I remember the day well. My mother had taken my children to a nearby park, and the sky was cloudless and brilliantly blue, and the valley was still green from spring rains. I had asked the missionaries if we could meet to talk about the spirit world, and their mission leader gave them permission. Elder Neilson and Elder Collins were friendly and eager to talk. They were both nineteen years old, with bright blond hair and ruddy complexions. They could have been brothers. At the beginning of our conversation, Elder Neilson told me that, "We usually don't talk about spiritual experiences, but we do acknowledge that they happen. We believe that certain spirits have been given permission by Heavenly Father or other leaders in the spirit world to have interactions with people in the physical world."[1]

Most spirit experiences among Latter-day Saints in northern Utah involve positive interactions with the spirits of helpful kin—those of the deceased and those not yet born. This chapter examines experiences with close kin, such as parents, grandparents, and future children, and the next chapter considers visits from more distant kin. The spirits of kin are nearly always benevolent, and they appear in human form and are thus identifiable as particular individuals. They always visit for a reason. The spirits of the deceased offer comfort and reassurance, impart useful knowledge, and even intervene in perilous situations. The spirits of future children are often prescient, providing reassurance about fecundity or implicitly guiding their future parents

---

[1] Some material from this chapter appears in an article I recently published in *JRAI: Journal of the Royal Anthropological Institute*, in which I situate these spirit encounters in recent debates on individualism and relationalism in the anthropology of Christianity (Stiles 2023).

along a moral path. Frequently, spirit children ask to be born into an earthly family (see also Brady 1987; Eliason 2014).[2]

The spirit visits show that the Latter-day Saint theological notion of the eternal family is not simply abstract or something to imagine and long for in the afterlife. It is certainly these things, but the eternal family is also active in the world of the living. The living and the spirits co-exist in a relationship of *mutual ethical responsibility* centered on assisting one another with spiritual progress. These spirits respond to those in need, and they offer encouragement and advice about living life in accordance with an ideal Latter-day Saint framework. For the living, the spirits of the deceased mediate between life *as it is* and life *as it should be*, and thus help to guide their living kin on a path of righteousness (Stiles and Davis 2018). The accounts discussed in this chapter show that anthropological understandings of kinship that foreground mutual ethical responsibility, as in Sahlins's conception of kinship as *mutuality of being* (Sahlins 2013), can be enhanced by including a consideration of spirit kin. Drawing on Rupert Stasch (2009), Sahlins has asked us to consider a kinship system to be "a manifold of intersubjective participations, which is also to say, a network of mutualities of being" (2013, 20).[3]

The spirit experiences discussed in this chapter show that the mutual, collective responsibility for kin that is such an important part of the Latter-day Saint framework, and has been addressed by the anthropologist Fenella Cannell in much of her research on Mormonism (Cannell 2017, 2013a, 2013b), includes responsibility to *all* kin—spirit kin as well as living kin. For Mormons in northern Utah, these spirit experiences provide evidence of the reality of the eternal family and the connections and responsibility between living and non-living members of that family. As noted in the previous chapter, the benevolent spirit visits described in this book are bound up in Mormon theological ideas about the eternality of the family, and in this chapter, I aim to show how the Latter-day Saint understanding of kinship that extends beyond the earthly realm becomes manifest in everyday experiences of the spirit realm. There is a great deal of anthropological research that describes the significance of ancestral spirits in different contexts and how they interact with their living descendants, and most of

---

[2] The folklorist Eric A. Eliason has examined memorates telling of encounters with spirit children and used the folklore term PBEs, or Pre-Birth Experiences (Eliason 2014). I do not use the term PBE, however, as it is not an emic term that project participants use.

[3] In a recent article, I address this issue with greater engagement with anthropological work on both Christianity and kinship (Stiles 2023).

this literature focuses on non-Western contexts. What seems particularly interesting about Mormon spirit experiences is, first, that they constitute a case study from the wealthy, industrialized Global North, and second, that the interactions between familial spirits and the living involves both ascendants and *future* descendants of the living. These relationships are ones of mutual aid and mutual ethical responsibility.

Cannell has argued that one of the distinctive aspects of Mormonism in the broader Christian tradition is an emphasis on "collective salvation"—salvation depends not on the individual alone, which she notes is comparable to early thinking among Puritans and in nineteenth-century American Christian thought (Cannell 2017, 154). Cannell argues against a too narrow view of what Christianity "is" that overstresses the individual (cf. Robbins 2004). Indeed, she draws attention to intriguing imperatives in Mormonism of both free agency/individual responsibility and the necessity of helping others achieve salvation (Cannell 2017, 165). Cannell finds that this possibility of collective salvation is one of the things that attracts converts to Mormonism, and she draws attention to the standard set of teachings (formerly called "discussions" and now called "lessons") that missionaries offer to potential converts (known as "investigators") that frequently begin with an emphasis on the eternal nature of the family (Cannell 2017). It is important to note that Latter-day Saints differentiate between *salvation* and *exaltation*. The latter might be understood as the culmination of salvation—the possible perfectibility of the spirit in becoming like God in eternal life.[4] And it is exaltation that relies so much on mutual responsibility. Considering this, throughout this book I strive to be clear when the specific goal is exaltation and eternal life, and so I use those terms more frequently than the somewhat muddier term "salvation."

The spirit visits described in this chapter show how, and how frequently, the cosmological idea of an "extended" eternal family plays out in the lives in the living. The spirits of deceased members of the family offer aid, comfort, reassurance, and guidance to the living, thus encouraging them along their path to religious fulfillment in the Plan of Salvation. In turn, the living offer aid to the spirits by providing the spirits with earthly bodies and performing ordinances on their behalf, which is the subject of the next chapter. Benevolent familial spirits are thus instrumental in mediating between the

---

[4] I would like to thank the anthropologist Adam Dunstan for discussing salvation and exaltation with me and for encouraging me to differentiate them clearly in my work.

living and the divine; the creation and fostering of the mutual moral community extends to the denizens of the spirit realm.

Benevolent Spirits and the Economy of Heaven

One afternoon I visited with Andrea, the elementary school teacher, and her father, Mr. Anderson, who was in his eighties at the time but has since passed away. Andrea and her father were eager to help me with my project. We met at Mr. Anderson's house in the southern part of Cache Valley, which was just a few blocks from Andrea's home. We talked about spirit visits, and Andrea shared her perspectives and her family's experiences with me. I asked them how one differentiates between experiences of the Holy Ghost and those encounters with individual spirits. Andrea's response illuminates the significance of the continuity of family love and care both in the pre-existence and after death.

> Sometimes the way I feel about it [spiritual experiences] is that it *is* the Holy Ghost. But then other times, I think that our family members who passed on before us are able to sort of— . . . you know, when I say these things out loud I'm like "Wait! Am I really saying this?!" because it sort of sounds corny and made up—but that family members who have gone before us can be used as kind of guardian angels to kind of lead us and help us to know what to do.

She shared an example from her own experience. At the age of three, Andrea ran into the street and was hit by a car. She was badly injured, and she was in the hospital recovering for over a month. When she was growing up, Andrea's mother had frequently told her about the accident and her time in the hospital.

Andrea explained, "My mom said she spent a lot of time in the emergency room praying to her dad who had passed away earlier that year in March, and she just she felt like his arm was around her. That her dad was there with her."

Recall from Chapter 2 that Brad, the high school seminary teacher, called the possibility of visits from kin spirits to be truly "the heart" of religion in practice for Mormons. However, he noted, the spirits do not just show up to offer casual greetings. Rather, they show up for a purpose—like Andrea's grandfather visiting his distressed daughter.

When I asked Brad why spirit visitations were nearly always from kin, he introduced me to the idea of the economy of heaven, which he attributed to Elder Jeffrey Holland. Why, he asked me, would God send an angel when a mother will do? He first used the phrase "economy of heaven" when we were talking about the likelihood of having a profound spiritual experience. As I did with several other people, as discussed in Chapter 2, I had asked Brad if there was anything one could do to encourage such a visit, and he reasoned that there probably was not, and questioned whether or not it was even appropriate to pray for angelic ministration in the form of a spirit visit. However, he capitulated that certainly God sends spirits, and that it made a great deal of sense for God to send someone close to the recipient of the visit:

> So let's just say God wanted to communicate something to you, right? Is he gonna just choose some random person up in heaven? Or doesn't it sound more reasonable that Grandpa Stiles would come down? Because there's a connection. There's a love, there's a concern, there's an interest. Yes, there's a family interest there. And so I think that most of the time that I hear these stories, it seems like it's familial. Its family connected, somebody passes away, they come back to them with a message.

Brad thus emphasizes the mediatory powers of the spirits, sent to those who need intervention by a God concerned with both efficiency and efficacy; hence, sending a family member is an "economic" heavenly choice.

Similarly, Andrea explained that she thought her grandfather, who had passed away right before the accident that landed her in the hospital, had been permitted to remain on earth to comfort his daughter in her time of need. Andrea believed that because her grandfather "hadn't been gone from Earth very long," he was allowed to be there to comfort his daughter—her mother was scared to death, and in Andrea's words, "she needed her dad and he was allowed to be there for her."

Spirits certainly visit to bring comfort, but they also appear with guidance and direction, and stories about such visits make up much of the "cultural kindling" (Cassaniti and Luhrmann 2014) of northern Utah. One narrative in the Utah State University Fife folklore collection relates a well-known tale that the writer heard in church. The story tells of a grandmother and her "smart little grandson" of only eighteen months old. The grandmother was looking at family pictures, and came across a photo of her deceased father, who had died many years before. The little boy pointed at it and exclaimed that he knew the man in the picture. The boy explained, "That is my other grandpa. He brought me first to Mommy and Daddy and he said he would also come and take me back some day" (Morris 1983). The writer relates that the grandmother "was sure her father had befriended and guided the spirit of her grandson to his earthly destination and would be there to greet him when he left this mortal life" (Morris 1983).

Grandparents and parents figure prominently in positive spirit visitations. Jake, introduced in the last chapter, shared a number of his family's spirit visits with me. The college essay that led me to get in touch with him related one of his grandfather's spirit experiences. Jake wrote:

> He [the grandfather] fell asleep [at the wheel of his truck] and says he remembers seeing his mother standing in front of the truck waving him over. When he woke up he was pulling on the wheel in the same direction his mother had been waving. He pulled over and got out and checked his tracks, and found out he was about a foot from going over the edge of the road. If that had happened the truck would have rolled quite a ways and probably killed them both. He felt like he was preserved for some reason.

In the same folder in the folklore collection, a friend of Jake's wrote about a similar event, but featured Jake as the driver and his grandpa as the helpful spirit:

> One night, driving home from his girlfriend's house, Jake found himself nodding off at the wheel, and had to remind himself of those repulsive films from driver's ed, like 'Death on the Highway,' . . . to keep himself awake. It didn't do any good . . . . His eyes were only closed for a split second because in that split second Jake saw his grandpa standing in the middle of the road. Waking with a start he looked up and found himself only inches from the edge of the road and a 10-foot ditch filled with water. After the initial shock of nearly rolling his car, a sudden realization caused him to shake uncontrollably—his grandpa had only recently passed away. (Maughan 1990)

When Jake and I met to talk a few days after I read these accounts, I asked about the stories of the truck—which story actually happened? Jake laughed and told me that his friend had the story wrong, and that his own version was correct: the encounter with the spirit while driving had happened to his grandfather—not to Jake himself. My goal in asking, of course, was not to ascertain who was right and who was wrong in relating the experience of the spirit guide. What I find significant about these tales is, first, that the two related accounts are an excellent example of how spirit experiences are shared and thus become an important part of local folklore. Clearly, Jake and his friend had discussed the incident, and his friend recollected it, if in a somewhat altered fashion, when asked to write about experiences of the uncanny in a college folklore class. Second, it is significant that both versions of the story illustrate the mediating ability of the spirits of the deceased to assist their living descendants and potentially protect them from physical harm.

Although Jake did not fall asleep at the wheel of his truck, he has had a number of spirit encounters himself. The first experience Jake described was a visit from the spirit of his grandfather when he was preparing for his mission at the Missionary Training Center (MTC) in Provo inn the early 1990s. whUntil 2012, young men served missions starting at age nineteen and young women served at the age of twenty-one; today, young men can serve at age eighteen and women at age nineteen. Like most young Mormon men in Cache Valley of his age, Jake submitted his mission paperwork around his nineteenth birthday. A few weeks later, he received a "call" placing him in a mission in the United Kingdom. Upon receiving the call, which can be very exciting, arrangements begin to be made and most missionaries spend several weeks at an MTC preparing for the mission. Before departing for the MTC, most missionaries will have a "farewell"—a special Sunday sacrament meeting in their ward at which the departing missionary and his or her family members give talks, and it may be followed by a lunch or other social gathering. Friends and family are invited; even as a non-Mormon, I have attended farewells. Jake's grandfather had been unwell at the time of his farewell, but, he still spoke lucidly and movingly at the service; the two were very close. Unfortunately, the elderly man's health did not improve and Jake told me that once his family assured him that Jake was safe at the MTC, his grandfather passed away. He died on Christmas Eve, only one day after Jake arrived at the MTC. Jake told me that he was consumed with grief and doubted whether he should go on the mission. That very night, his grandfather's spirit appeared.

Jake explained, "The same night after I heard he'd died . . . I'm in my bed . . . and my grandfather came, and he sat on the edge of the bed, and he said to me . . . 'Do what you need to do. Don't worry about me.'"

The day had been difficult. Jake had been permitted to call home, and he told his father he "just couldn't do it" and that he wanted his father to come get him so he could go home. He told me:

And my dad said, "If you want to come home, you're going to have to walk." He said, "because you know what, life is hard. And you gotta do hard things." ... And my dad's not a man of many words, but he's just direct and simple ... and he said, "You're thinking about yourself, and you're worrying about yourself." He said, "Think and worry about the other things you need to do, there's people where you're goin' that you're supposed to find and teach."

His father's words did not convince him. Jake spent the night praying for comfort and guidance, and then the spirit appeared:

So, anyway, later that night, you know, I'm praying for some comfort ... what should I do? I really feel like I should go home ... I'm not cut out for this, and then that's what happened [the spirit visit] .... You can look at it different ways, it's your subconscious telling you what dad told ya .... I *want* to look at it as, you know, "grandpa knew," and we were tight. Because that's how real it was. 'Cause I dream a lot of dreams and not many of them are that real.

Jake remembered that he had wondered whether he was awake or asleep when the spirit came, but eventually he determined that it did not matter. Either way, it was a profound spiritual experience in the form of a communication from his grandfather, and it convinced him to go on the mission.

Jake's conclusion that his waking state was insignificant is important. It illustrates the common perception in northern Utah that spirit visits can happen in many ways. As noted in an earlier chapter, throughout this book I do not make much of the difference between visits in dreams or waking because my research participants do not think this is of significance. For most, a spirit visit is a spirit visit whether it happens when one is awake or asleep.

A similarly moving account comes from Lyne, whom I have also known since we were young. Like Jake, Lyne is a highly educated working professional and a parent. We have talked numerous times about the project, and she generously shared her own experiences with the spirit of her mother, who passed away many years ago. Lyne seems particularly attuned to the presence of spirits. In 2019, while working on this project, I lost my own father after a prolonged illness. A few months after his death, when I told Lyne that I had not had any real sense of his spiritual presence, she expressed sympathy and said that she could teach me to become more aware of the presence of spirits. Her comment indicates an understanding that a sensitivity to spirits is something that can be learned, and is very much in keeping with anthropological arguments about receptivity to uncanny experiences in different cultural contexts (see, for example, Cassaniti and Luhrmann 2014).

Lyne's experiences are remarkable. In an excerpt from my fieldnotes below, I wrote about a conversation we had in 2018 when we were catching up over lunch at a café by the Logan River. I had already told her about my research, and I knew she was interested in it, and she shared the following experience with me. I wrote:

> Lyne was texting with a friend and they were talking about motherhood, and the friend had said something about mothers being our "champions and protectors." Lyne texted to her: "I wish my mom was still here." Right after that, she got a text that said, "Why didn't you tell me? I wasn't in the valley." She replied, thinking it was her friend, but then the friend texted back, confused, asking what she meant. *She had not sent the message.* Lyne is sure that this was a communication from her mother.

Lyne and I discussed the incident at length. In their confusion about the message, Lyne and her friend both took screen shots of the text conversation, which she showed me. Lyne's shot of their exchange clearly showed the "Why didn't you tell me?" message, while her friend's screenshot did not. Lyne was certain the communication was from her mother, who regretted that she was not available when Lyne needed her.

There are many accounts in the folklore collection at Utah State University that are similar to the experences of Lyne, Andrea, and Jake. Dozens of narratives describe the helpful spirits of deceased relatives making appearances in people's lives, and the narrators frequently stress the continuity of the eternal family. In some accounts, as we saw in Jake's experience, the spirits of the deceased will visit soon after their own death to comfort and guide their grieving kin. Spirits also offer other kinds of reassurance or promises of guardianship, such as in Andrea and Lyne's accounts. In one narrative, for example, a young woman relates a story from her mother's first pregnancy, which ended in miscarriage. Her mother was devastated, but the spirit of her grandmother visited, took her hand, and reassured her that she was watching over her and everything would be okay (Demke 2011). In a brief commentary included with her narrative, Demke writes that story is particularly moving for her family because "It helped me realize that families can be together forever . . . In the LDS church, we believe that if families marry in the temple then the family can be together forever. It helped me realize this fact and it brought me a lot of comfort."

Other accounts tell of guidance that is more specific. In one narrative, a woman describes her grandparents, Ellie and Ned, who were seemingly incompatible in their devotion to temple work. Ellie had been imploring Ned to do his temple work so that he would know what to do in the afterlife. He refused repeatedly, but eventually came around after a visit from his deceased parents. The granddaughter reports that:

> One morning, when they were a very old couple, Ned told Ellie that she would not need to worry about him not knowing what to do as far as temple rituals to be with her in the afterlife. He said, "My parents were here with me last night, and they have shown me what I need to know. You don't need to worry about it anymore." He died later that day. (Toone 1994)

When Ned's wife could not convince him to perform righteous action in the form of temple work, the spirits of his parents intervened, showing him what he "needed to know."

It is not solely parents and grandparents who visit from the spirit realm. In one narrative, a writer tells a story related by her friend about a deceased child guiding her parents toward conversion. The friend remembers an incident from her childhood, in which the deceased daughter of a neighbor tells visiting missionaries that her parents will eventually convert to Mormonism:

> The missionaries are out tracking [*sic.*, this is usually referred to as "tracting"], and this was in my neighborhood, and they went to my own neighbors who were the grouchiest old couple you had ever met in your entire life. Well, none of us even knew who they were . . . but we knew never to play on their grass, never walk by their house, 'cause we'd get yelled at. So, we all sent the missionaries over to their house, and we're like, and my one

friend said, "your [sic] never going to be able to talk to those people, they don't talk to anyone, they don't even talk to our bishop or whatever." So they went anyway, and they said that they went there and a little girl answered the door and said, "my mom and dad aren't home, they'll be back in two hours, please come back, because I know that you can get two baptisms if you come back." And so they came and told the family and they said, "No, you're wrong, they don't have a little girl, because we would know we would've played with her or whatever." So they came back. And what's her name, Doris, answers the door, and she says and first of all, she has a bunch of groceries in her hands and so the missionaries helped her of course... and she's like "well thanks for your help be on your way, I don't want anything to do with the Mormon Religion, it's not true, and all this stuff about being together forever as a family is fake, and I know that my daughter is in Hell, because somebody told us that." So the missionaries were like, "wow, wait a minute you said that your daughter is dead?" She says yes and there was a picture of the little girl that answered the door above the mantel, and they said, "Well, she was the one that answered the door and told us to come back." And so she started crying and of course they took the discussions, and that's it. And now they are faithful members, and he's in the bishopric. (Holt 1999)

This account clearly illustrates the importance of the eternal family and the ability of spirits to guide their living kin on the path to eternal life.

In addition to offers of comfort and spiritual guidance, spirits offer protection of various kinds. In one account, a student reports that the spirit of her deceased grandfather warned her living grandmother about the presence of the Devil. The grandmother experienced an "awful smell" and she saw a figure that "had a lot of hair on the body, and his eyes were bright red." Her husband died a few years later, but came back to her one night, awakening her from sleep: "Down at the end of the bed, she saw her late husband. He told her to get out of the house as soon as she could because she was in danger. He told her that the devil wanted her soul. She went back to sleep, and the next day she left the house and found an apartment complex" (Price 1991).

In other narratives, spirits of kin protect through healing. One student writer tells movingly of his own son's miraculous recovery from a devastating brain injury resulting from a car crash. The accident happened in Brigham City, which is just on the other side of the Wellsville range, on the western side of Cache Valley. The young man was in critical condition, and he had been flown from the hospital in Brigham City to the large children's hospital in Salt Lake City. The medical team, which included a neurosurgeon, told the young boy's parents that the situation was dire and, if he pulled through, he would have severe brain trauma. There was also damage to his lungs. The writer relates that he did not believe in God at the time, but he asked his deceased grandmother for help:

> My grandmother had passed away in January of the same year. Suddenly I felt a strange feeling, a presence in the room, my grandmother. I felt Tyler leave his body and I could feel their two spirits hovering above me, conversing, discussing where Tyler belonged. The feeling was so strong. I heard a voice, it was Grandma telling me Tyler would be okay and then there was complete silence. (Shearer 2001)

The writer, Shearer, reports that his son miraculously made a complete recovery. What I find particularly interesting about this account is Shearer's report of the deliberation between the grandmother and his son—the spirits were in conversation, discussing "where Tyler belonged." The use of the term "belonged" is telling, and given the cultural context, it seems likely that they were deliberating whether he belonged in the world of the living or the dead. The term references a degree of planning—the grandmother interceded, and they decided the young man belonged in the world of the living.

Latter-day Saint teachings indicate that once people are born with a mortal body, they do not remember the pre-existence. Spirits, however, have a more complete knowledge, and will sometimes impart this to their living relatives, usually by providing explanation and comfort in difficult circumstances. As we have seen, many of the accounts in this section emphasize the importance of knowledge: the spirits of the deceased know things that the living do not, and at times they intervene in the lives of their living kin to impart this knowledge for beneficial ends. We also see that spirits can be involved in planning and preparation in the lives of their mortal kin. Jake's grandfather encouraged him to go on his mission. Lyne's mother expressed regret that she was not present when her daughter needed her. In Shearer's narrative about Tyler, he reports that the spirits of his grandmother and his ailing son conferred and decided that he should stay among the living. Such narratives suggest a sense of planning and responsibility and lead us to consider next accounts that illustrate this sense of mutual responsibility even more closely.

Mutual Ethical Responsibilities of the Eternal Family: Planning in the Pre-existence and the Spirit Realm

The spirit visits we have examined thus far indicate that the eternal family is not important solely an abstract way, as something to hope for in the afterlife. As we have seen, deceased family members may be active in the lives of the living, guiding them on the path of righteousness and offering comfort and protection. The accounts that we will consider in this section offer an even more profound indication of the relevance of the eternal family in the lives of the living. As we will see, families make plans for their collective exaltation in the pre-existence. Those plans play out in the earthly realm and illustrate the mutual ethical responsibility that members of the family have for one another—both spirit members and living members. This is an excellent illustration of the collective responsibility that Cannell emphasizes as so important in Mormon Christianity: "kinship collectivism is identified as the nature of divinity, and in the sense that LDS can—indeed *must* for the sake of their own salvation—try to help others to be saved also" (2017, 165). And these accounts show that this collective responsibility extends to the spirit members of the family.

Both spirit and living members of the family weigh options and responsibilities in this world and the next: people certainly have responsibilities to the living members of their families, but we also see that there are ethical responsibilities in the spirit world that we might frame as the collective responsibilities of the family. The accounts also emphasize the importance of free will in weighing options and making decisions (see also Cannell 2017).

In the previous section, Shearer's account indicated planning between the spirit of his injured son and the spirit of his deceased grandmother. In a similar account from the Utah State University folklore archives, the spirit of a deceased woman intervenes to prevent the death of her seriously ill daughter:

> When Aunt Mary Anderson was a young mother, she became very ill. The doctor was called, and he told her that she might die. She had a dream and in her dream she saw her mother who had died several years before. Her mother was sitting by a granary sewing a white dress. Aunt Mary asked her what she was doing.
>
> She replied, "You are coming here unexpected and I must make a white dress for you."

Aunt Mary replied, "But I can't die! I must live to take care of my husband and children."

Her mother promised her that she would talk to someone to see if Mary would be allowed to live. Grandmother talked to a man for quite some time, and when she returned she informed Mary that the choice was hers. She could choose to live or die. Mary chose to live. Her dream ended and soon after that she was well. She lived to be 90 years old. (Keeley 1988)

The student writer, Keeley, adds context by explaining that her mother told her this story as a "faith-promoting device" to generate an interest in genealogy among her children. Importantly, Keeley emphasizes free will—Mary is given the *choice* to live or die and chooses to live so she can take care of her husband and children.

A similar account relates a measuring of responsibility in this world and the spirit world. A student shares a story from her grandmother, who related that when her own mother—the writer's great grandmother—was very ill with advanced diabetes, she was visited by the spirit of *her* mother, who called her to the next life. The writer's grandmother said that she told her mother (the great grandmother of the narrative), "You can't leave us, we need you," but the sick woman replied that her own mother—in the spirit realm—needed her more. She died a few days later (Reese 1991).

In one of our many conversations, Lyne shared some similarly intriguing accounts of familial responsibility in the spirit world. Earlier in this chapter, I described one of Lyne's profound experiences with the spirit of her mother, who sent her a text message. Lyne has had experiences with the spirit of her mother at other times, and she told me that led her to reflect on her mother's premature death in the context of Latter-day Saint teachings and theology. She told me that a few months after her mother passed away, her spirit visited one of her neighbors. The neighbor had been heartbroken at the woman's death and was "really mad at God." The deceased woman then appeared to her in spirit form:

And my mom actually came to her, and sat right in front of her—and this lady isn't religious so it's not like . . . —And she [my mother] said, "You have to let me go because I have work to do. There are so many children that need a mother." So it shows you, God really has a full [plan for] this because it isn't just who we are *here*, it's what we are also supposed to be doing *there*, to still bring [about], for lack of better terms, what needs to occur.

Here, Lyne emphasizes the necessity of her mother's work in the spirit realm—she refers to what she is "supposed to be doing" *there*—in the spirit world—rather than *here* in the world of the living. Her mother visited the neighbor to emphasize the importance of her work in the spirit realm—she had a responsibility to be mothering children *there*. Lyne described this as God's plan. Her use of the phrase "supposed to be doing" indicates the importance of her mother's duties and ethical responsibilities in the spirit realm. Lyne's interpretation of her mother's visit to the neighbor highlights the expanse of God's plan and the necessity of individual human and spirit actors in it, each of whom have the responsibility to perform certain duties for others.

Another visit from Lyne's mother similarly illuminates the significance of work in the spirit world and the eternal nature of the family. As we have seen, ethical responsibilities are incumbent on both the living members of the family and those in the spirit world. We see that although there is an understanding of a plan—the "supposed to"—there is also an emphasis on choice and agency: one can choose to follow the plan, or one can choose not to. When Lyne told me about another communication from her mother, she described not just God's plan, but also her own family's planning in the pre-existence:

> My mom . . . she didn't come to me actually, she spoke to me . . . . There was one time, I had a migraine, I was just walking through my room and I said [to myself], "Well, jeez, maybe I have a brain tumor!" . . . And, she [my mother] said back to me—and I already know it was her—she said, "Well, I already did that for you!" And I said, "What?"—because then you can talk to them [spirits] in your mind—and I said, "What?" She said, "It was better for me to go, and leave you . . . than it would be for you to be the one to go and leave your kids."

Lyne's mother explained that there was planning in her untimely death: she relates to Lyne that it was better for her to die young and leave her children behind than it would have been for something similar to happen to Lyne, who was at the time a mother with young children. Lyne's mother has knowledge of the pre-existence that Lyne does not have, and she shared it with her to comfort and reassure at a time of difficulty. Lyne had reflected on this frequently. She told me that the experience taught her that it was possible that all families had to come up with plans and agreements in the pre-existence, and that perhaps her family had agreed that her mother should be the one to depart the earthly realm early to do the necessary work in the spirit world. Because of this agreement, Lyne herself would not have to do it, and could stay earthbound to raise her children. The emphasis here is on the family's responsibility in the spirit world: Someone would have to do the work to fulfill God's plan, and the family had agreed it would be best for Lyne's mother to do it.

However, Lyne also emphasizes the importance of agency of members of the family in the pre-existence, which clearly reflects Latter-day Saint teachings about the importance of free will. These teachings are found in many parts of Mormon scripture, and they are relevant to both life as a mortal and the pre-existence, as we discussed in Chapter 2. For example, in the Book of Mormon, verses 15–16 of the Book of Nephi emphasize God's plan in creation of oppositions, such as the forbidden fruit in opposition to the tree of life, so that that humanity should have a choice: "Wherefore, the Lord God gave unto man that he should act for himself. Wherefore, man could not act for himself save it should be that he was enticed by the one or the other" (2 Nephi 2:16).[5]

In an excerpt from the interview below, Lyne uses the phrase "the success rate of having us all make it back," which indicates the collective nature of the journey toward eternal life. In the pre-existence, her family made agreements about the best strategy to ensure that everyone would "make it back." She explained:

> I learned that . . . even in the pre-existence we made agreements. Maybe there were certain things that we all had to go through, familial-line wise, maybe we did make agreements. And say, "Hey, I'll do this." It was all about agency, which is what we are always told. Maybe there was an option that it was either going to have to be her, or me, or a great-grandparent and *the success rate of having us all make it back* was better for her to go than for me to go. Isn't that crazy? (emphasis added)

---

[5] For a clear discussion of official teachings on free will, see the online resource at https://www.churchofjesuschrist.org/study/manual/gospel-principles/chapter-4-freedom-to-choose?lang=eng. Note the many sources cited for the teachings, for example, the books of Moses and Abraham from *The Pearl of Great Price*, Doctrine and Covenants 29, and the book of Helaman from the Book of Mormon, among others.

Lyne told me that she was certain that she was communicating with her mother, even though in this case she could not see her spirit form. She had no doubts that the message was from her mother. "Yeah," she said, "no doubt . . . who else would say, 'I already did that for you?'" Her mother's meaning was crystal clear.

Lyne's experiences illustrate a strong Latter-day Saint emphasis on agency and free will—she indicates that her mother and her family had control over her mother's early demise. However, she wondered aloud about the consequences of this premortal agreement, and she thought it possible that certain family members resented the arrangement and her mother's willingness to be the one to go early. Again, we see that the eternal family does not simply exist in an abstract way as a distant but reassuring possibility in the afterlife. Rather, the eternal family exists in the spirit world *now*, and makes plans *there* that impact life in this world, *here*, as Lyne put it. The premortal agreement indicates an *ethical responsibility* incumbent on the family in the spirit world. Lyne's mother indicated their family had decided that *she herself* would be the one to fulfill that responsibility through her early death—not Lyne—and that this was a means of ensuring the family's spiritual progress, which Lyne refers to with her comment on "the success rate of having us all make it back."

Lyne stressed the continual development and progress of spirits in the afterlife. "I mean, who knows?" she said, "We have no idea, because we are told that we die with the same spirit we have. We all grow . . . we are all going to move forward."

Like most everyone I worked with on this project, Lyne is a deep thinker. Her ruminations on the consequences of planning in the pre-existence are profound, and she elaborated on this when I asked her about the possibility of spirit rebirth. She explained that a spirit only has a body one time, but that when people think they remember moments from past lives, or in those experiences we refer to as "déjà vu," she believes they are having vague memories of planning in the pre-existence. She used Jesus Christ as an example:

Déjà vu, for me personally, this is what I believe . . . . So, Christ suffered in Gethsemane, so I look at it as a black hole. You know how condensed a black hole is? And there's a lot of energy and power there? So, through the atonement, being in the garden of Gethsemane, if he had to suffer everybody's sins, and their struggles and their cries, every part of humanness, he had

> to condense that in a twelve-hour period or whatever, so it was huge, right? Well, part of *really* suffering with somebody is that you experience it. So, to suffer, it means that you are fully empathetic with that situation but you can only really be fully empathetic if you've experienced it. I believe, like I said before, that when we made all of our agreements before we came here [in the pre-existence], [such as] who would take on what trials, in Gethsemane, that's when he experienced it with us. Before he even came [here] is when we would have made all those agreements so he had the opportunity to actually walk through them with us . . . in a spiritual realm. And then we had to come here to the earthly realm to experience [it]. So, I think déjà vu is maybe some of those memories we had that we already knew was going to happen because we already made that agreement.

She concluded by explaining that the reason we think we have experienced events before is because we already have but in the spirit realm. I asked her if she thought that although people forget most of what happened in the pre-existence, they were perhaps able to remember some of it. She said that this was probably the case. I asked if her thoughts on this matter reflected specific church teachings on the spirit realm and the pre-existence. Intriguingly, she answered that they did not unless you "take the things we teach and put them together." A lay theologian indeed, Lyne continued, saying she always wondered how Christ could experience our pains: "I thought to myself, 'Well, I get how he could suffer our sins, but how could he suffer our pains?' The only way he can is if he did it once with us already, you know?"

Prescient Spirit Children

I had reached out to Mrs. Williams, introduced in Chapter 2, on the recommendation of an old friend, who was her great niece. My friend suggested I contact her because she was particularly knowledgeable about spiritual matters. Mrs. Williams was in her early eighties, and her lively demeanor and boundless energy made her seem decades younger. She had grown up in Wellsville, the small farming village that was one of the first Mormon settlements in the valley. Mrs. Williams has many children, and dozens upon dozens of grandchildren and great-grandchildren. When Katryn and I visited her, we enjoyed hearing her stories of how she managed occasions like

Christmas—she told us her strategy was to sew and craft gifts all year, then invite all the children over to choose from a giant pile of homemade gifts.

We sat for an hour or two in her tidy living room and the conversation flowed easily. We talked a great deal about her large family, and the conversation eventually turned to *spirit children*. Mrs. Williams explained the subject this way: "Oh yeah, the spirits are there, they want to come to earth to get their body to have this opportunity. I mean this is a great opportunity to live on this earth, whether we believe it sometimes and not because there is a lot of evil on the earth."

I asked if there would someday be an end to this line of waiting spirits—would we eventually reach a point where all the spirits had been born into mortal bodies? Mrs. Williams replied, "Well, is there an end of spirits? Sometime? I don't know! I wondered . . . if all of a sudden none of us are able to have children anymore, we'll start thinking—is that the end of spirits in heaven? But people are still having babies, so I guess there's plenty of spirits." She laughed.

The mutual ethical responsibilities between mortals and spirits are perhaps most clear in experiences with and relationships to spirit children. The most profound ethical responsibility to spirit kin that is incumbent on mortals is to ensure that spirit children are born into earthly bodies. Women and men are frequently visited by the spirits of their unborn children; Latter-day Saints may also be visited by their future siblings or grandchildren, although this is somewhat less common. This seems to be a uniquely Latter-day Saint phenomenon, and it reflects aspects of Latter-day Saint theology that describe spirit children waiting for birth to mortal families.[6] As addressed in Chapter 2, Mormon cosmology teaches that all spirits exist in a premortal life, known as the pre-existence, or "life before life," and that God determines when spirits will be born into an earthly body, after which memories of the premortal existence are typically shrouded and "veiled." All people exist as spirit beings (i.e., "spirit children") created by God before they are born in human form. In a few accounts, in the USU folklore collection the spirits of future children offer aid—even physical aid—as in the following story in which the writer tells a story that her friend shared at church one day:

---

[6] This conception of spirit children is quite different from other understandings of spirit children, for example, in northern Ghana that Aaron Denham (2017) has recently described. Denham explores the conception of spirit children that are sent to cause problems among the living among the Nankani in northern Ghana, where young living children who are either ailing or have special abilities are sometimes thought to be "spirit children" sent to cause misfortune. In the Latter-day Saint tradition, all people were once "spirit children."

About ten years ago, my aunt was involved in a really horrible car crash. It was so bad that when the police and rescue workers approached her car they were sure she didn't survive. She had been t-boned directly at the driver's side door, completely demolishing it. As the workers approached though they found that my aunt wasn't anywhere near the front seat, but instead was tucked safely in the right corner of the back seat, not a scratch on her body. They called this a miracle. About six years later, my aunt was married and had a four-year-old son. She was going through some old things as they were preparing to move into a new house when she ran into a box full of pictures and information of her accident. As she was looking at one particularly gruesome picture of her wrecked car, her son took an interest in it. After looking at it for a minute her son said, "Hey, I remember that. That was the day I pulled you into the back seat of the car." My aunt just looked at him in awe. Her son hadn't been told any specifics of the crash and certainly not where she had been found once the dust settled. There has been no question in my aunt's mind ever since that her son was what saved her life in the crash that day. (Wilson 2011)

Although this account is intriguing in that the spirit of an unborn child saves his future mother in a devastating car accident, such accounts do not make up the majority of experiences with spirit children. More often, people experience visits from spirit children who are waiting to be born. These spirits typically visit the living to encourage the family to have more children and thus ensure their own birth, indicating the ethical responsibility of the living to provide earthly bodies for spirit children and so set them on their path to eternal life. For many Latter-day Saints, not having children is understood as denying spirit children the chance to be born, therefore robbing them of their chance to improve themselves in mortal life and progress in the afterlife. The ethical responsibility is thus clear.

In her research on ideas about blood and kinship among Mormon families in New York and Utah, Cannell recognizes that the distinction between spirit and matter in Mormonism is not the same as in other Christian traditions; for Latter-day Saints, the completion of spiritual progress requires a mortal body (Cannell 2013a, 2005; see also other scholars of Mormonism like Taysom 2017; Brown and Holbrook 2015; McLachlan 2015; Mitchell 2001). The spirit children wait for their turn to be born to their earthly families, and thus continue on the journey to the afterlife

(Cannell 2013a, 2005). As noted previously, Cannell finds the emphasis on the family in the pre-existence has been attractive to the converts to Mormonism with whom she has worked. Indeed, in her work on Latter-day Saint adoptions, Cannell observes that, "A genealogical sensibility is not confined to the present life for Latter-day Saints but stretches forward into an infinite future of post mortal existence" (Cannell 2013a, 227). This animates discussions over adoption and the nature of the adoptive family, where both birth mothers and adoptive parents conceive of the baby as a spiritually destined member of the adoptive family, but also potentially spiritually connected to the birth mother. Cannell writes of a mother who considered that one of her adoptive daughters, to whom she was sealed in the temple, might be more properly reunited with her birth mother in eternity (Cannell 2013a, 228–29).

What I find particularly interesting about the visits of spirit children is how clearly they illustrate the teaching that the responsibility for salvation rests not simply on the mortal members of the family, but also on those in the spirit world: spirit children, as well as spirit ancestors, are actively engaged in the project of salvation. Cannell describes the "collective responsibility for salvation," and the cases presented here clearly illustrate the imperative to expand this notion to include spirit kin, as well as the earthbound family. Spirit children often ask for the mediating help of their earthly kin. Their request is nearly always to be born and thus take on the responsibility and opportunity of a mortal body. The spirit children, who may appear as children or, more often, in their adult form, visit to confirm their future births, and thus provide reassurance to the unmarried and to those who are told they are unable to have children, or those who are unwilling or unable to have additional children. Spirit children frequently encourage couples to defy the advice of doctors who have warned women about the dangers of having more children. They might also plead to be born, thus changing the minds of those who thought they were done having children.

Shauna, remarked that she had frequently heard accounts of visits with spirit children in visions. She said:

[Someone] would be having a rough time, and think, "Oh I'm never going to have a baby!" and then they'd have a dream where they'd see themselves with this baby and they know. They know that they're going to have [a baby]. I actually have a friend who left the church around the same time as me. And she was telling me about seeing her daughter in a vision and she still believes that she had [the vision] and that her daughter, you know, was meant to be part of her family.

Shauna said that even though the friend in this account had left the church, the woman still firmly believed in the reality of her vision experience.

Spirit children are nearly always identifiable as individuals, and they most often identify themselves by name or parentage. People reporting visits also frequently include physical descriptions of the spirit, usually as a means of identifying the future parents. For example, while writing this chapter in the spring of 2021, I received a text message from Katryn, who was conducting her dissertation research in central Utah among members of a self-described fundamentalist Latter-day Saint sect that maintains the practice of polygyny. Katryn often shared fieldwork anecdotes with me via text, and in this case, she wrote to tell me that a close friend in the community, a young married woman, had confided to unmarried Katryn that her mother-in-law had been having dreams in which a spirit child kept visiting her to tell her she wanted to join her family. The spirit child had curly dark hair, and the spirit child told the older woman that she would be born to the next sister wife of her son. As she related the story to Katryn, the young woman smiled and looked knowingly at Katryn's curly dark hair.

There are dozens of reports of spirit children visiting in the student folklore collection at Utah State University, and many are firsthand accounts. In one particularly fascinating narrative, a student writes that she was visited at the age of twenty by the spirit of her future eldest son. She records that she was worried at the time about never having children, and the reassuring spirit took her to a beautiful white city where she saw four men and four women lined up in a row. He told her they were her other future children. She writes that she did indeed eventually have nine children in the order in which she remembered:

> The young man who had accompanied me left me standing about 10 feet from the group of people and took his place with them. I was told in my mind (not by words but by thoughts) that these were my children. The young man was my first child, and the others would come as I saw them lined up . . . I now have all nine of my children that I saw that night. (Smith 1992)

In a similar account, another woman writes about a dream in which her future children appeared to her. She recorded that at the time of their appearance, she was dating a man who was "not a very nice guy." She writes:

> One night, I had a dream in which four children appeared to me. They were three girls, and one boy. They never spoke to me, yet I knew they were the children who were to be born to me. One of the girls turned and walked away. After this dream, I began to wonder about the man I was dating and felt he would not be a good father to my children. I feel my children appeared to me to help direct my life. (Sorensen 1995)

In another account, a student writes that a spirit appeared to her grandparents, who had both been married previously and had nine children between them. The couple were not planning on having any additional children. The student writes:

> When Grandma and Grandpa were first married, they didn't think they would be able to handle any more children, being older and having so many already. But one night both of them dreamed they saw two little girls who wanted to come to them. One was a blonde, and one was a brunette. They discussed the dream, and had two more children, both girls, the same two who were in their dream. (Bair 1995)

Another account describes the future child of the writer's Aunt Linda, who had a recurring dream about a child in a long white nightgown with "an olive complexion" and brown hair and eyes. The woman was curious about the recurring dream, and she asked a friend for help. The friend, the writer's mother, told her simply to ask the child what she wanted, "Maybe she just wants a drink of water or to be told that everything is okay." Aunt Linda did so the next time she saw the girl, but she did not receive a reply. The writer reports that, "She didn't see the girl again in her dreams, but shortly after the dreams stopped, she was blessed with a beautiful baby girl with long brown hair and big brown eyes and an olive complexion" (Young 1994).

In yet another account, a student shares her mother's experience of a visit from the spirit of her younger sister. The narrative is similar to others in that the future child appears as an adult and indicates to the parent that she is ready to be born. The writer reports that her mother often told her children this story when they were growing up, so it was a familiar and loved family story. Her mother explained:

> I hadn't had the ultrasound yet so I didn't know what I was having. And I was asleep but I was not quite asleep, it was that in-between sorta state. And over by the window just next to me she was standing, she was wearing a white gown and uh, her hair was about shoulder length and it . . . was a real dark brown, really pretty brown; about the color of daddy's hair. I was surprised because the wind was blowing, and her dress was waving. She was beautiful, very pretty girl, looked about 25. And she said to me, "It's me, mother, Mary. Are you ready for me?" And I'd been thinking what I'd name my baby and I had been considering Mary so then I knew. (Wakefield 2011)

In a written commentary on the story, Wakefield notes, "At the end [of the tale] my sister Mary, now 15, happened to come up the stairs and my mom smiled at her with something more in her smile."

Although most accounts are of spirit children visiting their future parents, they occasionally visit their future siblings to ask for aid and mediation. One student writes that the spirit of a small boy appeared to her one night, telling her to encourage her parents to have more children: "I'm your brother," he said, "Tell mom about me. Don't forget about me." A few months later, her mother was pregnant and later delivered the very child that appeared to the student (Watts 1994b).

In some accounts, the spirit children are distraught that they might not have the chance to come to earth. For example, in an account simply titled "John," a student reports that her mother-in-law was visited by the spirit of one of her husband's siblings. Her husband related the following to her:

> My mom already had six children and was being pressured to limit her family because of her health. She wasn't sure what she should do and decided to pray about it. She knelt by her bed one night to pray. Almost instantly, she saw a beautiful garden with a boy sitting on a bench. He had a very sad expression on his face. He didn't say anything, but mom got the message. He wanted to be part of our family, and was sad because my mom was considering not to have any more children. Almost a year later, he joined our family when John was born. Both my mom and John survived the birth without any problems. (Hall 1994)

An older narrative relates the story of a woman who had recently died and gone to heaven, where she encountered two sad spirit children. The children told her, "We can't go down to earth; we don't have anyone to go to on earth because our parents won't take us." The writer then explains:

> She felt sorry for them, and she asked them who their parents were to be, and they said her name. She felt so bad, she asked the lord to let her go back and have however many children he would give her. She came back the next morning, and after a while she had the girl and then the boy and then she had several more children. (Hurst 1964)

In both accounts, we see that the mortal family member—the mother—becomes an intermediary. She meets sad spirit children who think that they will not have a chance to be born. In the first account, the mother prays about her decision to not have more children due to her health. Seemingly in response to her prayers, a spirit child appears, and she decides that she will have another child, and so John is born. In the second account, a woman asked God to bring her back from the dead to give birth to children that she met in heaven. Spirit children visits frequently reassure couples about the possibility of healthy offspring, and women report going against their doctor's advice due to the reassurance of the spirit children. In another account, a woman relates to the writer that the spirits of two of her daughters visited her. The writer relates the first experience, when the woman's daughter appeared to her after a visit to the temple: "Just a few years prior to this she saw her daughter, Gloria, in another dream. This was immediately after the doctor told her that she would not be able to have more children because of an Rh factor in her blood. Since that time she has had four children and only little Gloria was in any danger at all. They knew she would live because of the dream" (Hatton-Ward 1964).

In a similar narrative, a student writes that his mother was very depressed when she was in her thirties and not yet married. He relates that one day she was playing the piano, and "All of sudden, there was a little girl in the room. She told my mother not to worry because someday she would be hers, and then she disappeared." He writes that his mother was then called to go on a mission, where she met her husband. Hurst writes that they eventually had six children, but none of them was the girl who appeared to her, so his mother knew that one more child was yet to be born. Although her doctor had advised against any more pregnancies, his mother disregarded the advice and had another child—and this was the girl who appeared to her (Hurst 1989).

In her research on spirit child experiences in the 1980s, the folklorist Margaret Brady (1987) suggests that this is particularly the domain of women and a mode of women's spiritual experience. However, I have found that men are also visited by their future children, although seemingly not as often as women. In one narrative, a student writes that his father, a farmer in southern Idaho (at the northern end of Cache Valley), once heard a voice while on his tractor telling him "there was still one more child waiting to be brought to his home" (Talbot 2001). Talbot expresses how important children were to their farming family, and that they had a large family of six children already. His mother was getting older, however, and they were not expecting more children:

> My father would often run machinery in the fields on the family farm. One summer day, something would happen that had a lasting effect on him. As he was driving along a tractor in the fields, a strong feeling came over him. He kept driving along and the feeling kept getting stronger and stronger. As he stopped the tractor, a very strong impression came over him that something was missing in his life. The feeling continued and he heard or felt something telling him that there was still one more child waiting to be brought to this home. "Why are you leaving me out," he recalled the voice saying.
>
> With such a powerful experience, my father realized that one more addition to the family would be necessary. On September 3, 1978, his seventh and final child would be born. (Talbot 2001)

A student shares a similar story about her in-laws, who were from Cache Valley but had moved to New Hampshire. Her father-in-law, Ted, told her the following story one night after she had married her husband. Ted explained that he and his wife had three young children, and his wife's doctor had told her that she could not have any more. He said that his wife laughed at this, because all her children had been "surprises." The writer relates:

> One night, Ted woke up suddenly, and saw a little girl at the foot of his bed. Startled, he woke up Pat, who did not see anyone. He kept insisting he had seen a little girl. A few months went by, and he couldn't stop thinking

about her. One day, Pat wasn't feeling well, and went to the doctor, who announced she was going to have another baby. She was very surprised, and when she went home and told Ted, he just said, "That's my little girl." Their youngest child, Anne Marie, was born that summer. (Bair 1995)

Brady collected numerous stories shared by pregnant women in the 1980s and has argued that the visits from spirit children can be understood as way of finding meaning and exerting power in women's lives. She suggests that women interpret such visitations as communications from God through the spirit child about their special status as a mother (Brady 1987). More recently, Eliason (2014) reviewed explanations for the prevalence of visits from spirit children, including Brady's arguments. Eliason suggests that American Mormons may be hesitant to share such stories out of fear of being seen as "kooky," and proposes that as the church expands, perhaps Mormons will find themselves in more "enchanted" environments that are more culturally receptive to such narratives (2014, 27). However, my ethnographic work shows that Mormons in northern Utah are not really living in the disenchanted environment Eliason presumed—experiences of spirit children and other spirit kin are widely known and not infrequently shared.

Sharing the Experience and a Note on Skepticism

But when and why are such experiences shared? When I began this research project, I expected to find that spirit experiences would be locally framed in ways similar to what other anthropologists have found in recent research on contemporary forms of Christianity that emphasize the importance of spiritual authority and spiritual progress. Indeed, in her analysis of pregnancy narratives, Brady suggests that this is one of the reasons Mormon women share stories of being visited by spirit children: "The status derived from the telling invests the teller with a new kind of personal power, as the narrative effectively mediates between the personal, spiritual, and social domains" (1987, 467). More recently, in other Christian contexts, anthropologists Brendan Jamal Thornton (2016) and Naomi Haynes (2017) emphasize how certain spiritual experiences can be understood as marks of spiritual progress or as indicating a propensity toward spiritual aptitude. Thornton (2016), for example, describes how male Pentecostal converts in the Dominican Republic leverage both spiritual transformation and negative charisma into spiritual authority. In Zambia, Haynes (2017) shows how Pentecostal Christians spiritually "move" through charismatic aptitude.

Considering this, we might expect Latter-day Saint spirit visits to be leveraged as charisma, in the Weberian sense: not only understood as a mark of righteousness and "right living," but as a way of asserting spiritual adeptness or authority. And indeed, occasionally people told me about their *desire* to experience such a visit as a longing for confirmation of their spiritual aptitude or righteous worth. Shauna, for example, explained that when she was younger, she had hoped she was "spiritual enough" to have such an encounter. Recall that even though she was afraid of evil spirits, she "really wanted to meet a good spirit and just feel like . . . you know, like I was a good enough person to have a personal witness . . . . Like if you were spiritual enough that things could [happen?]." Similarly, Jeannette said that when she was young, she wanted to have "something happen" to confirm her righteousness but she never had such a spiritual encounter.

However, among people who have experienced spirit visits, there is much ambivalence about sharing them. Some view the visits as a special gift, and the sacred, special, and private nature of the visits was noted by many. In general, it seems that such experiences are not often shared, and if so, only with intimates or the occasional fortunate researcher. Jake, for example, claimed that he had never shared his experiences before telling me about them, Andrea and Elder Neilson told me that that they only rarely shared them, and many others emphasized their private significance and hesitancy to discuss them widely. Brad proposed that there was a fairly strong cultural norm of keeping such experiences relatively quiet. Reminiscent of Eliason's observation about "kookiness," he explained that if someone stood up in a sacrament meeting on Sunday and announced an experience of angelic ministration, people might roll their eyes and say to themselves, "Okay, here we go."

However, I think the hesitation to share is often attributable to concerns other than kookiness. The folklorist and anthropologist Tom Mould explored ambivalence among North Carolina Mormons who experienced the inspiration of the Holy Ghost, or what is known as "personal revelation." He identified two patterns, or norms, in sharing personal revelation: one was a norm of humility and modesty that discouraged people from sharing the revelations, and the other was a norm of the spiritual, in that sharing stories should glorify God (Mould 2011, 382) and confirm the truth of the church to others (Mould 2011, 240), *not* enhance the authority of the narrator. In the Latter-day Saint context of northern Utah, in the abstract, spirit encounters may sometimes be interpreted as a mark of "the spiritual" and may build one's sense of self-worth and confirm spiritual progress. However, those who have experienced these encounters do not tend to describe them in this way. Rather, they are more likely to interpret them as guideposts, as reassurance, or even as a redirection to the righteous path than they are to interpret them as a reward for righteousness. As we have seen, this is in some contrast to what anthropologists have observed about spiritual experiences in other Christian contexts, where people leverage experiences as a way to gain social capital, establish charismatic capacity, or to affirm one's spiritual progress in public.

Indeed, in this cultural and religious context, anyone might be visited by a spirit. Brad was particularly adamant that spiritually meaningful experiences could happen to *anyone*, not just a bishop or high-ranking person in church leadership. In Brad's view, spiritual experiences respond to need. Jake's grandfather visited him at a moment of crisis in the MTC, and the visit assured him that completing his mission was the right decision. Prescient children advise against this or that marriage partner, and deceased family members bring comfort about God's plan for the family in times of distress. In reflecting on her many spiritual experiences, Lyne said that, ultimately, they were the reason she decided to stay active in the church, even when faced with frustrations about the way she was treated by some members of her ward.

Andrea expressed a similar sentiment. She told me that when she was younger, she felt that sharing spirit experiences was something like a competition. I asked her to elaborate, and she replied:

> Well, a little bit, like people who have those things happen to them—it almost felt like they in some way were more spiritual or were more worthy to receive those kinds of things and those kinds of experiences. But as I've gotten older, I realize maybe they just come to people who need them and I'm good.... I don't know why they happen to some people and why they don't to others. Yeah, but I don't think that Heavenly Father picks someone and says, "You're my chosen one and so I'm going to give you this experience." You know, I don't think that happens. Honestly, sometimes people are way more in tune than others and since my mom died I have wished to feel her or to— ... I know that she's there. I know that she can see me, she can hear me. She's right here, you know, with us when we need her, and I don't think that I need to see her or hear her to know that she's here.

Our conversation continued in this vein, and Andrea suggested that sometimes she suspected people were saying they had been visited by a spirit when they had not been. I thought about why someone might say they had been visited, and I asked if she meant that people were fabricating such accounts to manipulate others. She quickly corrected me, in her gentle way, and said that was not what she meant. Rather, she said, "I think they just do it either to comfort themselves or make themselves feel better to convince themselves of something I don't think they're trying to hurt any people."

I would not call Andrea a skeptic, but there are of course other skeptics. They are similar to Andrea in that it is not the general possibility of spirit experience that generates skepticism, but simply an assumption that not all accounts of spirits are genuine. To readers who are familiar with classic work in anthropology, this might suggest a parallel to what the twentieth-century British anthropologist Edward Evan Evans-Pritchard observed when studying witchcraft among the Azande of what is today Central Africa that witchcraft is a real and present means of accounting for misfortune, but it does not mean that every poor outcome is because of witchcraft. Sometimes, a pot breaks just because the artisan was unskilled—witchcraft is not always to blame (Evans-Pritchard 1937).

It is important to note that skepticism was a far less common response from those learning about research than knowing affirmations that these experiences happen, and so I do not make skepticism a major theme in this book. However, I have heard people doubt the spiritual experiences of others as nothing more than attempts at gaining spiritual standing in a group. Although there is notable reticence about sharing these sacred experiences, there may be potential gain in sharing something. A man called John, who was at one point the bishop of a small ward outside of Utah, remarked that the emphasis on humility could be something of a feint, or perhaps we could call it the leverage of "sharing not sharing." By hinting at significant spiritual experiences, John argued, one can establish a righteous self and claim a certain authority among one's peers, while affecting modesty and humility.

Spiritual Progress, the Eternal Family, and Ethical Kinship

Perhaps the most profound insight shared with me by those who encounter spirit kin is that the visits confirm the reality of the eternal family—the cornerstone of Latter-day Saint theology. In the economy of heaven, as Brad explained, God chooses to send family members rather than other spirit beings, "Why send an angel when a mother will do?" The spirits of close kin are active agents in the lives of those on earth, and they have information and knowledge that the earthbound do not.

I find anthropologist Amira Mittermaier's (2012) research on "special dreams" among Sufi Muslims in Egypt to be helpful in making sense of these experiences. In most of the spirit encounters described in this chapter, an unsuspecting recipient is "acted upon," to use Mittermaier's term: they are *acted upon* because they did not seek out spiritual experiences, just like Egyptian Sufis who have dreams of spiritual significance did not seek out the dreams. Mittermaier shows that these Sufi dreams initiate relationships with special beings, who are otherwise out of reach.[7] Latter-day Saint spirit visits are similarly purposive. Spirits visit people, who are typically unsuspecting, for a reason and often in response to needs (and thus "not just to say hi," as Brad remarked). Spirit kin are both mediators and guides on the journey to eternal life. And in turn, the living assist the spirits along their path toward the same goal. To be sure, some spirits visit with particular requests of the living, as when spirit children ask to be born. Together, the encounters reinforce the importance of continual spiritual progress that Latter-day Saints undergo from the pre-existence to the post-existence, to salvation, and, possibly, exaltation.

All these visitations reinforce Mormon cosmological ideas about the nature of the individual and spiritual progress in the Plan of Salvation. What seems particularly important about the encounters described in this chapter is the recognition of the *active* nature of members of the eternal family in advancing one another's spiritual progress: the individual is inherently connected to others, both living and non-living. Spirits of the deceased visit to advise and direct. Spirits of those not yet born implore future parents to ensure the mortal body required for salvation by giving them birth. And all spirit kin seem to have knowledge that the living do not.

Anthropological literature abounds with accounts of ancestral spirits actively involved in the lives of the living. This research spans the globe from the Americas to Africa to Asia. Indeed, in a comparative article from the 1990s, Steadman, Palmer, and Tilley proposed that "ancestor worship," by which they simply mean communication between the living and ancestors,

---

[7] This work forms the basis of Mittermaier's argument (2012) about the limits of the "self-cultivation" model that has been so prominent in the twenty-first-century anthropology of Islam.

should be recognized as universal aspect of religions (1996).[8] More recent research illustrates the inherent mutuality of these relationships, such as Hylton White's (2013) recent work on ancestral spirit relations in KwaZulu Natal, Jacob Hickman's (2014) work on ancestral personhood among Hmong people in Thailand and the United States, Heonik Kwon's (2016) work on ancestral spirits in Vietnam, and Kate Glaskin's (2005) work on ancestral spirits bringing revelation in indigenous Australian communities. In some ways, the model of ancestral personhood that Hickman (2014) develops is a useful parallel to spirit experiences in Utah. Hickman observes that the knowledge that one will be an ancestor one day undergirds Hmong moral sensibilities: "this form of subjectivity underpins certain types of moral discourse, particularly with regard to responsibilities and obligations to one's clan and ancestors" (2014, 332). In the Mormon tradition, there is a similar conception of the mutuality of being and mutual responsibility, and we will return to the Hmong example in the next chapter. Anthropologist Bradley Kramer (2014) has described a Mormon theory of intersubjective kinship centered on temple rituals. Another anthropologist, Jon Bialecki, has observed that spiritual experiences during temple activity "knit the Mormon Dead and the Mormon living together into a kinship system of literally cosmological scale" (2022: 138)

As noted previously, Cannell (2017) observes that converts are attracted to the idea of the eternal family and the knowledge held by spirit members of the family. She argues that this indicates a sense of collective responsibility that stands in contrast to some other contemporary understandings of salvation in Christianity, and particularly processes of conversion to Christianity, as anthropologist Joel Robbins (2004) articulated in his work on Urapmin conversion in Papua New Guinea. We see this frequently in various aspects of church culture, for example in the common exhortation "every member a missionary" that has been part of everyday Mormon discourse since the 1950s, when then-church president David O. McKay used the phrase in a talk (McKay 1961).

I have written more extensively elsewhere about how this research contributes to recent anthropological work on kinship that emphasizes

---

[8] It should be noted, however, that the authors only consider indigenous societies, and argue that the importance of ancestors in these religions—as opposed to "world religions"—is because they are "kinship based." I take issue with some of the claims of the article, and the material presented here should certainly show that the role of ancestors is prominent in "world religions" as well, although one wonders if they would characterize Mormonism as a world religion (being a Christian religion) or an indigenous religion.

mutual ethical responsibility (see Stiles 2023). Similarly, several chapters in the recent collection *New Directions in Spiritual Kinship* (Thomas, Malik, and Wellman 2017), which houses Cannell's chapter on collective salvation, emphasize kinship as an ethical relationship. Don Seeman's contribution argues against the utility of a notion of spiritual kinship as it is too biased toward Christian conceptions of kin. Alternatively, he proposes that like Sahlins, we consider kinship an ethical relationship (Seeman 2017). Rose Wellman's chapter similarly describes a set of ethical practices in Iran as a way of collectively cultivating an ethical family: the family is thus an *object* of ethical cultivation (Wellman 2017). In addition to her chapter for this volume, Cannell has similarly argued elsewhere, in her work on hobbyist genealogy in the United Kingdom, that the mutual bonds of dependence with family in the modern West complicate "atomistic" notions of the contemporary self (Cannell 2016, 216).

Kin relationships in the Mormon tradition are similarly ones of ethical responsibility, and we must extend our conception of kin to include to spirit kin. Several researchers have started to consider how non-human agents, like spirits or deities, in their own right contribute to the ethical formation of living subjects (Mittermaier 2012; Scherz 2018; Pina-Cabral 2019; Itzhak 2021; Lambek 2010). Mittermaier (2012) considers how Egyptians are "acted upon," China Scherz shows how the ethical formation of Ugandan nuns is dependent on God as much as on the individual, which necessitates ethnographic focus on "spiritual others" (2018, 110), and João de Pina-Cabral describes a "participatory personhood" involving the living and spirits among Brazilian Candomblé practitioners (2019, 310). And in northern Utah, this mutuality of kin similarly extends to the spirit world, particularly with the spirits of ascendants and descendants. As we have seen in this chapter, and as we will explore in the next chapter, there is a pronounced interdependence between living and spirit kin, as responsibility for collective spiritual progress lies with both.

Although it might be easy to argue that the Mormon notion of kin can be construed as "spiritual kinship," perhaps what is notable is that the sense of genealogical and spiritual kin are not distinct and are not in opposition. This is similar to what Joelle Bahloul has observed about Judaism in the same volume on spiritual kinships. She writes that the matrilineal rule in Judaism "points to the fact that religious identity operates as a kinship relationship: the genealogical is formulated in religious terms; the spiritual is formulated in bio-genealogical terms" (2017, 112). In Mormonism, we could expand this to include spouses, to whom one is sealed for eternity in a temple marriage, and adopted children to whom parents may also be sealed for eternity (see Cannell 2013b). And, eventually, in Latter-day Saint teachings, when the temple work is complete, all of humanity will be sealed together.[9]

Spirit and living kin help one another on the path to glory. Just as the spirits of deceased relatives guide their descendants on the path of righteousness, perhaps by encouraging a mission or a return to active membership in the church, the spirits of family members yet to be—spirit children—may ask the living to mediate in requests to be born. In Latter-day Saint northern Utah, it is not just the living who have ethical responsibilities. Rather the entire family works together—from the time of the pre-existence—on the path of salvation and possible exaltation.

---

[9] Thanks to Adam Dunstan for pointing this out to me.

4

Where the Veil Is Thin

Temple Work, Posthumous Baptism, and the Gratitude of Spirits

"Yeah, because to us, [the temple] is the nearest place to heaven on earth.... If you're going to be where the veil is thin, it's in the temple." Jake, interview in Logan, Utah, June 2018.

Most of the instances reported in Mormonia of visitations from deceased persons pertain to the vicarious temple rites that must be performed by their living descendants before they may proceed along the paths of enteral glory and progress (Fife and Fife 1956, 222).

Often, the temple is referred to as a place "where the veil is thin" between this world and the other world of deity and the departed. This expression is interestingly metaphorical in that the temple does possess a veil, the veil of the temple. In ritual, this veil symbolizes the division between the earth and the Celestial Kingdom of the heavenly realms, and initiates do, literally, pass through it as they gain new status as endowed Saints invested with divine potential. Veil symbolism condenses these varied meanings so they come to influence each other (Davies 2000, 80).

Active Latter-day Saints have a formal obligation to perform various ritualized forms of *temple work* on behalf of the dead. Numerous accounts show that spirits of the deceased may appear to encourage temple work or express gratitude for it. Like the familial spirits discussed in the previous chapter, spirits who appear during temple work are consistently benevolent, although they may be more distantly related (or not related at all) to the recipient of the visits. In Chapter 3, I proposed that we should understand human interactions with the spirit world vis-à-vis the mutual responsibility for eternal life that is inherent in Latter-day Saint theology. Both living and spirit members of the family work together to achieve this, and this chapter considers the formal ritual obligations the living have to the deceased, which are performed in the temple. The most central of these obligations is posthumous proxy baptism, known more frequently among Latter-day Saints as "baptism for the dead." Many people tell of encounters with eager or grateful spirits of the deceased before, during, or after temple work. Spirits seeking baptism or other ordinances request the proxy rites directly or guide the living in the genealogy research that leads to proxy baptism. Grateful recipients of posthumous baptism may appear in the temple to give thanks to those performing their temple work or may even save the living children of their temple workers from physical harm. Nearly everyone I worked with on this project could tell me about a temple encounter with spirits, and such experiences have been a part of the Latter-day Saint experience for a long while, as evidenced by the similar narratives collected by Austin and Alta Fife many decades ago (1956, 222–227). Some people told me about their own such spirit experiences or those of close family members, and others related their desire to see spirits while doing temple work. Brad, the seminary teacher, told me that "the closer you get to temple worship, and family history, and death, the more likely you are to have these experiences." When we discussed the many stories of spirit encounters in the temple in Logan, the largest town in Cache Valley, Brad explained that while such experiences should be considered "stories" rather than "doctrine," they are certainly an important part of the rich "fabric" of what Latter-day Saints believe.

The spirit visitations in this chapter have much in common with those discussed in Chapter 3. Indeed, Latter-day Saints who receive visits from spirits in the temple always recognize them as spirits of the deceased (unlike the spirits we will explore in the next two chapters), and they are consistently benevolent. Their visits highlight the interdependence of the living and spirit worlds in their mutual quest for eternal life. In the previous chapter, I considered how this mutuality was evident in spontaneous, unpredictable encounters that frequently happen in times of emotional, spiritual, or physical need. As discussed previously, such visitations are not sought or solicited, and the recipients of the visits are thus "acted upon" by spirits, to adopt Mittermaier's (2012) term from her research on dreams among Muslims in Egypt. As we have seen, spirit kin support their living family members by offering comfort to the grieving, reassurance to those concerned about fecundity, and advice and direction at times of crisis. Spirits also encourage the living to have more offspring to give spirit children the chance to have a mortal existence. The living recipients of these visits frequently interpret them as welcome aid or support from the spirit world, which guides and directs them toward a path of righteous action. This chapter examines another dimension of spirit visits by considering how the living formally aid spirits through ritual action on their behalf, which sustains their mutual dependency. I have found that those who experience visits in the temple tend to interpret them not as guidance but as confirmatory: the spirit encounters index the reality of the eternality of the family as well as the righteousness of the ritual action and the ritual performer.

Temple Work and Spiritual Progress

Temple-based ritual obligations to the deceased are central to Latter-day Saint religious practice. In the temples, the living mediate directly on behalf of the dead by performing proxy rites for them, and these constitute most of what is known as "temple work." As noted, a key ritual is baptism, which is the primary ordinance in the church. The recipients of the proxy ordinances are sometimes, but not always, deceased ancestors of living members of the church, and they are identified through genealogical research. The deceased are baptized into the church by proxy, and then may receive other ritual ordinances by proxy, such as family sealing or temple endowments. All these rites assist the spirits on the path to salvation. This emphasis on the possibility and efficacy of performing ordinances for the dead is, of course, why the church so strongly emphasizes the importance of genealogical research—the living must identify their ancestors before they can assist them on the journey toward salvation through temple rites. As mediators, then, the living bring the dead closer to salvation through ritual action. It is important to note that this chapter does not attempt to comprehensively discuss temple rituals in history or practice. Indeed, temple rituals are sacred and private and, as I am not a member of the church, I am not privy to details of rituals. Rather, through analyzing narratives about spirit encounters in the temple, this chapter aims to show how Latter-day Saints in northern Utah understand and experience the mutuality of the spirits of the dead and the living in temple rituals.

As discussed in previous chapters, a central organizing theological idea in The Church of Jesus Christ of Latter-day Saints is the Plan of Salvation, and the culmination of salvation is eternal life in exaltation. Per Latter-day Saint teachings, a primary aspect of understanding the human person is that persons can essentially *become like* gods. A key source is from the Doctrine and Covenants 132:20–32, and a brief excerpt follows here: "Then shall they be gods, because they have no end; therefore shall they be from everlasting to everlasting, because they continue; then shall they be above all, because all things are subject unto them. Then shall they be gods, because they have all power, and the angels are subject unto them" (D&C 132:20).

Latter-day Saints recognize three kingdoms of heaven: the Telestial, the Terrestrial, and at the highest level, the Celestial Kingdom. The most righteous, meaning those who marry in the temple and receive all the ordinances, will inherit the Celestial Kingdom and exaltation, achieving perfection, eternal life, and thus becoming like God. The official church website defines exaltation as "eternal life, the kind of life God lives. He lives in great glory. He is perfect. He possesses all knowledge and all wisdom. He is the Father of spirit children. He is a creator. We can become like our Heavenly Father. This is exaltation" (www.churchofjesuschrist.org).

Former church president Joseph Fielding Smith's (1876–1972) explanation of this potential for human perfectibility is also helpful, in that he emphasizes the connection between God's state of being and humanity's potential: "The Father has promised through the Son that all that he has shall be given to those who are obedient to His commandments. *They shall increase in knowledge, wisdom, and power, going from grace to grace, until the fulness of the perfect day shall burst upon them*" (*Doctrines of Salvation*, comp. Bruce R. McConkie, 3 vols. [1954–1956], 2:36; italics in original). Many Latter-day Saints embrace this theological notion that the person is thus inherently transformable and perfectible through righteous actions.

The nature of exaltation has been discussed by the anthropologist and theologian Douglas Davies in *The Mormon Culture of Salvation* (2000). Davies argues provocatively for acknowledging the centrality of mortality and the dead in Latter-day Saint thought, writing that "the rise and success of Mormonism as an increasingly distinctive religious tradition can be interpreted as inextricably grounded in its conquest of death" (2000, 4). This is somewhat reminiscent of what the Fifes proposed decades ago when they wrote, "The real cult of the dead consists not in monuments of stone but in reminiscences that have been steeped in the brew of folklore until they come forth as images, more of that men aspire to be than of what they are" (Fife and Fife 1956, 263). Davies refers to exaltation as the "foundational Mormon process of salvation" (2000, 65), and suggests that the "distinctive" Mormon fixation on and means of conquering of death through the emphasis on the eternality of the family is "part of the ritual process of exaltation" (2000, 65). Davies asserts that, historically, the church moved away from "the grammar of a discourse of grace" in Protestant Christianity in favor of what he calls a "new vocabulary" (2000, 60; see also Brooke 1994). This "new vocabulary" generated the "Mormon culture of exaltation, grounded in the soteriological lineage, fostered by temple ritual, which combined to empower the profound religious belief in the transcendence of death" (Davies 2000, 60).

This achievement is predicated on righteous action, and temple rituals are thus the key to exaltation. Davies identifies "temple Mormonism" as one of the three primary modalities of Latter-day Saint life, along with "domestic Mormonism" and "ward Mormonism" (2000). He proposes that it is in temple Mormonism where the focus on mortality and the status of the dead is so evident, and "temples house the prime rites of endowment that assure an identity for eternity subsumed within a family bonded for cosmic togetherness" (2000, 67). Further, "it is this realm of experience of eternal persons that established the Mormon Temple as a *domus dei*" (2000, 74). Davies references historian Jan Shipps's argument that while the individual is the "unit for salvation" in Mormonism, it is the family that is the "unit for exaltation" (Shipps 1985, 148).

Spirit Assistance with Genealogy

The responsibility for the journey of the spirit is inherently collective. Members of the church strive not only for their own righteous perfection, but also for that of others, starting with their family members. This includes the immediate family and the ancestral family, some of whom may be residing in spirit prison, as discussed in Chapter 2, where they wait to receive the teachings of the church and the blessings of the ordinances. Latter-day Saint interest in genealogy stems from this imperative to help others achieve salvation and exaltation: one must identify one's ancestors before they can be baptized, and they must be baptized before they can receive other ordinances. Although this outreach effort begins with the family, as noted earlier, there is an understanding that when the temple work is eventually complete, all of humanity will be sealed together.

Importantly, in everyday Latter-day Saint understanding in northern Utah and in mainline church teachings, the spirit can accept or reject the baptism.[1]

---

[1] Outside of the church, baptism for the dead is controversial, even with the emphasis on choice. I recall my mother, a committed Episcopalian, frequently announcing to Mormon friends and

In a conversation with Mrs. Williams, she reflected on this, and explained the importance of genealogical research in preparing for temple work by telling us about one of her sisters. The sister had led a challenging life and had never had temple work done for her, so after her death her family decided to perform ordinances for her. Mrs. Williams first emphasized a spirit's ability to choose whether to accept the rites:

> If I would be searching my genealogy and I find I have a great-great-grandmother who has never been to the temple to have her work done or anything, [then] I can take her name. I have to record her genealogy. Who her parents were, where she was born, and all that . . . and I could take her to the temple and . . . do her work for her . . . . She can either accept it in the spirit world or reject it. Now I have a sister who . . .

Here, Mrs. Williams trailed off and paused for a moment while she reflected on her sister's life. She continued, saying:

> Her life becomes sad. She had a lot of problems, she ended up with divorce and sadness in her life, and her [temple] work was never done. So after she passed away we did her work—my sisters and I. I was baptized for her, one of them did her endowment work . . . . We sealed her to mom and dad. So this was all done, but now it's her choice.

Mrs. Williams notes the importance of genealogy research to temple work. In northern Utah folklore, spirits frequently help when genealogy researchers run into difficulty finding particular ancestors or family connections. In one of our first conversations, Brad remarked that one of the main areas where people are likely to receive help from the spirits of the deceased is in doing genealogy research. Shauna, the graduate student, made a similar comment when we started discussing spirit visits:

> So a lot of times it [spirit visits] has to do with genealogy. And so I've heard people say, "I was doing genealogy and I couldn't find this name and then

---

neighbors that they did not need to bother baptizing her spirit after her death because her spirit would certainly reject it! The baptisms of those killed during the Holocaust have been soundly criticized. In 1995, the church agreed to stop these baptisms, although it has been reported that they continue in various temples (see Perreault, Duffy, and Morrison 2017 for an analysis of media coverage of this controversy).

my ancestor came to me in a vision," or in a dream and said, "you need to look here or you need to go to this place and then I found their information" and they're able to be sealed to their family . . . . older people say that they were doing their genealogy and an ancestor pointed them in a direction in order to get their work done.

In one account from the Utah State University folklore collection, a student writes of hearing a voice that urged her to keep searching for the birth certificate of a troublesome ancestor. The writer relates that she had been frustrated in doing genealogy work, and she was thinking about this while she was at a temple endowment session. She heard a voice that insisted that the genealogical information she was searching for was indeed available; she attributed the voice to her Aunt May. The voice explained that a relative, one James Hall, was born in Brooklyn, New York. She writes, "However, the impression was very clear that the information WAS available and I felt the way I'd be able to find out if it was a real conversation with Auntie May or not would be the fulfillment of her admonition" (Fox 1986). Fox explains that she had never before been able to find a birth certificate for James Hall, and she tried one more time. Although she did not find the birth certificate, she did find death certificates for both James Hall and another important relative. The death certificates were sufficient to submit their names to the temple. She writes, "I could almost hear Auntie May saying, 'I told you so!'" (Fox 1986)

In a similar account, a student relates a story she heard from her mother-in-law, Sue, who converted to Mormonism when she was in her early twenties.

A close friend of Sue's was asleep next to her husband one night. She woke up suddenly because she thought she heard someone call her name. This movement woke her husband up and he asked her what happened. She told him what she heard, but they both thought it must have been a dream and they settled back down. Before she fell asleep she heard her name called again. She told her husband she heard it again and the voice sounded like the voice of her Aunt Opal, who had passed away only two weeks prior to this. Jokingly, her husband said, "Well, ask her what she wants." He then fell asleep. The third time her name was called, Sue's friend identified the voice of her aunt and did ask her what she wanted. She said she was not afraid to hear the voice of her Aunt Opal, who had not been a member of the Church. Her aunt simply told her that she wanted her to do the family's genealogy work (Hodgkinson 1995).

Interestingly, the writer of this account interprets the story as "an attempt to convert her." She notes that although she was "now LDS," she was not at the time her mother-in-law told her the story, when she and her husband had just been married for a few weeks.

Ordinances, the Priesthood, and the Temple

The temple is the primary site of the rituals performed by the living on behalf of the dead. The Church of Jesus Christ of Latter-day Saints builds impressive, architecturally distinct temples wherever the church membership is large enough to support the ritual work that must be performed in the temples. Although the grand appearance of the temples may suggest comparisons to cathedrals or Friday mosques, the activity of the temple is not large-scale collective worship, but rather "work" on behalf of the dead, and as such temples are not constructed with large, central worship halls as one would find in cathedrals. Many of the visitations described in this chapter took place at the Logan Temple (see Figure 4.1). The temple was completed in the late

Figure 4.1 Logan Temple, photo by Erin Stiles.

nineteenth century, and it sits on a hill on the eastern side of the valley, visible from nearly everywhere in the valley. It is architecturally impressive—indeed, the Gothic style gives the temple the look of a medieval European castle, save for the two white towers on either end.

The work of the temple redeems the dead through proxy baptism and the subsequent performance of other church ordinances on their behalf. As noted in an earlier chapter, ordinances are required acts of religious practice, and they are performed under the direction of members of what is known as the Melchizedek Priesthood. The first ordinance is baptism, and children growing up in the church are usually baptized at the age of eight years, which is considered the age of accountability. Other essential ordinances that are necessary for salvation and exaltation are confirmation, ordination to the Melchizedek Priesthood, temple endowments, and the sealing of marriages in order to render the marriage eternal. In my conversation with Elder Neilson and Elder Collins, the young missionaries identified these five as the key ordinances. Because only men can be ordained as members of the priesthood, I remarked that it seemed that women have four essential ordinances and men have five. However, they countered that, actually, the priesthood ordinance is for everyone. In Elder Collins's words, "everybody is a beneficiary of the priesthood." We will return to questions of gender and the priesthood in Chapter 6.

The ordinances are not just for living members of the church. Spirits of the dead sometimes request temple ordinances to be performed on their behalf. Baptisms, sealings, and temple endowments are performed to redeem the spirits of the dead so they can embark, or continue, on the path to salvation. The temple endowment has been part of church activity since the mid-nineteenth century, and is a sacred, private temple rite that is not shared publicly. In general, it involves receiving special knowledge of a religious nature. According to the official church website, "To receive the endowment is to receive a course of instruction together with all the keys, powers, and ordinances ordained and revealed by God to prepare his children for eternal life" (The Church of Jesus Christ of Latter-day Saints 1974). Young Latter-day Saints will often receive their temple endowments when they are ready to go on a mission or when they marry. Sealings are rites that are performed in the temple that ensure the eternality of the family. Marriages that are sealed in the temple are eternal, and children born of such a union are automatically sealed to their parents; this is known as being "born in the covenant." If a couple is married before becoming Mormon, they can be sealed to each other and their children at a later tie. As noted in Chapter 3, adoptive children can also be sealed to the family. I have found spirit encounters in the temple are nearly always with benevolent spirits who appreciate the ordinances being performed on their behalf. Indeed, as discussed in Chapter 2, I only came across one or two accounts that could be construed in any way as a non-benevolent spirit kin intervention, and with both, the spirit's actions might be understood as a result of loneliness rather than malicious intent.

A holder of the Melchizedek Priesthood always performs baptisms (and other ordinances), although any Latter-day Saint in good standing may stand in as a proxy during the rites. The ordinances cannot be done without members of the priesthood, and priesthood holders thus make the divine present for others.[2] The institution of the priesthood is thus a mediator par excellence. In Latter-day Saint teachings, the priesthood passed from Jesus to Joseph Smith to worthy males aged twelve and over. Many view this as a key difference between The Church of Jesus Christ of Latter-day Saints and other churches. Mr. Anderson, Andrea's father, who was in his eighties at the time of our interview, stated this explicitly and assured me that although he knew that other churches certainly do good things, the distinguishing factor between all the Christian churches was that the Latter-day Saints traced priestly authority back to Jesus Christ.

Mr. Anderson explained, "We feel that we have the priesthood authority and our religion is the true religion. That's not to say other religions don't have part of this truth and some others might have most of the truth but they don't have the actual priesthood authority. That's our belief now, and so people and sometimes you'll get [people thinking] we're people that condemn the Catholics, [but] that's a bunch of crap."

The priesthood consists of boys and men over age twelve who are in good standing. It is tiered, and the historian Stephen Taysom has proposed that "Mormon attitudes about the sacredness of hierarchy" are evident in the body of priesthood (2017, 59). The two major branches are the Aaronic and the Melchizedek. Members of the priesthood are called "priesthood holders" because the term "priest" is used to refer to one specific leadership position within the Aaronic Priesthood.[3] Priesthood holders of various leadership

---

[2] There is also an important Latter-day Saint emphasis on personal inspiration from the Holy Spirit (Mould 2011). This is akin perhaps to the "live and direct" that Engelke discusses in his work in Zimbabwe among the Masowe apostolic Christians (2007).
[3] William Hartley analyzes the changing role of the Aaronic Priesthood from the early church to the late twentieth century, showing that the roles of leadership positions in the priesthood changed in response to the growing church (Hartley 1996).

positions have different "keys," or powers, in their arsenal, and these correspond to certain ritual duties. The historians W. Paul Reeve and Jeffrey Johnson have argued that, historically, the conferring of the priesthood on all Mormon men meant that the priesthood was "democratic" as well as hierarchical, in that all men were granted titles and were allowed to "pronounce gifts of the spirit upon their posterity" (Reeve and Johnson 2010, 300).

The lower, or Aaronic, priesthood is conferred upon boys when they are twelve years old, and it has three levels: Deacons, Teachers, and Priests. Young men in good standing are ordained into the Melchizedek Priesthood at the age of eighteen, the first step of which is that of Elder. Once a young man becomes an elder, he may give *priesthood blessings*, and thus "bestow the gift of the Holy Ghost by the laying on of hands" (The Church of Jesus Christ of Latter-day Saints, 2023a).[4] The priesthood blessing is an example of a "key" in the priesthood. In essence, holding a specific key provides the priesthood holder with the authority to preside over or enact certain ritual actions and ordinances such as distributing the sacrament, baptism, or directing temple work (see The Church of Jesus Christ of Latter-day Saints 2012). Higher up in church leadership, priesthood holders have more keys. As those in the Melchizedek Priesthood hold more keys than their Aaronic counterparts, higher-ranking leadership positions of the Melchizedek Priesthood have more keys than other leadership positions. For example, a bishop holds more keys than a ward member, and the Quorum of the Twelve Apostles, a leadership body second only to the First Presidency, holds even more keys; only the president/prophet of the church holds all the priesthood keys.

Baptism for the Dead and the Gratitude of Spirits

Much temple work involves baptism for the dead, in which the living are baptized by proxy on behalf of the deceased. Baptism by proxy typically prioritizes distant ancestors of living member of the church,[5] identified

---

[4] It seems that sometimes baptisms were used to exorcise spirits (Stapley and Wright 2008). In the words of church elder Dallin Oakes, "In a priesthood blessing a servant of the Lord exercises the priesthood, as moved upon by the Holy Ghost, to call upon the powers of heaven for the benefit of the person being blessed" (The Church of Jesus Christ of Latter-day Saints 1987).

[5] In their intriguing look at baptisms for healing and health in the early church, Stapley and Wright observe that baptismal healings were very common in the early days of the church, and these took place in early Utah temples earlier than the proxy baptism (Stapley and Wright 2008); for a period of time, baptisms for health were the most common ordinance for the living in the Utah temples in

through genealogical research. Thus, we see that the collective ethical responsibility for salvation extends far beyond close kin. Many Latter-day Saints in northern Utah begin performing this temple work in their teenage years, and outings may be organized the church auxiliary associations for teenagers known as Young Women's and Young Men's.[6]

Those serving as proxies for the baptisms are subject to full immersion baptism performed by a holder of the Melchizedek Priesthood. The vast majority of the accounts of spirit visits during ritual temple work describe the visits occurring during or after posthumous baptisms; few accounts relate spirit visits during other temple rites.

Shauna identified baptism for the dead as a common site of spirit visitations, and she reflected on this in remembering her own experiences of proxy baptism as a teenager. She noted that unlike other temple work, such as receiving endowments, baptisms are quick, and it is easy to do multiple baptisms in one session. The proxies may be baptized several times in one session, and the success of the activity is often counted in "names," as in "Jennifer did thirty names [i.e., was baptized for thirty people] today." Shauna explained:

> Yeah, a lot of times [spirits will visit] when people are doing genealogy or baptism or endowments, which are the other things you do in the temple. Those ones [the latter two] you do older; younger, twelve to eighteen, or twelve and up can do baptisms in the temple . . . . You get endowed before you go on a mission or before you get married. So I got endowed a week before I got married . . . that's when you start wearing garments and those sessions are like an hour and a half long, so they're big. You know, when you go do a baptism it takes like five seconds for each person, and you just get dunked like thirty times.

I asked, "You do the full immersion baptism?" She replied:

> Mm-hmm. They have this baptismal font in the temple and, the guy's like, "I baptize you for and on behalf of" and then reads the name of the person

---

the nineteenth century, and the majority of those receiving healing baptisms were women. However, baptisms for health also took place in many other locations outside of the temples.

[6] When I was young, I recall friends frequently baptizing for the dead as a church activity. As in, "Can you come over today?" I would ask. "No, I can't, our Young Women's is baptizing for the dead."

who is dead, and then you know, baptizes you. And, anyway, so you can do a whole bunch of those. But when you go for endowments, it's like an hour and a half session and you're doing it for one person, so it takes an hour and a half for each person who's died. So, Mormons have to . . . the first time you go for [endowments] yourself, but after that it's always for someone who died.

Shauna recalled that, as a young girl, she really wanted to have a spirit experience. Because so many stories circulating in northern Utah told of spirits appearing during temple work, she expected that this might happen when she was performing baptisms for the dead. She said, "It was my hope that [I would get visited]. Well, not [by] an evil one, obviously . . . like you'd hear about when you go to the temple, to do . . . baptisms for the dead as a teenager, you would maybe see the person that you were gonna do the work for and they would thank you for helping them to become a Mormon after they died."

She laughed at the memory, and I asked her why she wanted to see a spirit, "Did you think you would receive some special knowledge? Or that a spirit would befriend you?"

Shauna's answer emphasized both the confirmatory potential of such a visit and the importance of helping spirits achieve salvation. She said, "[I thought it would] just confirm everything for me. And that, you know, I'd go to the temple, and I would see a spirit that's like, 'Thank you for being here and helping me not be damned. Because now I'm baptized with the proper authority and now I can go to heaven. So thanks for that!'"

Shauna is not the only one who hoped to see a spirit while performing baptisms for the dead. In account in the Utah State University folklore collection, a young woman named Karalee recalls a story her grandfather told her when she was young. She writes:

He said there was a man who had gone to the temple to do baptisms for the dead. And he said that his heart was prepared because he wanted to have a special experience. Well, he did it seems like 32 names and so he went into the font and was baptised [sic] and he noticed each time he was baptised [sic] he noticed that in the viewing area (for some reason he could see it) there was a large group of people. And each time he was baptised [sic] he noticed one of them would smile and kind of nod their head and walk away. And after he had gotten through about half of his names, he realized, because the spirit was with him very strongly at that time [this means the Holy Spirit], that he was seeing the spirits of the people was being baptized [*sic*] for. After that, when I first had my chance to do Baptism for the dead, I tried to see my people, too, but I was doing them at the Provo temple, and your back is to the viewing area and I couldn't see. (Pugmire 1996)

Karalee's account is somewhat similar to Shauna's memory of wishing to see the spirits she was baptized for. Karalee hopes to see her "people," like the devout young man in her grandfather's story, but she is not able to do so. Interestingly, she attributes this not to a lack of righteousness or doubt about the possibility of spirit manifestations, but rather to the structural arrangement of the space in the Provo temple: those performing baptisms have their backs to the viewing area, and so cannot see the grateful spirits.

Although Shauna and Karalee did not encounter spirits when being baptized for the dead, narratives about such experiences are plentiful. Numerous accounts in the student folklore collections tell of as-yet-unbaptized spirits appearing to an attentive living proxy to request baptism. The accounts vary in detail, but the general line of the story is as follows: (1) a young person, usually a teenager, is being baptized for the dead at temple (the account often emphasizes the teen's sincerity and faith); (2) when the temple worker tells the teenager that he or she is at the end of the list of "names" to be baptized, the teen questions this and asks the temple worker to review the list of names; (3) the worker finds that one name has been missed, and asks how the teen knew one was missing; (4) the teenager reports being able to see all of spirits of those being baptized, and that one remained for her baptism. Three versions of this story follow, all from the student folklore collection:

Kay and his ward members were performing baptisms for the dead. Kay had been baptised [*sic*] for 30 names and was stepping out of the water when he noticed a little boy in the corner crying. He walked over to the boy and asked him what the matter was. The little boy looked up at him and said that he had been waiting so long to be baptized, yet they had forgotten to baptize him. Kay went back and asked the man overseeing he baptisms that day to check if any names had been missed. After looking through the list they realized that one name had been overlooked. Kay went back into the water and was baptized for this little boy. As he emerged from the water he looked to the corner to see the boy, but the boy's spirit disappeared. (Watts 1994a)

In another version of the story, the voice is heard saying, "Don't forget me..." (Alder 1984).

In another narrative, Jamie, a young girl performing proxy baptisms for the first time sees a line of spirits, all "ladies dressed in white," standing around the baptismal font, one of whom would leave each time she was baptized. When the man performing the baptisms said that she was done, Jamie did not believe him, and gently urged him to read the list of her "names" again. He had indeed forgotten someone, and then they performed that baptism. When he asked the girl how she knew he had missed someone, the account reads "Jamie very humbly replied after every name one of the ladies in white standing around the faunt [sic] would leave the room, and when you said we were finished I knew we weren't because one woman was still left in the room" (Boman 1984).

In a similar account, the writer notes that the girl says, "I saw each of the people that I was to be baptized for standing around the edges of the font. As I was baptized for each person, they smiled and left the room. When the Elder told me that I was finished I could still see one person waiting for their baptism" (Page 1982).

A related set of narratives involves grateful recipients of posthumous baptism repaying the favor by helping their living proxies. One well-known tale follows this pattern: (1) a woman (or sometimes a married couple) goes to the temple to perform baptisms for the dead; (2) at some point, either before or during the temple work, she has an ominous feeling, and she consults a bishop or temple worker, who encourages her to complete the baptisms; (3) when she gets home, she finds out one her children fell into a canal but was rescued by a mysterious stranger; (4) when the child relates the stranger's name, the mother realizes the stranger was a spirit and the recipient of her temple work that very day. I remember hearing this story in my youth, and there are many versions in the folklore archives. Student writers report hearing it from parents, at sacrament meetings, at firesides (informal evening church meetings on particular topics), and while driving home from basketball games. William A. Wilson, in an article from the 1990s, notes that this particular story is one of the most widely known in "Mormon country," and one that his own folklore students brought to class frequently (Wilson 1995). What follows is a version of the tale from the 1970s that I found in the student folklore collection:

> A lady had gone to the temple for an afternoon session. While in this session, she felt very uneasy and felt like she should return home. She approached one of the temple workers and told him how she felt. He reassured her that if she would just finish the session everything would be alright [sic] at home. She did just that. After the session, she returned home as fast as possible.
>
> As she approached her neighborhood, she saw police cars and fire engines all over. She stopped and asked what had happened. They told her that a little girl had fallen in the canal. In a rage of panic, the woman hurried home. She ran to her little girl's room. Standing in the room with water dripping from her was the woman's little girl. When she asked the little girl what happened this is how she responded, "I felt into the canal and then a lady picked me up out of the water and carried me to my room." The little girl told her mother the woman's name. It was the same name as the one this mother had done temple work for that afternoon. (Hardman 1978)

In another version of the story, the mysterious woman who performed the watery rescue is the child's deceased grandmother:

> A little boy was left with a babysitter while his parents were at the temple (in Logan) doing work for the dead. The little boy wandered off and fell into a canal. When the babysitter found the little boy she asked him what happened and why he was wet. The boy said he had fallen in the canal and was struggling until a lady in a long white dress had pulled him out. He said she looked like his grandmother who was dead.
>
> After returning home his parents showed him a picture of his dead grandmother and he said that it was the lady that had helped him out of the canal. It was for his grandmother the little boy's parents were doing Temple work for [sic] when he fell into the canal. (Abrams 1980)

Still another version tells of a couple who wanted to do temple work, but they had no babysitter. Mysterious visitors, who turn out to be the spirits of the recently baptized, show up and offer to watch the children:

> Have you heard the one about the couple who wants to go do work for the dead? Well, one night this married couple feels a sudden urgency to go to the temple. The only problem is that their three children will have no one to watch them and they're all too young to stay home alone. Well, there's a knock at the door when the couple is discussing this. She opens the door

and finds a cute little old couple who says that they are relatives of their next door neighbors who aren't home and they were wondering if they could stay at their house until their relatives got home. The young couple had a good feeling about the couple and told them that they were more than welcome to stay. After talking with the old couple, the young ones felt that they would be okay if they left their children and went to the temple. The old couple said that they would be more than pleased. Anyway, the couple goes to the temple and when they get back, the kids are safely tucked into bed and the cute old couple's faces were glowing. As the couple was leaving the young ones asked their names. Once the couple was gone, the young ones realized that the names they had sealed at the temple were the names of the old couple. The next day, they asked their neighbors about the old couple and the neighbors said they had some ancestors by that last name but they had died over 20 years before and no relatives had shown up by that name. (Toelken 1997)

After relating the narrative, Toelken provides context for this account by explaining the significance of temple ordinances to achieving the highest level of salvation. Toelken concludes that the spirit couple showed up so that the young couple could complete their sealing in the temple that evening.

Tales such as these circulate widely in the community, and people report similar heroic rescue outside of the context of temple work, too. Lyne explained to me how a spirit rescued one her children:

> I know there was one time, my little boy when he was little, my oldest son, he got out of the house, like he went to my room for some reason and I didn't answer so he didn't think I was there. So he was like three or four, he went outside and was wandering around all by himself and a spirit brought him back into the house. He said that somebody, well it kinda scared me, because he said somebody in a black robe and I was like, "What do you mean a black robe!" but maybe it was so it wasn't all bright and scary, who knows, but it brought him back to the house.

As we have seen, spirits occasionally ask for help from the living, and some may request baptisms or other ordinances. Elder Neilson shared a fascinating personal account in which he had an encounter with the recipient of a proxy baptism. We had been discussing spirits in general, and at one point the young man paused somewhat dramatically. We were all silent for a moment, and then he told me that he felt prompted to share an experience with me. The encounter had happened just a few months before our conversation, when he had been paired with another mission companion.[7] Elder Neilson explained that he and this companion had a run-in with a troubled spirit who was trapped in a church building:

> Me and my companion, we were going to a church building just to use the restroom and outside there was a lady and her children. She came up to us and told us that somebody from inside the building had called 911 and the police came and looked all throughout the building, but they couldn't find anything. So, she asked us to go inside and maybe see if there was somebody in there. So, we did that and when me and my companion went inside we just felt something very . . . it felt mysterious to me, it felt really weird.

I asked if the mysterious feeling was frightening or compelling, and he said that it was neither, it was "just mysterious." He continued:

> My companion didn't really notice it at first but eventually, as we were going throughout the building, he also eventually noticed it. He was like, "You're right, something's weird here," and eventually we went to one side of the building and we finally just went into the basement because it was the last place that we hadn't checked and we did encounter— . . . we didn't really see it, but we *felt* something. We felt that there was a spirit around us and we felt that it was literally right in front of us and we didn't know why.

They started to leave the building, but then felt a prompting from the Holy Ghost, encouraging them to return to pray for the spirit. They did so, and "asked for ministering angels to be sent." When they left the building again, once again the Holy Ghost prompted them to return to the distressed spirit. They returned and prayed for the spirit again, but when they left the building, the spirit followed them. Elder Neilson explained:

> We kept walking, and then eventually we started receiving inspiration as to who this spirit was . . . . eventually we started having really weird stuff

---

[7] Missionaries always work and live in pairs, and every three months or so, a missionary gets a new "companion."

happen to us. Animals kept following us . . . as we were going in neighbors' houses, the spirit wouldn't go in with us but would wait out at the front door and then as we came back out, the spirit would start following us again.

He said they kept praying:

And then afterwards, eventually we were looking at a mailbox, I think I mentioned to my companion how weird it would be if we saw something move. And then, to my surprise, there was mailbox to my right, right on the doorstep and bing it flicked, all by itself. Both me and my companion jumped and were wondering what the heck just happened?

. . . and then . . . I was struck, like my whole body started tingling really weird. We eventually we made our way back to that same church building and we knelt down upon our knees and we prayed for the spirit to have peace and comfort, asking for it to stay here so that the [ministering] spirits could come and help it out. [Then] we . . . noticed that the spirit wasn't following us anymore . . . We believe that it was a spirit who had already been baptized by proxy in the temple, had already received the ordinances by proxy, but just hadn't accepted it yet.

Elder Neilson's account is compelling, and I was grateful that he felt comfortable sharing it with me. I find his experience intriguing in that he describes an interaction with the spirit of a deceased individual and personal revelation—a prompting—from the Holy Ghost. The spirit seeks their assistance, and the Holy Ghost instructs Elder Neilson and his companion to serve that spirit through prayer. Even though the young missionaries did not perform the ordinance of baptism for the spirit, through their righteous action—prayers on the spirit's behalf—they were eventually able to "release" the spirit by encouraging it to accept the baptism performed on its behalf. As he explains, Elder Neilson presumed that the spirit was troubled because it was unable to understand, and therefore accept, posthumous baptism.

A number of narratives from the student folklore collection are similar requests from spirits. In the following account, Maria, a middle-aged woman who recently became a member of the church, is nervous about performing the baptisms for her father and brother, who died a few years earlier in their home country of Italy. The writer, Maria's neighbor, says that Maria prayed about it, and then went to sleep:

At about 4 a.m. (12 noon in Italy), she received a telephone call from her mother. Her mother told her that she dreamed with her husband and son, and that they told her that they were very happy because Maria was going to do something very special for them. They told her to tell Maria it was okay, that they wanted her to do the work. Maria's mother is not a LDS member, and had no idea what Maria was doing. When Maria went to the Temple that morning, she felt secure and happy, she knew that what she was doing was right. She says that the warm presence of her father and brother were there with her throughout the ceremony. (Shelton 1995)

Framing this feeling as the "presence" of those baptized is quite common; Davies (2000), although he does not describe spirit encounters, has also noted that Latter-day Saints often comment on feeling the "presence" of ancestors when performing temple work.

In a similar account, a student writes about her grandmother, Martha, who joined the church when she was a young woman in Denmark, around the year 1900. Martha's father was not happy that she had converted, and she eventually left Europe and settled in Cache Valley. When she was much older, she was doing temple work and did not know if she should be baptized for her father, so she consulted with president of the Logan Temple. They decided she should wait, but after a few days, Martha had a "strange visitor" who turned out to be her deceased father:

> Her father came three nights in a row and stood at the foot of her bed in the nighttime. Nothing was said in these visitations. Martha was now assured that her Father was no longer bitter towards the gospel and the L.D.S. [sic] church. He had accepted the gospel in the spirit world and was now prepared to have his work done for him here on earth. (Peterson 1984)

After this, Martha visited the temple president again, and they decided to do his temple work as soon as possible. In both of these accounts, a convert to the church expresses concern about baptizing deceased family members who were not church members. Their worries fade away when the spirits of the deceased visit and ask to be baptized.

Another narrative comes from a student's interview with a friend, Karen, who was particularly devoted to genealogy and temple work. Karen told the writer that when her father had visited Wisconsin for genealogy research, he came across a young boy's grave from the 1970s. He realized he had done the temple work for the boy's parents, but he did not know they had had a son. The writer's father then took down the information from the grave so his daughter could do the temple work to seal the young man to his parents. Karen explains:

> Anyway, I busy at Scout Camp all summer cooking for the little scouts and I did not get this boy's work done before I left. When I got back I was busy and I kind of ignored my responsibilities to family history. One night as I was sleeping I felt the presence of two or three people beside my bed, kind of impatiently wanting me to do something for them. I recognized them as the parents of this little boy and in my sleep I promised them that tomorrow I would get his work started. Well, the next day came and went and then it was the weekend and I still hadn't done this little boys' work. On Monday morning I woke up to the sound of a little boy saying, "You promised me. You promised me." I didn't delay after that. I got up the next morning and got that little boy sealed to his parents and I haven't been bothered by voices since. (Allred 1994)

This account is telling in that Karen specifically emphasizes her "responsibility to family history" when she expresses regret that she had not yet done the temple work for the boy. Clearly, she understands the work of genealogy and subsequent temple work as a responsibility to her family.

Finally, let us consider an amusing tale about a posthumously baptized spirit that involves the spirit of Lady Godiva. The student writer explains that her Aunt Sheila found the name of Lady Godiva when researching her family history. Aunt Sheila had been having dreams about "a beautiful woman riding naked on a white horse through her neighborhood. After Sheila did Lady Godiva's baptism for the dead, she never dream [sic] about her again" (Moffit 1996). The writer contextualizes the account by saying that her mother, Aunt Sheila's sister, frequently told this story at family gatherings even though she was doubtful about the veracity of her sister's dreams. In the writer's words, "I guess everyone has to have a claim to fame."

Other Temple Visitors

Not all spirits who make appearances during temple work are those who have recently received posthumous ordinances or those awaiting the ordinances.

Sometimes, the spirits of those who have died premature deaths appear in the temple to comfort their living relatives. Mrs. Williams shared the following experience from her family:

> I had a cousin who was killed in the Korean War. He was just . . . you know . . . [one of] these young men whom they dearly love. And he lost his life. And they [his mother and father—Mrs. Williams' aunt and uncle] were attending the [Logan] temple one night. They had mourned so over his death. And after that the session was over, one of the officiators came up and said, have you lost a son? And they said "yes" and he says, "He was with you tonight in the temple." And she said during the session you know that she just felt just a warm feeling all at once. And I just kind of took it as it was maybe him visiting her to reassure him that he was okay.

Mrs. Williams explained that they "just went to do a session, to do some temple work for people beyond the grave. In our church we do temple work for those who pass on." I asked how the officiator saw the young man, and although she was not clear on exactly what happened, she explained that, "You know, it made a total turnabout in their lives because from then on they felt like, you know, he [their son] was okay, that he was where he needed to be and things were all right."

Accounts such as these are common, and many families share stories of meeting spirits of loved ones who died prematurely in the temple. Unlike the accounts described in Chapter 4, these visitations happen not in times of obvious need or distress, but when the recipient are doing temple work for others. Consequently, the recipients of the visits often interpret them not simply as the spirit proffering comfort but also as a special blessing confirming the righteousness of the ritual activity.

Jake and his family have had numerous experiences of spirits, and he told me that many members of his family had encounters with deceased ancestors when they were doing work in the temple. The first encounter he described happened to his wife's father and sister. He told me:

> So, my wife comes from a family of eight that are living, she had an older sister who died at childbirth . . . . She died when she was born, I think she may have been stillborn. I can't remember. So, she was either stillborn or

died, they didn't even get out of the hospital, so they never knew her. My father-in-law has talked openly about seeing her as a grown adult in the temple. And knowing it was her, you know, knowing exactly who it was, I don't know that any words were spoken or anything . . . . I just remember hearing a story where, "Yeah I've seen her. I've seen her in the temple." My father-in-law is a convert. At twenty-one he was baptized.

He talked a bit more about his wife's family, and he told me that his sister-in-law had also seen the spirit of this child when she was doing her own temple work. This was particularly significant to Jake because even though his sister-in-law later left the church, she would not deny the temple story—she was convinced it had truly happened.

I remarked that many spirit encounters seem to happen in the temples, and Jake said, "Yeah, because to us, that's the nearest place to heaven on earth . . . in the temple, if you're going to be where the veil is thin, it's in the temple."

Jake shared another story about an aquaintance who had a similarly profound experience in the temple after he and his wife lost a baby:

> They lost a baby. She was playin' on the floor on a blanket, the wife walked out of the room, and then she walked back, she was not breathing and non-responsive. She was out of the room for two minutes. And [she] was, you know, just a baby . . . . it just devastated them . . . . And I ran into him, I can't remember how long it was after this happened. And I was askin' him how he was doin'. Cause I'd been hearing he was really struggling. And he said, you know, I'm doing good now. And I said, "Now? What happened that you're finally just getting over it?" And he said, "I saw her." I said, "You saw her?" He said, "Yeah, we went to the temple." You know, you go to the temple to try to find some peace and solace. He said, "We went to the temple and I saw her." I said, "You saw her?" He said, "Yeah. I saw her."

When I asked if the spirit of his friend's daughter appeared as a baby, Jake said that he had asked the same thing. His aquaintance told him that he saw her as a grown woman. Jake related, "And he said, 'She was in there, and she was in the room, and she smiled at me, and then she wasn't in the room anymore . . . . And it was her, and she was fine, and I knew she was fine, and everything was okay, and I've been fine ever since.'"

Jake explained that this friend was "not a guy who would make something up." He said, "You know, some people make stuff up 'cause they want some attention. He's not that. He's not that. He's very serious-minded . . . . he's also not one of these, you know, every time a bird flies it's miracle of God, you know?"

I observed to Jake that these two encounters were somewhat different from other temple experiences because they were visits from lost children who appeared not when their families were performing proxy baptisms for *them*, but when doing temple work for *other* people. Jake affirmed that this was what happened and that they were indeed different kinds of encounters. He said that he did not know what his father-in-law and sister-in-law were doing in the temple when they saw the spirit, but he knew that his friend was "just doin' his regular temple session. Doin' work for someone else."

However, Jake said, he himself had also felt the presence of recipients of temple work, "This is different because it's a family member. I have been in the temple before doing work, and doing it for somebody else, and having a feeling that, 'Yeah they, this person is here, and they are accepting this work.'"

I asked, "Really? You could feel it?"

Jake clarified that sometimes when the dead visit you just get a feeling, but sometimes you see the spirit. He said:

When my grandmother passed away, we lived in her house for a while, never saw her, but knew she was there a couple of times. One time I woke my wife up at night and said, "Grandma's here." "Are you sure?" And then my daughter had been born, she would have been the first grandchild, my grandma died before she was born, and she was in the other room, and she was yappin' and talkin' and all the sudden she was real quiet. We go in there, and she's sittin' there just starin' over in the corner. She's just starin'. And she you know, she kinda smiles like someone's talkin' to her. And then you know, eventually, and then like, they're gone! And she starts back to what she was doing. And it was right around that same time that I'm having these feelings that Grandma's come to visit. And you never saw anything. You just, you feel it and you know it. You just feel it and you know it. It's like I just knew it: "Grandma is here." "What?" "Yeah, she's here. I don't know why. I just feel it. I know it. She's here." Out of the blue.

Visits from Jesus Christ and Joseph Smith

I conclude this chapter by considering two very unusual encounters: visits to the living from Jesus Christ and the spirit of Joseph Smith. I have not found many accounts of visits with such prominent religious figures.[8] Folklorists have recorded accounts of visits from biblical and Book of Mormon figures such as the benevolent Three Nephites (Fife 1940; Lee 1949) or the menacing Gadianton Robbers from the Book of Mormon (Reeve 2011), and numerous sightings of Cain, who in recent history is often equated with Bigfoot (see Reeve and van Wagenen 2011). In my interviews, no one reported encounters with these legendary figures or even discussed them, but there are numerous accounts of Cain legends in the university folklore collections. Visits from figures with the stature of Jesus Christ and Joseph Smith are even more rarely reported, yet two of my interviewees had experienced their presence. Unsurprisingly, the visits were profoundly significant for both recipients.

As mentioned briefly in Chapter 3, Andrea told me that as a toddler she ran into the street and was hit by a car, which resulted in serious injuries and a lengthy hospitalization. The spirit of her recently deceased grandfather comforted her mother while Andrea was in the hospital, and Andrea also had a profound spiritual encounter at the time. She told me, "I woke up and told my family they needed to call me Sweet Andrea Child, and they wanted to know why, and I guess I told them that I had gone and talked with Jesus and that I sat on his lap." When I asked her to tell me more about the experience, she said, "He told me that it wasn't time for me to come to be with him yet because my mom needed me." The tale was beloved by her family, and they called her Sweet Andrea Child for a time. She does not remember much about the accident or the experience, but the encounter became part of family lore and history.

Andrea made a point of explaining to me that her family was not going to church at the time of the accident. Both of her parents were "inactive" at the time (this term is used to describe Latter-day Saints who are not attending or participating in church), and Andrea had not yet been sent to Primary, the Sunday school program for very young children. Andrea referenced the fact that they were inactive to emphasize the profound nature of both encounters—her own with Jesus Christ and her mother's with the spirit

---

[8] Of course, this does not mean that they do not occur, and it is possible that many people would choose to keep such significant encounters private.

of her grandfather—and to attest to the reality of her visit with Christ. She explained that because she had not yet gone to church at all, she would have had no idea about Jesus. Thus, she could not have fabricated or imagined the experience.

Andrea quietly explained, "I don't think I had been to Primary. So, it kind of solidifies the experience for me and makes it so that I didn't make it up. How would a three-and-a-half-year-old make that up?"

She told me that she rarely talked about this experience, and she had only shared it with close family members. Personally, it was very significant to her. She said that it gave her a sense of purpose in life: "I don't remember anything about it or anything, but it's a neat story for me to hear, especially when I get frustrated, and you just remember *you're here for a reason.*" In this, Andrea emphasizes Christ's explanation that her mother needed her. This is reminiscent of some of the near-death experiences discussed in Chapter 3, when a decision to live is made because of a sense of obligation in the world of the living: families need one another and are interdependent. What is so intriguing about Andrea's account is that this interdependence was communicated to Andrea by Jesus Christ, not a family member, and that, even as a child, Andrea had an obligation to care for her mother.

Jake also had an uncommon experience with an important visitor. When he was serving his mission in the United Kingdom, Joseph Smith appeared to him. As we learned in the previous chapter, Jake had some doubts about serving his mission, but he was convinced it was the right thing to do when the spirit of his grandfather appeared to him in the MTC. The uncertainty returned while he was on his mission. He determinedly prayed for answers, which resulted in a visit from Joseph Smith himself. I include a rather extensive excerpt from our conversation because Jake has a gift for verbal expression, and his account is worth reading as it was originally related to me. Jake explained that, as a missionary:

> I'm askin' people to pray [about the truth of the church], I need to do this myself.... it was a lot like the one with my grandpa. While I'm studying this [church teachings], and doing all this [talking to potential converts, known as *investigators*], and every day and every night I'm prayin' about this and I'm asking, "I need to know. I need more than just well 'yeah I feel like it is....' I need to know."... That night, I prayed about it... and I look out my window, and there's somebody standing outside. My companion is over there asleep in his bed. And there is somebody standin' outside.... And

they're standing outside this big bay window. And they're standing there. And I'm lookin' at him. They're looking at me. And I look, and I look a little harder, and I'm like, "That looks like Joseph Smith."

When I invited him to continue, he told me that he had never told anyone this story before. He said that he had alluded to it with his family members, and expressed to them that he was sure of the teachings of the church because of a profound spiritual experience, but he had not told them exactly what happened.

He continued, "And I'm looking and he does this [gestures to him to come]. And I walk out the front door, I go out . . . and you're not supposed to go away from your companion."

"Really? Never?"

He answered:

Well, I mean when you go to the restroom and stuff like that. But you're not supposed to leave the building, right? I walk out, and walk out the front door. And I stop on the step and I'm a little bit . . . this is weird and I'm a little bit nervous . . . and they're [the spirit] all in white . . . .it's not like glowing or anything like that . . . and it's very calm. And I said to him, I said, "So it's true?" [laughs]. I couldn't think of what to say, I said, "So it's true?" And he didn't speak, he just nodded his head. And I said, "So, this, the Book of Mormon is true?" And I don't remember like what his face looked like, I just remember what he looked . . . . I just remember he nodded his head. And then, and I just thought, okay I'm going back inside. Like it was really weird. 'Cause I just, I turned around and walked back inside and looked out and he wasn't there. You know, it's ten steps from door to the window, and there was nobody out there. It snowed, there was no footprints, no nothin'. And I was awake for that one. You know, I'm in my bed, I don't know what sit up, I sat up and I looked out. No words spoken, no nothin'. Just, only words spoken by me. And then, "So it's true?" or "It's true? The Book of Mormon is true?" And just a nod of the head, and it was really weird because I just felt like, "Okay, that's all I needed." And I turned around and walked, it was like, there was nothing else I need to ask and I'm going to bed now. Which to me later I thought about it and I'm like, "why so casual?"

Jake chuckled a bit at the memory. I also laughed at the thought of this "casual" interaction, and commented that there were so many other things that he could have asked! Jake laughed again, and he agreed that it was a missed opportunity. He said that he was so quiet the next day that his mission companion asked him what was wrong because he was not his usual loquacious self.

Jake told me again that he had never shared that experience. I asked if he was confident it was Joseph Smith, and he said it certainly looked like him—"not like some guy from the neighborhood." The spirit was dressed in white, in pants and a shirt, but Jake said he did not recall more details about the style of clothing. He explained that the apparition was not transparent or glowing, as depicted in so much of pop culture, and he just had a *feeling* that it was a spirit being. The experience was not at all frightening, but rather soothing and comforting. He explained, "Like the whole feeling of it was just, everything's fine.... You know, it was like everything's fine. Just let's ask the question and, okay, and now back to our regularly scheduled programing."

Of all the accounts I have analyzed, this is the one that seems most profoundly confirmatory. The gentle nod from the mysterious visitor—Joseph Smith himself—answered Jake's questions and assuaged his doubts about the work he was doing on his mission. To understand Jake's interpretation of the encounter, it is helpful to return to the idea of the *economy of heaven* discussed in the previous chapter. As noted, Brad first taught me about this idea when reflecting that it made sense for God to send the spirit of, say, someone's mother rather than an angel. We learned that during one of Jake's first experiences with doubt, when he was at the MTC, the spirit of his recently deceased grandfather came to him, which convinced him that going on the mission was the right thing to do. Jake's experience with Joseph Smith, which happened while he was on his mission, also suggests questioning and, perhaps, doubt. Jake indicated that, at the time, he was praying to know the truth of what he was learning and teaching to investigators. This time, in the economy of heaven, it was not a relative who visited, but rather Joseph Smith. The first visit, by the spirit of his grandfather, convinced Jake to remain at the MTC and to go on his mission. The next visit, from the spirit of Joseph Smith himself, convinced Jake about the truth of the church's teachings.

Personhood, Mediation, and Divine Distance

The spirits described in this chapter and in Chapter 3 are always benevolent or beseeching, and they are frequently kin to the living persons they visit.

This chapter considered spirits who appear during temple work. The spirits express gratitude for baptisms or other ordinances or request that temple work be done on their behalf. The living perform prescribed ritual actions to advance the spiritual progress of the deceased. Temple work is a time that is ripe for the visits of spirits because the veil between worlds is indeed thin in the temple. As with the encounters described in the previous chapter, these visitations connect the realm of spirits with the wider Latter-day Saint mortal body and suggest that the mutuality and collective responsibility for salvation that is a part of the Latter-day Saint tradition (Cannell 2017; Stiles 2023) must extend to all members of the eternal family—including spirits. Those who encounter spirits in temples frequently understand them as *confirming* in some way: they confirm the necessity and righteousness of the mediating ritual work performed for the dead.

I have written about the eternal family elsewhere (Chapter 3 in this volume; Stiles 2023), and so here I would like to focus on how spirit visits also suggest something compelling about the nature of the righteous *person* in Latter-day Saint thought and practice. As we have seen, the living are key mediators for the dead in that they bring the spirits of the dead closer to salvation. The moral community must be maintained, grown, and strengthened through the performance of proxy ordinances on their behalf. Compelling recent anthropological research on religion has considered various forms of mediation, and prominent anthropologists of Christianity, such as Birgit Meyer, have proposed that religion is, essentially, mediation between the divine and the profane (Meyer 2006). Drawing on Meyer's understanding of religion as mediation, anthropologist Joel Robbins (2017) has observed that the necessity of mediation assumes a separation of the divine and the sacred from the mortal world of the profane, and he reflects on this by asking why this distance seems so necessary in religions. In reflecting on Hubert and Mauss's early twentieth century work on sacrifice (1981) and his own fieldwork among the Urapmin in Papua New Guinea, Robbins observes that the way people construct religions reflects their thoughts on human social relations. For example, Robbins proposes that traditional Urapmin religion and social structure emphasize differentiation between mortals and the divine, which reflects the cultural focus on maintaining distance between humans. When most Urapmin became Pentecostal Christians in the 1970s, these values came into conflict to some extent with the new "Christian" emphasis on closeness and mutual sharing. Robbins (2017) suggests that new Urapmin practices involving the Holy Spirit thus reflect both the new and the old: elements of "traditional" religion that maintain distance and elements of Christianity that emphasize closeness.

Robbins (2017) thus argues that the way in which people in various cultures construct religious worlds that focus so much on mediation between the divine and the profane reflects cultural understandings of social relationships and how people should relate to one another. A consideration of spirit visits among Latter-day Saints provides insight on this question of "divine distance" in a very different Christian context. In Latter-day Saint cosmology, we might understand distance from the divine as merely a preliminary state, as the end state in the quest to perfect the soul is something like divinity itself. The Plan of Salvation is a quest to become like God, which suggests the possibility not just of closeness to the divine, but of becoming divine.[9] Mortals and their immortal spirits are thus ultimately *perfectible* and the reward of righteousness is becoming gods, or like God.[10] Distance between the divine and the mortal is achievable and should be the ultimate goal of the righteous and, as we saw in Chapter 3, there is a mutual responsibility to help one another toward this goal—particularly within the family. The mutuality of spirits and the living collapses the distance between the divine and the mortal spheres. As Davies writes, "the progressive development of the family, following its Melchizedek and patriarchal head constitutes a process of deification.... it is not a question of the human family adoring God, lost in the beatific vision of traditional Christianity, but of an active fostering of salvation for self and kin in relation to the personages of deity" (2000, 83). Similarly, in describing the characteristic architecture of temples, Davies writes that the space known as the celestial room "expresses the *divinization of the family* as the goal of being" (2000, 83; emphasis added).

---

[9] On the official church webpage, a response is provided in the "Frequently Asked Questions" section to a query about whether Latter-day Saints become gods. As in much of the official media of the church today, the response suggests many parallels with other Christian teachings, de-emphasizing difference and citing the New Testament: "Latter-day Saints believe that God wants us to become like Him. But this teaching is often misrepresented by those who caricature the faith. The Latter-day Saint belief is no different than the biblical teaching, which states, 'The Spirit itself beareth witness with our spirit, that we are the children of God: and if children, then heirs; heirs of God, and joint-heirs with Christ; if so be that we suffer with him, that we may be also glorified together' (Romans 8:16–17). Through following Christ's teachings, Latter-day Saints believe all people can become "partakers of the divine nature" (2 Peter 1:4)."

[10] I reference here an abstract idea of the perfection of the spirit, although it is important to note that there is also a strong emphasis on perfection in action in earthy life as well. However, Douglas Davies has pointed out that what constitutes perfection in the Latter-day Saint sense changes over time: "To be perfect in 1840 did not mean the same thing as to be perfect in 1940 or in 1990.... to be perfect in one era does not mean the same thing as to be perfect in another, even within a single religious covenant" (Davies 2000, 57).

In Latter-day Saint understanding, then, the distance to the divine is ultimately collapsible but not in the way that we might understand with the practices of Holy Spirit possession that Robbins discusses among the Urapmin. Nor is it the same as the goal of annihilation of the self within God that we find in various mystical traditions. Rather, it is a journey to *become like God*. And, ultimately, this is dependent upon other people and other spirits, who help each other along this path as mediators. Spirits help the living along their path to salvation, and mortals help the spirits through performing ordinances on their behalf. What strikes me as most significant about these spirit visits is the inherent and necessary reciprocity between the living and those in the spirit world.[11]

As introduced Chapter 3, an intriguing parallel comes from a model of ancestral personhood among Hmong communities in Thailand and the United States (Hickman 2014). Although a very different cultural context, the model provides a useful framework for understanding what is happening with benevolent spirit visits. Hickman argues that in Hmong communities, "a cultural ontology of personhood drives the more conscious moral justifications that Hmong employ in their moral discourse" (2014, 319), and the notion of ancestral personhood revolves around the understanding the one not only has a relationship with ancestors but will become a future ancestor. "In other words," Hickman writes, "ancestral personhood denotes a particular view of the life course as eternally embedded in kinship-based relationships and hierarchies that are enacted through ritual and discourse" (2014, 323). The knowledge that one will be an ancestor one day undergirds Hmong moral sensibilities and sense of obligation to the kin group (2014, 332).

This model of ancestral kinship bears some similarity to the Latter-day Saint conception of ancestors, in that they are both cultural models of personhood that recognize mutuality between the living and ancestral spirits. Drawing a distinction from Meyer Fortes's explication of personhood as *achievable* rather than *inherent* among the Tallensi of Ghana, Hickman argues that for Hmong people, "Ancestral personhood is a cultural model of the self and its eternal life course and not an end to be achieved in one's life" (2014, 324). Latter-day Saints similarly have an enormous responsibility

---

[11] The historian Manuel Padro has similarly discussed the living and the dead as mutually dependent in his exploration of the influences of various nineteenth century Christian ideas of treasure hunting, ghosts, and the nature of the dead on Joseph Smith's thought. Padro argues that "folk Christian practices of redeeming the dead is his [Smith's] most likely early exposure to the idea of the dead and the living as a common body, engaged in acts of charity across the divide" (Padro 2020, 79).

for kin and distant ancestors who were not baptized into the church, and this responsibility is met through the obligation to perform temple work, the core of ritual activity for church members in good standing. As noted in Chapter 3, what is so intriguing about encounters with benevolent spirits is that they indicate the *active* nature of this engagement, which is illustrated in the ways that spirit and living kin are engaged in helping each other achieve advanced spiritual states. In the temple, where the veil is thin, spirits appear to those doing the work on their behalf. They watch over the families of those doing their temple work. And, sometimes, spirits appear to ask that temple work be done on their behalf.

In the Hmong case, Hickman writes that "deontological prescriptions can be based on a set of ontological beliefs about personhood" (2014, 322). I take this to mean that the way people think about their duties and obligations and then act on them—those deontological prescriptions—is informed by ideas about the nature of what it means to be a person. Latter-day Saints think about their obligations to the temple work—as a kind of righteous action—is based on religious conceptions of the person as something inherently *perfectible*. This perfectibility can only be achieved, however, vis-à-vis one's relationships to other people—both living and non-living. Indeed, Latter-day Saint teachings are explicit in this regard, and a good illustration of this is in contemporary teachings on the priesthood. The bestowal of the priesthood, as we discussed earlier in this chapter, is one of the key ordinances. In addition, although only men can become members of the priesthood, the ordinance is understood (as we saw with the comments of Elder Neilson and Elder Collins) as being incumbent upon all—women access the priesthood through men in their family, fathers, husband, and brothers.[12] Exaltation depends on these relationships, and only those married and sealed to each other in the temples can expect to reach the highest level of heavenly reward. This sense of mutual dependence and responsibility extends to spirit members of the family, including distant ancestors and, ultimately, to all of humanity itself when all temple work is complete. In a conversation about this project, Dr. Adam Dunstan, a colleague who is a both a Latter-day Saint and an anthropologist, noted to me:

---

[12] This dependency on men is one of the reasons Shauna left the church, and she described temple endowments in which a man is pledged to God and a woman to her husband.

Mormonism sees all of humanity as a family which could be sealed together. Thus, in a sense the pan-human responsibility of collective salvation is itself an outgrowth of kinship-oriented exaltation, and vice-versa: kinship-oriented exaltation is the application of Christ's saving work within families. In Mormonism, it's families all the way down, to mis-use an old phrase. (personal communication 2022)

Deontologically speaking, then, righteous responsibility includes helping others advance along the road to salvation and, possibly, achieve perfection in exaltation. Once again, we see that righteousness is *action* and a righteous person, then, is one who acts in accord with these goals. The benevolent visits of spirits described in this chapter reflect this mutuality, and the obligation of the living to ritual action on behalf of the dead. Righteous action collapses the distance between the divine and the profane.

5
The Devil Sat on My Bed
The Slippery Edge of Righteousness

Shauna, the graduate student introduced in earlier chapters, told me that when she was growing up in northern Utah, she was very conscious of the power of malevolent spirits:

> You gotta be careful about evil spirits . . . like, don't talk about them, 'cause they might possess you . . . if you talk about them too much you're kind of inviting them . . . . at sleepovers we'd talk about that kind of stuff and if people were getting possessed, and how you'd have to raise your arm to the square and say "in the name of Jesus Christ I command you to leave!" We were prepared if that happened.

Shauna has never encountered an evil spirit. However, her comments illustrate the pervasiveness of the idea that evil spirits are constantly present, and that certain actions, or even thoughts, can attract their attention. She drew on her memory of childhood slumber parties, and she remembered practicing what to do if evil spirits made an appearance.

In northern Utah, encounters with evil spirits are not uncommon, and they usually take the form of harassment. A threatening spirit might whisper in someone's ear, thwart a missionary's righteous activity, or even physically attack a sleeping youth. As described in Chapter 2, evil spirits are those who followed Lucifer in the War in Heaven, and thus were never born into mortal bodies. Consequently, evil spirits are never identified as individuals, although they are sometimes gendered as male or female. Those who are harassed by malevolent visitors often frame such experiences as occurring on the edges, so to speak, of their religiosity. Negative visits are typically understood as a consequence of unrighteous, anti-religious actions or, importantly, as impediments to exceptionally righteous action. The way people talk about these experiences illustrates a local conception of "evil" among northern

Utah Mormons that must be understood in the context of righteous action and the grand cosmological narrative of the Latter-day Saint tradition.

The folklorists William A. Wilson and David Hufford have noted that stories of encounters with demonic beings are a major part of the rich heritage of oral narrative in Utah and wider "Mormon country" (Wilson 1989; Hufford 1982; see also Fife and Fife 1956 and Hand 1983 for an overview of devil narratives). Wilson has characterized Latter-day Saint evil spirit narratives as "cautionary tales" that "show what happens when one surrenders to the alluring powers of evil" (1989, 101). However, there are few previous accounts of lived experiences of evil spirit encounters. As noted in Chapter 1, Hufford's cross-cultural comparative book *The Terror that Comes in the Night* (1989) includes a brief section on "night terrors," "sleep paralysis," and "Old Hag" stories in Cache Valley, in which he proposes "Mormon culture" provides an excellent context for understanding such experiences as evil spirit attacks (Hufford 1982, 223).

My research confirms that experiences which might be categorized using the etic concepts of "sleep paralysis" or "night terrors" are accommodated in the robust local cultural framework for spirit interactions. However, in northern Utah, evil spirit harassment is not limited to physical attacks like sleep terrors: a shadowy spirit may lurk in a dark corner, an unseen spirit might whisper temptingly in the ear of the unsuspecting, and a threatening presence could disrupt a home through unsettling sounds or atmospheric disturbances. Most negative visitations take the form of such external harassment, and accounts of what anthropologists typically classify as overt "possession"—when a spirit takes control of the consciousness and the body—are very uncommon, although not unknown.[1] In general, then, contemporary Latter-day Saint experiences of evil spirits are more like the Catholic Church's designation of spirit "obsession," as described in de Certeau's *Possession at Loudon* (1980), and are similar to what the anthropologist Thomas Csordas has described among American Charismatic Catholics, who frequently report harassment, yet very rarely describe such encounters as "possession" (Csordas 1997). It is important to note, however, that Latter-day Saints do not have a complex, classificatory demonologies along the lines of charismatic

---

[1] Latter-day Saints certainly recognize possession as a possibility to be feared and avoided. Possession is never understood as benign or beneficial, and a possessing spirit is always evil, and must be expelled rather than accommodated. The few accounts of possession will be described in the next chapter because they center not so much on the act of possession but on the power of the Latter-day Saint priesthood to expel spirits.

and evangelical churches in the United States that are described by a number of contemporary scholars (McCloud 2015; O'Donnell 2021; Csordas 1997).

Latter-day Saints in Utah explain negative visitations as sensory manifestations of a metaphysical, cosmological evil that is licentiously attracted to human unrighteousness *and* actively engaged in thwarting exceptional righteousness. Since the late twentieth century, anthropologists have gradually taken up the general question of evil (Taussig 1980; Parkin 1985; Meyer 1999; Clough and Mitchell 2001; Sanders 2008; Caton 2010; Csordas 2013;) and devil beliefs in Christian contexts (Taussig 1980; Meyer 1999). An initial comparative foray into the subject of evil was David Parkin's edited collection *The Anthropology of Evil* (1985). In his introduction, Parkin distinguished between three modes of evil: (1) a moral evil, or that enacted by humans themselves; (2) a physical evil, which refers to "destructive elemental forces of nature"; and (3) a metaphysical evil, "by which disorder in the cosmos or in relations with divinity results from a conflict of principles of wills" (1985, 15). Two foundational studies by Michael Taussig (1980) and Birgit Meyer (1999) examined Christian devil beliefs in the context of colonization and cultural change. Taussig considered how miners and plantation workers in Colombia and Peru used devil narratives to process a capitalizing economy, and Meyer's work showed how devils and demons are means of drawing boundaries between Ewe religion and emerging Christianity in Ghana. Both works suggested that local understandings of the devil and demons or evil spirits are a means of grappling with rapidly changing social contexts.

More recently, anthropologists concerned with evil have shown increased interest in understanding evil through cultural frameworks of morality. Todd Sanders, for example, provides an update to earlier work on "devil beliefs" as critiques of capitalism by examining how narratives about the Devil, evil spirits, and wealth generated through private bussing business (2008) provide an opportunity for people in Dar es Salaam, Tanzania, to reflect on—not simply critique—the different types of relationships between individuals and society and wealth and moral values. Thomas Csordas has proposed that "evil is fundamentally implicated in morality and ethics" (2013, 526) and argues that anthropologists should consider evil as an "analytic category" within the study of morality (2013, 523). In this, Csordas heeds Stephen Caton's call to move beyond a consideration of "ethics" to a recognition of "evil" in understanding the atrocities committed at Abu Ghraib prison, which Caton argues "exceeded what we might call 'unethical'" (2010, 166).

Looking cross-culturally and at Parkin's classificatory framework, Csordas proposes that anthropologists might think of "evil" as falling into two general categories: evil as a human phenomenon and evil as resulting from a cosmological force. Csordas views the conceptions of evil as manifesting from within—as a human phenomenon—are "less murky" (2013, 529) and are thus a better means of making the argument for evil as an analytical category, which he does through using comparative studies of witchcraft as primary examples. Csordas proposes orienting evil along dimensions of "internal/external" and "passive/active" and, essentially, as in most of these other works, evil is centered on persons doing evil things. This is similar to Parkin's suggestion that we might understand evil as "morality reflecting on itself" (1985), and to Jean DeBernardi's claim that in the West, Christian "spiritual warriors" in the evangelical tradition orient on perceived vices or "social bondages" (1999, 78).[2]

However, the narratives examined in this chapter show that evil as a cosmological force is far more relevant to the Utah context: conceptions of evil and wickedness are centered less on evil persons doing bad things than on Satan's grand attempt to disrupt the moral order through exerting influence and temptation. This seems somewhat similar to what Csordas observed in his earlier work with Charismatic Catholics in the United States, which showed a conception of evil that is similar to what we find in contemporary Latter-day Saint practice and understanding. He writes, "in this conception of evil there is a decentering of agency and responsibility: diabolical evil originates outside the individual even though a person must to some degree collaborate with and consent to it; sin opens one to the influence of evil, and evil tempts one to sin" (2013, 528).

I find that in Utah, conceptions of evil ultimately focus on the moral order—the community. Even though unrighteous action or compromised morality attract the interest of Satan, Latter-day Saints do not simply gloss evil as bad human tendencies, the human potential to do bad things, or as a means of displacing blame for bad actions to spirit entities. Devil beliefs are not necessarily a way of mediating cultural change (Taussig 1980; Meyer 1999) and grappling with excess (Clough and Mitchell 2001). Rather, Satan is

---

[2] Elsewhere, I have drawn more substantial connections between Latter-day Saint beliefs about the Devil and evil spirits with other American Christian communities (Stiles, 2022). I do not rehash those connections in full here, so suffice it to note that there are significant parallels, for example, in the idea of ongoing spiritual warfare with the adversary, but also very significant differences, such as the lack of a classificatory schema associating spirits with vices or an idea of demon inheritance (McCloud 2015; DeRogatis 2009).

a powerful and real adversary. Interestingly, Satan and evil spirits are not usually described as responsible for bad actions (although this is certainly possible). Bad actions are problematic because they attract the *attention* of Satan or his minion spirits, which are understood as cosmological forces that have been active in human affairs from the pre-existence, thus giving them a foothold in disrupting human affairs and the moral order. Moreover, as we will see, cosmological evil targets righteous action with the same ends in mind.

Recent scholarly treatments of evil in the field of Mormon Studies emphasize opposition and agency and reflect the cosmological grand narrative at the heart of the tradition. In *Joseph Smith, Jesus, and Satanic Opposition: Atonement, Evil, and the Mormon Vision* (2010), Davies provocatively argues that Jesus, Satan, and Joseph Smith make up a trinity of sorts: Jesus is the antagonist of Satan, and Joseph Smith inherited Jesus's priestly authority. Davies shows that in early Mormon writings which report troublesome evil spirits, authors identify the Devil as the source of evil and describe "the devil and Jesus as combatants" (2010, 216). The historian Stephen Taysom argues that Latter-day Saint views on an "incorporeal yet physically powerful Devil" and his army of spirit minions distinguished early Mormonism from Protestants of the era (2017, 20). Taysom writes that Joseph Smith seemed to understand his early encounters with Satan, addressed here in Chapter 2, as "A battle set against the cosmic backdrop in which two individuals with special powers fight over the fate of humankind" (2017, 73). And in a recent essay on evil in Latter-day Saint thought, James McLachlan similarly observes the importance of opposition in Mormon conceptions of evil: "Perhaps the key passage in LDS scripture that reveals the Mormon understanding of the existence of suffering and evil is found in the Book of Mormon assertion of the 'Opposition in All Things'" (McLachlan 2015, 280). McLachlan emphasizes Latter-day Saint ideas about temptations of the body and the necessity of agency and resisting temptations; thus, evil comes from freedom to choose one's path to do good or not. Drawing parallels to Davies's central argument, McLachlan observes that Christ is the model of "moral self-sacrifice and Lucifer is the archetype of self-will" (287). McLachlan thus emphasizes rejection of sociality as the essence of evil, and *sociality* as the key to problem of suffering and a "prefiguring of the perfection of sociality that we experience in the next world" (288).

As we will see throughout this chapter, the framework of agency is key in Latter-day Saint teachings in practice. In her work on what she refers to as the Mormon moral economy, anthropologist Hildi Mitchell similarly notes the importance of free agency in religious understanding. She writes that an "essential feature of evil for Mormons" is "this attempt to restrict free agency" (Mitchell 2001a, 166). The accounts that follow show an unequivocal local Latter-day Saint cultural consciousness of the cosmological opposition mentioned by the previous scholars. As an active, real presence, Satan and evil spirits interfere in people's lives and disrupt the moral order by both luring people away from the path of righteousness and attempting to thwart righteous action. I find that conceptions of evil in popular theology focus more on Satan's ability to lead one astray than the more abstract conceptions of sociality emphasized by McLachlan. However, the focus on agency is paramount to how people reflect on these encounters: evil is a test and must be resisted.

This focus on agency will be evident in narratives throughout the chapter, but let us begin an account from Sandra, a young mother in her late twenties, who related a story about beliefs in the temptations of the Devil as her explanation for why she stopped going to church as a teenager. I should note that I contacted Sandra for an earlier project on gender, religion, and marriage (Stiles 2014), and I interviewed her in 2014 in her charming one-hundred-year-old farmhouse in a small town at the north end of Cache Valley. I had not mentioned any interest in spirits or the devil to Sandra since I had come to talk about marriage; however, the subject came up, showing the local cultural salience of evil as an active force in the world. Sandra told me that she was raised Mormon, but her family was not very active, and she only went to church "off and on" as a child. Even so, one summer, she attended a Latter-day Saint Girl's Camp. The church-run youth camps for girls and boys are popular, and many people attend them as youngsters. Sandra told me about her camp experience, which would have taken place around the year 2000:

> I had a really bad experience, and I just didn't feel comfortable anymore going back. We were at a Girl's Camp . . . we had a girl that would come up and visit us at the girl's camp, and she went to a Spanish [speaking] ward and she was just visiting her sister, and we were sitting in the tent one night and singing songs and playin' and she was singing in Spanish . . . "I am a Child of God" in Spanish. And some other girls . . . it was a stake camp and so there were lots of different girls . . . reported to the counselors that we were chanting and devil worshipping. And so they called their parents at 1 or 2 o'clock in the morning and they came and got us and they didn't explain why we were being sent home. But it was a bad experience because nobody

said anything to us about what we were doing . . . we were just looked at as "they are devil worshipping." And they went and they washed our tent in the water and they blessed it and it made me feel if they are going to think like that then why should I feel comfortable coming to church?

For the purposes of this chapter, what is most notable about Sandra's account is not her disgust at what transpired, but rather her recollection of the other campers' characterization of speaking Spanish as devil worshipping, and the immediate concern of the parents and camp directors with devil worship and their resulting actions of washing and blessing the tent.[3]

The Slippery Edge of Righteousness: Evil and Moral Boundaries

In the introduction to an edited volume on good and evil, anthropologist Jon P. Mitchell writes that, "Demarcating moral acceptability therefore involves elaborating transgressions," just as "elaborating transgressions involves the demarcation of a moral boundary" (Clough and Mitchell 2001, 1). In Utah, negative spiritual experiences nearly always happen at slippery edge of righteousness, or what Mitchell might term the "moral boundary." As I have explained in previous chapters, in Latter-day Saint vernacular, the term *righteous* is used widely as shorthand for appropriate religious action and interviews and archival materials indicate that people in northern Utah frequently frame negative spiritual experiences as something that happens when one inadvertently slips or deliberately steps off the path of righteousness, which attracts the attention of evil in one of two ways: one might unintentionally attract a negative visit through engaging in dangerously unrighteous behavior or one might deliberately "invite the experience" through reaching out to spirits. However, negative visitations are not limited to those leaving the righteous path. Confoundingly, evil spirits also harass the exceptionally righteous. These scenarios indicate that the slippery edge is always close, and most people are very aware, even from childhood, of the lurking dangers of Satan and his minions. Thus, one should constantly be on guard.

---

[3] I expect that such a dramatic reaction would be far less likely today. Cache Valley has become more diverse, and Spanish is much more widely spoken.

Unrighteous Actions: Bad Spirits, Bad Morals, and the Body

As numerous anthropologists have shown in other contexts, the body is a key locus of righteous boundary markers (Lester 2005; Thornton 2018; Mahmood 2011; Dawley 2018). In Latter-day Saint practice and understanding, the body is a profound site for moral engagement and the formation of religious subjectivity. The significance of the body is clear: God was once human, and human spiritual progress is dependent on the body in many ways. As noted, humans have the potential to become like God, and divine embodiment is a key aspect of formal church teaching (McLachlan 2015; Brown and Holbrook 2015; Taysom 2017).

As Mitchell notes in her work on the Latter-day Saint moral economy, the body is seen as ultimately a force for good, and thus gives rise to what she describes as the "Mormon engagement with materialism," which plays a "central and positive role" (2001a, 162). As we discussed in Chapter 2, the followers of Satan in the War on Heaven were denied a physical body. Taysom notes that Joseph Smith taught his followers that the body was a reward for siding with Jesus Christ (2017, 60). In his work on the development of angelology in the nineteenth-century church, Park (2010) argues that ideas about embodiment influenced early Latter-day Saint understandings of evil spirits, who of course never had a body. While these evil spirits may take possession of a body, Park shows that early teachings from Joseph Smith indicate the power of the corporeal body. "Thus," writes Park, "while Smith confirmed that evil spirits sought to take control of human tabernacles, he assured the Saints that they had the innate power to resist them by virtue of their bodies as well as the endowed power to resist by virtue of the priesthood" (Park 2010).

In practice today, engaging in "unrighteous" behavior might draw the attention of a bad spirit, and most accounts of unrighteous behavior focus on the body (such as a person's unsanctioned bodily engagement with alcohol, tobacco, or drugs, and illicit sexual activity) rather than the harboring of problematic thoughts or cruel action toward others. It is notable that Latter-day Saint women and men are generally held to the same standards of righteous physicality, as anthropologist David Knowlton (1992) has observed; what is bad for the goose is also bad for the gander. This is similar to what recent ethnographic research in other Christian communities has described in contexts of new "emerging masculinities" that focus on comparable forms of sexual propriety for men and women. For example, in his work on Pentecostal conversion and masculinity in the Dominican Republic, Brendan Jamal Thornton (2018) writes about "ambitious moral self-making" among men who convert from Catholicism to Pentecostal forms of Christianity. Drawing on the work of Michel Foucault and Kathleen Stewart, Thornton argues that, for these converts, "the renunciation of sexual desire represents an important site of ambitious moral self-making, especially for devoted male converts, a decisive cog in the constitution of gendered church subjects" (2018, 163–164; see also Dawley 2018, on Christian men in Costa Rica).

As noted earlier, when Shauna described her childhood memories of learning about spirits, she told me she was "super afraid" of the evil spirits. As a child, she clearly sensed the slippery edge of righteousness, and the bad spirits were a constant threat. In Shauna's view, church teachings about evil spirits were ultimately about the body. She surmised that because the spirits who followed Satan never got bodies, they are thus both jealous of and attracted to human bodies, which could easily lead a careless person to the edge of righteousness: "[I was taught that] they're [the spirits] here, and they're listening, and trying to take your body. Or at least, get you to use your body in bad ways." To illustrate, Shauna referenced "Satan's slippery slope" in the context of dating.[4] As a teenager, she had been very conscious of the dangers inherent in going out with boys. She explained the hazards of the intensifying scale of intimacy:

> It starts out with an arm around, like you'd put your arm around him, and then, holding hands, and then first kiss, and then French kiss, and then, petting, and then, you know, it's just like, a slippery slope, and you're going to accidentally have sex. And I honestly thought you could accidentally have sex! I thought you would get to a point where you were out of control and like not really in your mind, and it wasn't until after I was married and I was like, "Wait a minute! I never lost consciousness!"

Shauna grounded this comment in scripture by referring me to a teaching from the Book of Mormon about the "natural man being the enemy of God," which reads as follows:

---

[4] The "slippery slope" is trope that is frequently used in describing the dangers of certain kinds of bodily activities (see also Bowman 2011).

> For the natural man is an enemy to God, and has been from the fall of Adam, and will be forever and ever, unless he yields to the enticings of the Holy Spirit and putteth off the natural man and becometh a saint through the atonement of Christ the Lord, and becometh as a child, submissive, meek, humble, patient, full of love, willing to submit to all things which the Lord seeth fit to inflict upon him, even as a child doth submit to his father. (Mosiah 3:19)

Shauna continued, "And so I just thought my natural—my bodily—instincts would take over. And that my spirit would be subdued and I wouldn't be in control of my body." In Shauna's view, "the evil spirits are always there trying to bring you down."

Although Shauna always hoped that she would encounter a good spirit, she perceived that evil spirits were far more likely to interfere in people's lives. As she explained, there are many of them, and they are just waiting for an opportunity to mess with people. Shauna expressed that, as a young girl, it seemed to her that Satan and the evil spirits were more powerful than God.

"It seems in some ways that the evil spirits can be more powerful because it feels like they're more present. There're *sooo* many of them. You know a third of the host of heaven, which is a third of all the spirits that will ever and have ever existed."

She then commented on the "other team"—the side of good—and commented on the good spirits only coming in times of need.

"So, you know the number here is huge, and then on the other team we've got the Holy Spirit, who can visit us. But everyone else is kind of in this other realm. Like God and Jesus, you know they'll visit you if there's a real need. And maybe ancestors if there's a real need, but usually those'll be in dreams because good spirits aren't going to try to appear to you and trick you."

In one of our several follow-up conversations a few months later, this one via email, Shauna echoed this sentiment. She had recently been reviewing Joseph Smith's account of his early experience with spirits, and she noted how much more he wrote about the evil spirits than about God. She wrote: "It really fits the way I viewed evil spirits and why we had to be so careful. They were more numerous and more present than God (and almost as powerful, like JS [Joseph Smith] indicated), so you really didn't want to attract their attention, even if you could get rid of them."

Malevolent spirits are attracted to those using the body in the wrong ways and can tempt people to use their bodies in the wrong way. As righteousness or worthiness is essentially about action, so is unrighteousness or unworthiness. The spiritual dangers of an indulgent, licentious lifestyle are a prominent theme in local folklore, as evidenced in numerous didactic tales shared at social gatherings and church functions. One narrative, collected by a folklore student in the 1980s, tells of a young man who went on mission even though he had some unresolved "moral problems." The brief account, titled "Unworthy Elder," reads as follows:

> An elder in the mission field had some moral problems that were not resolved before he left on his mission. One night, he and his companions were asleep and the beds started shaking and the lights started going on and off. The elder with the problems wouldn't wake up.
> .... The other elder called the mission president and the president went to the apartment and went through each room of the house casting out evil spirits. He then made arrangements for the elder with the problems to go home. (Thompson 1985)

In this edifying tale, the mission president[5] assumes the young man's unresolved "moral problem" attracted the evil spirits. As noted in Chapter 2, references to morality or moral problems nearly always refer to sexual licentiousness; as Brad explained, "We usually define that [morality] as being somewhat connected to sexual sin." Thompson's tale about the "unworthy elder" clearly instructs young people on the necessity of resolving moral issues before serving a mission, and the spiritual dangers that might ensure if they do not. The mission president sent the young man home (likely in disgrace!) and cast out the evil spirits (see Chapter 7 for more on "casting out").

In addition to inappropriate sexual activity, drinking and smoking, or "partying," are also attractive to spirits. As we have seen, Shauna was very aware of the dangers of unworthy actions because bad behavior tempted evil spirits, and she recalled being alarmed by her older brothers, who were "bad dudes" who drank and smoked: "And so I kind of went the other way and kind of became *extra* righteous." Similarly, Jake told me about his teenaged daughter's recent experience with a harassing spirit, which his wife attributed to her wild, partying behavior; in Jake's words, "She gave us a rodeo." We will return to her experience later in this chapter.

---

[5] The mission president is the supervising authority figure of a group of young missionaries in a particular mission. Like being a bishop, Relief Society president, or similar, the role of mission president is a calling for Latter-day Saints in good standing.

In an folkmore account from 1990, a student tells of a returned missionary speaking at a church "fireside" gathering.[6] The missionary described what happened in his youth when he had "gone off the path of righteousness." He had been at a party where the "atmosphere wasn't good"—people were drinking and smoking. The party was in the small town of Deweyville, on the west side of the Wellsville Mountains in the Bear River Valley, which is just west of Cache Valley.[7] The youth's parents had told him not to go to the party, but he defied them. He soon found himself getting hot and dizzy and slurring his speech: "Finally, I lost all of my means to speak, and I started to become red. I was so hot that no one could touch me, and everyone knew I was possessed with the devil" (Brown 1982). His drinking and smoking attracted the Devil, and a bishop was summoned to cast him out. After this terrifying experience, the young man explained that he realized the error of his ways; he returned to the path of righteousness and went on a mission.

In a similar didactic tale from the 1960s, the writer describes a divorced young mother, who "no longer loved the Gospel" and was living a wild, partying lifestyle in Salt Lake City. One night, the young woman awakened and saw a man in a suit standing in the corner, whom the writer identifies as both a spirit and the Devil. The writer describes the atmosphere as very "heavy," noting the young woman could barely get out of bed and walk. When she reached the living room, she prayed, but it "took a long time for her to *get the spirit* so that she could [know] that her prayers were being heard" (emphasis added). After praying for hours, the young woman finally felt a sense of relief. The writer concludes that, "this experience of the devil made Bobbie think of the wickedness in the way she was living. She is now happily remarried to her first husband in the L.D.S. [*sic*] temple, and they are both active in their church assignments." Like the returned missionary in the previous narrative, the experience frightened the young woman back to the path of righteousness. Just as the young man's service as a missionary indexes his righteousness, the young woman's decision to remarry her first husband *in the temple* and become *active* in the church indexes hers. Through prayer, the young woman was able to "get the spirit," referring to the Holy Spirit, and return to the path of righteousness. When the young woman is in touch with the Holy Spirit, she is able to drive the harassing evil spirit away through

---

[6] Firesides are informal church gatherings, often on weeknights, that are of an instructional nature.
[7] The writer notes that Deweyville is known for evil spirits, although I have not heard this elsewhere.

prayer. In a similar didactic tale, a student recalls a Sunday school story about a woman who experienced a visitation from a spirit identifying itself as Christ. However, because the woman was "in tune with the spirit" and she knew that it was a false spirit (USU 11, 1966); we will return to this theme in Chapter 6.

Inviting the Experience

Many people I spoke with described the ways in which one could "invite the experience," and the phrase assumes a preoccupation with or an intentional courting of bad spirits, unlike engaging in unrighteous behavior, which attracts evil as an unintended consequence. Elder Neilson, one of the young missionaries I spoke with, referenced both mechanisms—unintentional and intentional—when he told me reassuringly that a person could absolutely avoid negative spiritual experiences: "You can do that through living a righteous life. You can do that through not purposefully trying to draw those spirits to you.... Sometimes you can unintentionally invite them, just through being a very vile sinner. But for the most part, you have to invite them into your life."

Taking too much of an interest in Satan and the spirits is a particularly slippery spot. Recall Shauna's comments from the opening of this chapter, "... you gotta be careful about evil spirits. Like, don't talk about them, 'cause they might possess you, and yeah if you talk about 'em too much you're kind of inviting them." Greg, in his early fifties, is a professor of history on the east coast. We discussed spiritual experience on a number of occasions. At the time of our first interview, he had recently stopped going to church, although he had been active his entire life up to that point and had served a mission. Greg grew up on the west coast, but he lived in northern Utah for many years as student and young adult, and he served his mission in Salt Lake. Like many others, he referenced "inviting" the spirits by taking too much of an interest in them:

> In my Mormon experience of spiritual visitations, [it was] mostly good. I remember as a teenager in the church we were told we were all born with protection, and that we could not be possessed. But there were spiritual beings that did have malicious intent, and we could invite them to invade our boundaries, if we were to think about them or actively talk about these

things; it was one of these things we were supposed to not talk about because it would invite an awful visitation.

As we will see later in this chapter, Greg had an "awful visitation" in his twenties, and he was wracked with anxiety about why it had happened to him—had he unintentionally invited the spirit?

In addition to a preoccupation with spirits, particular actions can invite them in. In one narrative from the 1990s, a student recorded an experience her roommate, Angela, had while attending Ricks College[8] in southern Idaho. In the account, Angela attributed an evil presence in her shared house to a séance held by her roommates. Angela had gone to bed early while her roommates stayed up to play board games (or so she thought). She woke suddenly, and she felt a presence in her room. She called out but there was no response. She wandered the house and reported a "strange phenomenon." Looking downstairs to the basement, she noted that even though the stairwell light was on, halfway down the staircase the stairs were black, as if the light from the lightbulb had not penetrated that part of the stairway. The writer reports that, "Seeing this strange phenomenon, her fears only increased and she ran into the kitchen and prayed." Angela and a male friend called their bishop, who came to investigate, and found that her roommates had conducted a séance in the basement. During the séance, Angela reports that a young man had hypnotized a girl and commanded an evil spirit to enter her body.[9]

A more common problem is the use of Ouija boards, which figure in numerous didactic tales and personal accounts. Elder Neilson and Elder Collins agreed on the dangers of the Ouija board, and when I recalled playing with one as a kid, they advised against this. Elder Collins remarked, "Sometimes they'll do those things [playing with the Ouija board] and if you have no idea what the heck it is, it won't mean anything, but if you're doing it for the intent

---

[8] Ricks' College, in the small town of Rexburg, in southern Idaho, has a long history as an educational institution. After existing as a secondary school, it became a private two-year junior college affiliated with the Latter-day Saint church. In 2001, Rick's College became a four-year college and changed its name to Brigham Young University—Idaho. It is now a large private university.

[9] Séances are particularly problematic in that the explicit aim is to contact spirits. However, very few people mentioned them. Shauna, who studied spiritualism in a graduate school, explained that, in her view, holding a séance was not worth the effort because a good spirit would never bother to come at the request of those holding the séance. Why would they, she queried, when they were in a much better place? "You're not going to do a séance or try to contact the spirits because they're happy to be wherever they are, since it is so much better than here. Why would they bother coming here?"

of summoning a spirit, bad things will happen." Elder Neilson agreed, and said that when you use a Ouija board, "You're probably not going to get a good spirit."

A narrative from the Utah State University folklore collection tells of a girl who was playing with a Ouija board at a party. The student recorded this tale in the early 1990s, and she said it had circulated frequently at her high school. The Ouija board was not working, and so the girl's friends told her to take off her CTR ring. These embossed rings are popular among young Mormons, reminding them how important it is to "Choose the Right" (CTR).[10] After the girl removed the ring, the Ouija board started working. However, when she went looking for the ring the next day, she found it in a corner, "twisted up in a knot." The writer offers an analysis of the tale and its impact on her peers. In her view, the story:

> serves as a warning against putting aside religion and engaging in questionable activities. None of my friends in high school dared play with a Ouija board after hearing this story. This fear is also commonplace in Logan. On a recent camping trip, one of my friends pulled out a Ouija board. Two of the girls started screaming hysterically and threatened to leave if we played with it. (Giles 1991)

In an account from the early 2000s, the writer describes her aunt's experience at a party (the aunt in question happened to live down the street from me when I was growing up, although I did not know her well). The partygoers were playing with a Ouija board, and the aunt said that "a young man came down the stairs screaming things like you would hear if he was possessed and biting chunks out of his forearm." The woman reports that they had to call the bishop to come and "release it out of his soul," and she tells her niece that she believes in spirits because she witnessed a spirit attack firsthand (Larsen 2004).

---

[10] The CTR rings are widely available and come in many more styles today than they did in the past, when the only available option seemed to be a dainty silver ring with a green shield holding the CTR letters. In high school, I remember certain Mormon iconoclasts and one or two non-Mormons wearing the ring to "Corrupt the Righteous."

Pushing Away the Holy Spirit

Although most interviews and narratives discuss "inviting the experience" as an intentional or near-intentional engagement with the spirit world, certain problematic behaviors can invite evil indirectly by "pushing away" the Holy Spirit. A woman I call Michelle told me how her ex-husband's behavior had put her entire household in spiritual danger. It had been a difficult marriage. Her husband was not leading a righteous life, which she believed tempted bad spirits. She likened her feelings during marriage to her childhood fears of evil spirits. In the following excerpt from our conversation, she described playing at the home of a childhood friend whose family had been troubled by spirits as analogous to how she felt when she was married to her husband:

> I was always so scared to go over to her house and play . . . because she always talked about seeing two evil spirits in her basement one night . . . . I felt [similarly] especially when I was married, and my ex-husband . . . was not doing good things, and so in our house I felt that it wasn't filled with a good spirit. I didn't even dare go to sleep at night. I would just sit and watch the doors. And the minute I moved out of that house, I was fine. I could feel that there was something not good in there, but I never saw anything. I just felt it.

When I asked if her views reflected specific church teachings, Michelle told me that she had never been taught that certain behaviors "invite" evil spirits. Rather, she said, she had learned that certain behaviors could *push away* the Holy Ghost: "Well, we're kind of taught it in a more positive way kind of, like certain behaviors can push away the Holy Ghost. I really don't remember being taught in church that certain behaviors can invite bad spirits." In Michelle's framing, unrighteous behavior does not invite evil directly, but opens the door to evil by "pushing away" the Holy Ghost.

Exceptional Righteousness: Spirit Attempts to Thwart the Worthy

It is not only unrighteous behavior that invites the attention of evil spirits. Exceptional righteousness also draws their interest. I was first aware of this when Jake told me that he and his wife disagreed about why a threatening spirit was harassing their teenage daughter. The girl reported an evil presence in her bedroom over the course of several months. She could see the spirit, which she described as a shadowy, dark shape and as male. The spirit never physically attacked her, but she often felt like it was about to grab her. However, when she realized the spirit was there, it would always depart. Jake and his wife debated whether the girl's wild, partying behavior had attracted the spirits; recall that Jake said, "She gave us a rodeo!" Jake's wife was certain that the girl's behavior had attracted the threatening spirit. Jake disagreed, however, because even the most righteous can attract the attention of evil. As examples, Jake noted that he had been harassed while he was being "super good" on his own mission, and that the spirit who harassed his daughter also threatened his son as he prepared to go on a mission:

> I don't necessarily think it's because [of her behavior], because I had something like that happen over on my mission, and I was being super good . . . And my son was bein' real good getting' ready for his missionary papers and everything, knowing he has to behave a certain way, and he had described some similar things.

Jake and his wife's disagreement shows the local understanding that both unrighteousness and exceptional righteousness attract the attention of evil spirits. Spirits may visit the unrighteous in an effort to experience the pleasurable physicality of a licentious lifestyle, or they may aim to thwart the righteous behavior of the exceptionally good. In many ways, narratives of evil spirits harassing the righteous reflect foundational narratives in the sacred history of the church. Recall that in Chapter 2, we discussed Joseph Smith's first vision narrative. In the account, when Joseph Smith was searching for guidance about the true church at the age of fourteen, he was accosted by Satan, who tried to keep him from praying by tying his tongue. The young man was victorious in the struggle and continued praying, and then God and Jesus Christ appeared to him.

In his contribution to Parkin's *Anthropology of Evil*, David Pocock argues that evil as a general category can be understood as an "inversion of the ideal order itself" (1985, 47). This is similar, of course, to how anthropologists have typically characterized witchcraft. Certainly, Pocock's idea is useful in understanding the Utah experiences. When demonic visitors threaten righteous religious activity—missionary efforts, temple work, conversions, or efforts in religious teaching—they are attempting to invert the ideal order. Mitchell argues that her Latter-day Saint research participants in England tended to explain misfortune as the result of Satan's interference in good works. She gives as example comments made by the director of the Institute program[11] in the Manchester Stake, who explained their difficult finding buildings to lease for the young adult education program as indicative of Satan's attempt to stop their good works (Mitchell 2001a, 170).

Mormon folklore is rich with edifying tales of missionaries, new converts, and devout Latter-day Saints on their way to do temple work who are impeded by evil spirits. Shauna explained that the spirits will "get in the way of things if they know you're trying to do something good. And if you talk out loud, if you talk about evil spirits out loud, and if you talk about, good things you're going to do out loud, they might try to thwart you." She recounted a well-known story shared by a general authority in the church: "[And in the story] he would say, 'I'm going to go to the temple tomorrow,' and something would *always* happen that would make it so he couldn't go. And so he realized that by saying it out loud, he was notifying the spirits that he was going to do something good, and they would conspire against him." Similar stories abound, and many people report hearing such stories during Sunday school or at church meetings. In one such tale from the Utah State University folklore collection, the writer recalls a speaker at a meeting telling a story about an ancestor who would always be prevented from going to the temple if he announced out loud that he was planning to go: "Something would happen to prevent his going. An example—if we can finish this fence I will go to the temple. The ax broke, then after the ax is fixed it would start to rain. The man decided that he wouldn't ever mention his going to the temple aloud. He would milk his cow and then rush to the temple" (Hunsaker 1983). Another writer reports a story her roommate learned from an Institute teacher at Snow College in central Utah. The teacher told her of a young student experiencing a threatening presence in her dormitory: a malicious spirit pushed her down on her bed and silenced her. The event happened during the time when her father, who was not a member of the church, had begun "taking the teachings" of missionaries, and the student had been "fasting and praying" that he would accept the teachings and join the church. The evil presence was thwarting her righteous actions aimed to help her father accept the teachings and be baptized into the church (Fryer 1983).

---

[11] The term "Institute" refers to church educational programs aimed at young adults.

The Logan Temple

One well-known piece of Cache Valley folklore recounts Satan's attack on the Logan Temple. Many versions of this tale can be found in Nolan P. Olsen's history of the temple (Olsen 1978), and there are several retellings in the student folklore collection, and they are all very similar. The collectors note hearing them at Sunday school, in church meetings, and from older relatives. Austin and Alta Fife observed that such legends are associated with the construction of many Mormon temples, and their book includes a version of Logan Temple story (1956, 219–222). The general structure of the tale is as follows: Satan visits the temple to thwart the righteous work of the good people within. Through righteous power, the temple president drives Satan away, and eventually temple work returns to normal. One such narrative from the folklore collection, which the student notes that he heard from his father, reads as follows:

> After the completion of the Logan Temple, people came and did work for the dead inside. One particular day, some members were traveling up the hill to the temple to do some work. As they crested the hill, they saw a number of different looking people. People they did not recognize who acted different than they. After taking care of their horses in the livery stable, they came out and asked why all these people were out milling around outside the temple gate. Their leader, who answered their questions, was Lucifer himself. Him [sic.] and his hosts had come up to stop the work inside the Temple, he said. President Merrill of the Logan Temple, then proceeded to dismiss Satan and his hosts. Raising his right hand to the square and by the power of the Priesthood, he sent them away. As Satan and his followers were leaving, Satan said: "We'll be back. This isn't over yet!" Despite Lucifer's threat, the work has not stopped, proving that Satan cannot stop the work of the Lord. It will go on without him. (Allen, 1997)

This account specifically states that the "work" being done at the temple is "for the dead." As noted in the previous chapter, Latter-day Saint temples are spaces of righteous action, or "temple work," rather than sites of collective worship, and only church members in good standing may enter and perform temple work. In Allen's version of the tale, Satan's attempt to thwart righteous action was counter thwarted by the temple president. As in many temple tales, the president drove Satan and his legions away with the *power of the priesthood*, which we will return to in Chapter 6.[12]

In several versions of this story, Satan is able to stop the work of the temple for a short time. However, this is not because he was able to enter the temple. Rather, Satan specifically tells the temple president that if he cannot enter the temple to stop the work within, he will tempt people in the "temple district." In one account, for example, the "The man [Satan] said all right then, I'll have my people whisper to the people in your district to stop coming to the temple. So for about three years all the Temple [*sic*] work ceased" (Sondrup 1974). In another, Satan tells the temple president:

> If you do not stop this work, I will send all these people around to the people of this community. They will whisper in the ears of all the people not to come to this temple. This work will be stopped!" With these words, President Marrell [*sic*] commanded Satan to leave in the name of Jesus Christ. Satan and his followers departed. However, for a number of years following this incident the attendance to the Logan Temple decreased dramatically. (Hunsaker 1983)

Collectively, these well-known faith-promoting narratives are part of the local cultural kindling (Cassaniti and Luhrmann 2014) that clearly shows the possibility of Satan's interference in righteous action. In the temple narratives, we see that Satan and his minions consciously try to thwart the righteous action of the good by impeding temple work.

Righteous Action in the Pre-Existence

Other narratives show that righteous action in the pre-existence may also be targeted—and punished—by Satan and his minions. A number of accounts in the student folklore collection describe *patriarchal blessings* that connect an individual's role in the pre-existence to circumstances in the present life . A patriarchal blessing is an intriguing aspect of church practice, and I will not do its complexities justice here. In short, it will suffice to explain that

---

[12] Some versions of the tale name the temple president, President Merrill, and some date the incident specifically to 1914.

it is a blessing administered by a church officer known as a "patriarch" and conveys special information to the recipient about their personal lineage in the House of Israel as descendants of Abraham, and special counsel, guidance, or information for the recipient.[13]

What is so interesting about patriarchal blessings for our purpose in this chapter is that they can convey information about why things are the way they are in this life. Sometimes, for example, a blessing might convey that a person's disability in this life is a consequence of triumphant battling against Satan in the previous life. Extraordinary righteousness seems to inspire the wrath of Satan, and disability can be interpreted as a protective measure against Satan's influence. In one student narrative, , a young woman with a physical disability tells her friend, the student writer, about her patriarchal blessing. She said,

> As I sat there and the blessing was given to me tears came to my eyes as I listened to the words that were being said. I was explained to in detail the reasons that I had been placed in a wheelchair for my entire life. In the war in heaven, I had played such an important part in helping with the overthrowing of evil and defending good that Satan vowed to search me out and tempt me and test my faith. I was placed in this wheelchair almost as a safeguard against him. So I guess even the worst situations can turn out to be a blessing in disguise once you know the whole story. (Simpson 1991)

Other accounts of patriarchal blessings similarly explain mental or physical disability as the result of extraordinarily righteous action in the pre-existence. In one beautifully written account, a young man's "limited capacities" were described as a "protective harbor for this very special spirit" (Johnson 1997). In another, a mother seeks a blessing for her disabled son, and "While he [the patriarch] was giving him this blessing, he told him that he had been a great leader in the pre-existence, and that he had been one of people that had helped lead Satan out of heaven. He told him that God had had to send him in this protected form so that Satan would not be able to tempt him and lead him astray" (Paulsen 1997).

---

[13] An official description of the patriarchal blessing can be found online at https://www.churchofjesuschrist.org/study/manual/gospel-topics/patriarchal-blessings?lang=eng.

Experiences in the Mission Field: Satan and Those "Actively Living the Word of God"

Some of Satan's most dramatic attempts to thwart the righteous seem focused on a particularly righteous yet particularly vulnerable population: missionaries. Young Latter-day Saints immersed in the throes of righteous action by serving the church and teaching its message as missionaries are prime targets for Satan. This most righteous of junctures is perhaps the most slippery.

Young people frequently serve as missionaries in their late teens and early twenties. Missionaries receive a divine call to serve a mission in a particular locale after submitting paperwork. One might be called to serve in Brussels, Boise, or Buenos Aries, and at present the church has four hundred missions around the the world. Families are expected to contribute to the expenses of a mission, and many young people save for their missions for many years. In Utah, there is enormous pressure for young men to serve, and although young women also frequently serve, there is less social pressure to do so. For decades, the age for young men to serve their missions was nineteen, and twenty-one for young women. In 2012, however, the age for missions was lowered, and young men may now serve at age eighteen and young women at nineteen. Men typically serve a two-year mission, and women serve for eighteen months.

When I was growing up in Cache Valley, most young men in my age group went on missions. Young women were far less likely to go, and an oft-heard explanation was that a mission was something women did only when and if they were not married by age twenty-one. However, many young women were (and still are) eager to go on missions, as were several of my female friends. One acquaintance told me that her father was shocked and disappointed when she filed her mission paperwork in the early 1990s, just weeks before her twenty-first birthday. In his view, only young women with limited or no marriage prospects needed to go on missions, and he thought his daughter was much too attractive to need to go on a mission. A strong cultural framework is evident in this woman's memory: while a young man's righteous duty requires him to serve a mission, the priority for a righteous young woman should be marriage. Today, with the 2012 change in missionary ages, more young women are serving missions, and the path to righteousness for young women might be understood as changing with more emphasis on serving missions; we will return to this in Chapter 6.

Many instructive tales about spirit harassment focus on new missionaries at the MTC in Provo, where missionaries reside for several weeks before the official beginning of the mission. Time spent at the MTC is carefully structured, and few visits with outsiders are permitted. At the MTC, missionaries learn what they need to know to offer teachings to those in the mission field, and those who are called to a non-English language mission undergo impressively intensive language training.

Many tales focus on Satan's attempts to tempt the missionaries at the MTC. In the late 1980s, a folklore student collected three versions of one MTC story. In the tale, an elder started to experience difficulties and temptations once he was called on a mission. Prior to his calling, he had been an upstanding young high school student who did not have trouble "living the standards," and he was concerned about the various temptations that began to plague him at the MTC. In a dream one night, the young man was instructed to look out the window. He went to the window twice, and he saw nothing other than the view of the Provo temple. He was mysteriously pushed to look a third time, when he saw angels "four deep" outside the walls of the temple, trying to keep Satan and an "army of devils" at bay. In one version of the tale, the narrator concludes that the vision taught the troubled young man that, "no matter how hard Satan tried to get to us, or to tempt us, or to enter, so to speak, into our temple, he can't. If we prepare ourselves and are worthy Satan won't hurt us because there are angels guarding us and they are ready to protect us" (McKee 1988). In the two other versions, the narrators similar conclude that the vision "settled the mind" of the missionary and he was no longer tempted. What I find particularly interesting about these stories is that they all attribute his temptations to his status as a missionary, and all associate his temptations with Satan's attempt to breach the walls of the temple—clearly a metaphor for his person.

Missionaries who are preoccupied with Satan may attract evil. Another narrative from the student folklore collection describes the powerful influence of Satan as an "active force in the world," and the "special interest Satan has in people who are actively living the Word of God." In the tale, which the writer had heard several times, some missionaries at the MTC were spending their free time discussing how the Devil tries to "influence and tempt people." This mere discussion of the power of Satan attracted an "evil presence" and "one guy went to look out the window and saw the Devil looking in with all his demons." "Somehow," the writer notes, "their talking about the Devil summoned him." The missionaries called a superior and they prayed together to drive the Devil away (Speth 1997).

In other tales, missionaries at the MTC intentionally invite the experience. A common thread in these narratives is the danger of hubris: missionaries who are over-confident in the power of their righteousness invite evil. In one narrative from the late 1980s, the writer tells a story of a fellow missionary preparing for his mission in the MTC. The writer describes the MTC as "a very spiritual place, and place where many miracles have occurred in the past." While they were living together in the dormitories, the missionaries shared many stories with each other, including the following "miracle story." Two rather self-assured young elders decided to invite the Devil into the room so they could use their priesthood powers (special spiritual authority men in good standing have in the church—see Chapter 6) so they could cast him out. They successfully summoned the Devil, and "the room got very dark and they could feel the power of Satan crowding around them." Unfortunately, however, the missionaries could not cast him out. The MTC president was called to their aid, and he explained that, "their priesthood power was not effective in casting out Satan because they had invited him in" (Erickson 1988).

A similar, fantastically evocative narrative from the 1990s features a zealous missionary who was frequently angry at Satan's attempts to tempt the righteous (Hurst 1992). The missionary was frustrated at the "wickedness" of the people in his mission site (the location is not named), and he blamed Satan for tempting them and not repenting. The zealot would regularly yell at Satan, "How dare you tempt these people?!" (The writer is not impressed by his zealotry and calls him "very psycho"). In his fury one evening, the young man lashed out at the Devil: "He yelled to Satan that he wanted to get it all out in the open. He challenged him, screaming 'I know I can win!! I have the power of the priesthood, and good always wins over evil!!'" As intended, this swagger attracted an evil spirit. The young man and his companion[14] could feel the spirit's presence, and the two tried to pray the spirit away. However, it did not go as planned. The next morning, the zealous missionary was not in his bed, and his companion found him on the roof, with "every bone in his body broken."

---

[14] When serving a mission, missionaries are paired with a series of companions. The two live together and serve together for a period of about three months, and then are paired with a new companion.

Together, these stories indicate just how slippery the edge of righteousness is, and perhaps the most profound connection between them is the danger of excessive pride among missionaries, some of whom are consumed with pride in their righteous power, which leads to spiritual danger. My conversations with missionaries and former missionaries show that the power of Satan is not simply in the realm of folklore and faith-promoting tales. Many missionaries have told me about negative visitations during their missions, and a particularly intriguing account comes from Jake. During our conversation, I recounted some of the stories about the MTC. I then asked if he had heard any of these stories before and whether his training in the MTC prepared him for this kind of intense spiritual experience. I told him about the anthropologist Tanya Luhrmann's (2012) research on the power of prayer in American evangelicalism to facilitate certain kinds of attention to the uncanny, and I asked him if perhaps so much emphasis was placed on spiritual experiences in the MTC that missionaries were "extra kindled," so to speak, and thus highly attuned to spiritual events. Jake listened politely, but then quashed that idea. He told me that, actually, it was just the opposite: the missionaries were prepared to expect quiet and calm spiritual development, not dramatic or fantastic spiritual experiences. "Listen," he said:

> Don't think that you [the missionary] are going to pray for things or your investigators [those who receiving the missionary teachings] are going to pray for things and that angels are going to show up and tap dance on the end of their bed, and say, "Yes . . . ! Come on, join us!" You know, [you] don't set that expectation for people because, yes, it happens sometimes, but more often than not it's a very quiet conversion . . . . So I was never expecting anything like that. And, you know . . . I was raised to understand these kind of things happen, but not necessarily.

Even so, despite Jake's training to expect nothing dramatic, he had a very intense negative visitation while serving a mission in the United Kingdom. The didactic tales just discussed illustrate the dangers of missionary preoccupation with Satan, particularly over-confidence in their righteous power to combat evil. In Jake's experience, however, we see the potential danger of great success in mission work. Exceptional righteousness draws the attention of evil, and as we saw with Logan Temple stories, Satan takes an active interest in preventing righteous work.

As is evident in the earlier chapters of this book, Jake is exceptionally intelligent and charismatic, and he is a gifted storyteller with a sharp sense of humor. His oratorical gifts extend beyond humor, however, and I was captivated with his recollection of his missionary experience with an evil spirit. Jake set the scene by describing the home he lived in with his companion, two other male missionaries, and the mission leader of their ward. Their flat was in an old house, and two of the bedrooms, each shared by two missionaries, were at either end of a long hallway. Jake explained that the trouble started with odd noises and creaking in the house that seemed to happen when the missionaries would pray together in the evening. The creaking sounds would be followed by footsteps going down the stairs, but never back up. And then, the light in the hallway would flash on and off.

At first, each pair of missionary companions thought the strange happenings were a joke played by the other pair. Eventually, however, a spirit started whispering their names. Jake explained that one night his companion had gone to bed early, but then came out of the bedroom "lookin' like he'd seen a ghost." The companion told him that he heard someone saying Jake's first name:

> My *Christian* name, not "Elder." Because we call each other Elder and our last name.[15] Somebody's sayin' [he whispers] "Jake, Jake, Jake." And [the other missionary says] "I wake up, and there's a woman standin' next to your bed. And I'm like *what* are you doin'? And she's sayin' your name." And he said, "and I roll over, and I say, 'get her out of here!' And then I kind of realize, and I turned around, and I roll back over and she's not there. And then I ran in here."

The others seemed to think Jake was hiding a girl in the flat, which naturally met with the stern disapproval of the mission leader. Dating is not permitted for missionaries. But there was no girl. Jake said that a few days later:

> I woke up one night because I heard my name. And I'm facing the wall, and I hear my name . . . and it's a woman's voice, and I hear it again. And

---

[15] Here, Jake explains the common practice of calling male missionaries by the title "Elder" and the last name, which we discussed earlier in the book (as in Elder Jones). Female missionaries use the title "Sister" (Sister Smith) as they cannot be elders in the church. The spirit's use of Jake's first name suggests both a lack of respect for his status as a missionary and the tempting nature of her harassment.

I turn over and look, and this one's not dressed in white or anything like that. I didn't see a face or anything. It was just a shape. And I perceive that it was a woman. It was a woman's voice, maybe that's why I perceived that it's a woman. And this one was more—the first one that I saw that I told you about out on the yard, that was like you and I . . . a real person—this was more like what you'd think of watchin' Hollywood.[16] . . . . And I turn over and I look, and it turned around, and it just kinda drifted over, out the door, and up the steps. The steps creaked. And I look over and my companion is sitting there like this [Jake made a face of jaw-dropped astonishment]. Yeah, he saw it too. And I'm pointing to the door, and he's like, "It's gone, it's gone, it's gone, it's gone."

After seeing the spirit, Jake and his companion contacted their mission president, who advised them to "rededicate" their flat through a priesthood blessing, which they performed right away (this will be described in more detail in Chapter 6). Jake told me that he did not know much about the spirit itself, but he explained that the Devil knows human weaknesses, and so he sent a menacing spirit in female form. He laughed a bit as he said, "Lucifer knows all of our weaknesses. You know, he knows me, and I liked girls so maybe I'd pay attention if I heard some whispering girl."

I asked Jake how he interpreted the experience, and his explanation shows just how slippery that edge of righteousness is when one is on a mission.

He said, "That [happened at] a point in time [when] we were having a lot of success in different areas. And this particular area, there hadn't been a family baptized in this area in fifteen years . . . . we baptized the first family in fifteen years there!"

In a five-month span, he explained, the missionaries had baptized six or seven people, which was a great number for that region and, as he said, Jake and his companions had baptized the first family in fifteen years. Missionaries sometimes move from location to location during a mission, and they rotate in and out of towns and neighborhoods at different times. Of all the missionaries in his region, Jake had been there the longest, which he explained was probably why the spirit targeted him.

Modestly, he added that he did not think that *he* was the reason for all the baptisms, "I'm not sayin' 'Oh, I'm great,' or anything, but I just had been there longer and seen more of these [baptisms] happen." In Jake's interpretation,

---

[16] Here, Jake refers to the story from Chapter 4 when he experienced a visitation from Joseph Smith.

then, their success as missionaries—their exceptional righteousness—was the reason the spirit harassed them.

The final account in this chapter comes from Greg, the history professor. Greg's negative experience happened after his mission when he was a "returned missionary." The term "returned missionary" is used to describe people when they are recently returned from a mission. Greg had moved from Utah to a Midwestern college town to pursue a PhD. He described himself as active in the church at the time, and he was living with a family in his ward. The man of the house was a former stake president and a professor at Greg's university. It was in their home that he had a negative experience so overwhelming and powerful that he could not think or speak. It happened when he was lying in bed, and he experienced a presence so terrifying that he said he "could not formulate a thought." Although Greg could not see anything unusual in the room, he had no doubt he was being harassed by an evil spirit. He explained:

> I woke up at some point, but eventually it felt as if the spirit was trying to confound me. It was trying to take away my capacity to even speak. What I remember doing was following my training in the LDS church, which was to order the bad spirit to leave in the name of Jesus Christ. I managed to think this, and articulate this thought in my head, because I didn't say it, because I was still in this semi-conscious state. And that's when the feeling, the presence, the spirit, just departed.[17]

Greg found the encounter terribly disturbing, and said he felt "violated." Desperate to talk to someone about it, he approached the man he was living with. Greg described the older man as a senior priesthood holder, and he assumed he would be able to help. However, the man did not take the event seriously and told Greg to forget about it. In Greg's view, the man was more worried about Greg's sanity than the evil spirit, and he seemed concerned that he was going to be a mentally unstable presence in their home. Greg's impression at the time was that the older man had never counseled anyone about such frightening spiritual matters. He reflected that maybe it would

---

[17] A student writer, Sierra Mackelprang, records an interview with a missionary that is similar, but the missionary was able to see the spirits: "I saw shadows floating around like just like everywhere in the room and they were like taunting me" (Mackelprang 2018).

have been different if the man was "formal priesthood leader," like the bishop of his ward.

Greg thought for many years about why the spirit attacked him. When he discussed the incident with his brother years later, they both reflected on the negative spirit experiences of Joseph Smith as a possible explanatory framework for what had happened. Latter-day Saints are generally familiar with Joseph Smith's account of being harassed by Satan and evil spirits when he was young,. Greg asked himself, "Why me? Why now?" In questioning why he had the experience, he used the same interpretive typologies and linguistic frameworks as others we have discussed in this chapter. "I wasn't playing with a Ouija board," he told me, "I wasn't *inviting* the experience." After speaking with his brother, whom he described as a devout, "orthodox Mormon," he also considered that maybe he had a particularly important destiny to fulfill, as Joseph Smith did: "Did it mean that I was a person of destiny? That I had some sort of role to perform for good or bad? That this evil power knew it . . . ? I never thought I was going to be a prophet."

Greg referenced righteous standing as a possible explanation for the spirit visit, providing another example of the connection between spiritual experiences and righteousness or the lack thereof. In his research on inspiration from the Holy Spirit among Latter-day Saints, the folklorist Tom Mould has similarly found that "spiritual knowledge and divine knowledge are intensified for church leaders, those men and women who have proved themselves particularly righteous and worthy" (2011, 40). Greg pondered whether his experience of evil had marked him as "a person of destiny." Perhaps he was especially worthy, and the attack was intended to thwart that righteous destiny. Or perhaps he was especially prone to unrighteousness or even evildoing, which drew the spirit to him.

When I asked Greg if he thought that certain events in his life had triggered the evil visitation, he said no. However, he described his status at the time as that of the "late-twenties-single-Mormon-male-conundrum." Greg was a few years past the desirable age of marriage in Utah, as missionaries are encouraged to marry as soon as they return from their missions. He was also dating non-Mormon women at the time. Greg recalled that he was "pretty concerned" about being unmarried. In a follow-up conversation about two years after our initial interview, Greg referenced the words of Brigham Young, who had stated that any unmarried men aged twenty-five or older were a "menace to society." However, when I asked if he thought that his unmarried status was a mark of unrighteousness that attracted the spirit, he stated unequivocally that this was not the case. Over twenty years after the awful visitation, and at a time when he was inactive in the church, Greg still remembered the attack vividly. He did not doubt that he had been targeted by evil, yet he remained confused about why it happened.

Conclusion

In earlier chapters, we saw that one of the ways that Latter-day Saints in northern Utah interpret positive spirit visits is as guidance on the path of righteousness. In this chapter, we see that people tend to understand visits from the Devil or evil spirits as moral indexes of righteousness, or the lack thereof. These negative visitations reflect a cultural framework of evil as a cosmological force—Satan—attempting to disrupt righteous human life. Humans must thus be conscious and wary of the ever-present menace. Just as unrighteous actions attract evil, exceptional righteousness also attracts the attention of Satan. As I have argued elsewhere, "As righteousness is action, unrighteousness is also action, and it is actions and behaviors that attract evil more so than interiority and states of mind" (Stiles 2022, 15).

The accounts discussed in this chapter show that for many Latter-day Saints in northern Utah, evil is not simply a human phenomenon. Rather, evil is the result of cosmological interference. This is somewhat different from one recent study of evil in the broader field of Mormon Studies by the historian Matthew Bowman, which analyzed Mormon folklore about the biblical figure of Cain. Accounts of Cain appearing and causing havoc among Mormons began in the nineteenth century. Bowman argues that in the late twentieth century, Cain becomes equivalent to Bigfoot in Mormon folklore. Indeed, the narratives in the Utah State University folklore collection that mention Cain describe a large, hairy being.[18] Bowman ascribes this transformation to a twentieth-century change in Latter-day Saint conceptions of evil, in which evil was no longer understood as a threatening, personified cosmological power but as the consequence of poor decision making, not external malicious forces (2011, 38). The narratives in this chapter show, however, that evil is certainly still regarded to a significant extent as an external,

---

[18] I have not encountered any contemporary references to Cain in my ethnographic research and interviews; only a handful of late-twentieth-century narratives in the folklore collections report Cain sightings.

cosmological force, and seems more in keeping with Bowman's characterization of evil in nineteenth-century Mormon thought. My exploration of these accounts shows that, in northern Utah, Latter-day Saint understandings of righteousness and the lack thereof index the potential agency of an external, cosmological force—Satan and his malevolent minions, and show that these personified forces are part of the broader moral landscape.

As noted in the previous chapter, we must also regard these malevolent meta-persons as active agents in the lives of the living. As I argue elsewhere (Stiles 2022), exploring the lived experience with negative visitations shows that Latter-day Saint references to Satan and evil spirits are not a shorthand for or merely symbolic of vices or the broader human tendency to do bad things. Furthermore, in all these accounts, we see that *the potential to attract evil spirits*—even through exceptional righteousness—is more significant than the unrighteous action of the human subject. Therefore, we cannot understand these accounts simply as attributing culpability for bad human actions to spirit beings (e.g., "the Devil made me do it"), or as blurring the lines between spirit and human persons, as Parkin has described in his commentary on Csordas's article on morality (2013). In this Latter-day Saint community, poor decisions and unrighteous actions are consequential not simply because of their potential negative outcomes, and such decisions and actions are not necessarily attributed to the influence of Satan. Rather, they are significant because they might draw the attention of Satan. Exceptionally righteous actions, such as mission work, might do the same. And thus, all these actions—righteous and unrighteous—might possibly invite evil to disrupt righteous human progress and the moral order. Here, we find a profound cultural understanding of a belligerent, agentive evil that is persistently encouraging people to be bad. Recall Shauna's comment that when she was young, she always thought that it seemed that Satan was more powerful than God because his presence seemed so present in daily life. The conflict of good and evil in foundational understandings of the War in Heaven is still being waged. In the next chapter, we explore how people wage this "spiritual warfare" through the power of the priesthood.

6
The Power of the Priesthood, Gender, and Evil Spirits

In the *History of the Church*, the prophet Joseph Smith writes, "Wicked spirits have their bounds, limits and laws, by which they are governed . . . and, it is very evident that they possess a power that none but those who have the priesthood can control" (*History of the Church*, 4:576).

Certain aspects of dealing with malicious spirits are gendered. This is not because spirits seem more or less attracted to gendered beings, but rather because spirit harassment requires a specific righteous action administered through the power of the priesthood. Many accounts highlight the power of male priesthood holders to drive away evil spirits through gendered practices of righteous masculine action. In this chapter, I examine how a form of righteous masculinity, constructed in both folklore and lived experience, centers on the power of the priesthood to cast out demons. In doing so, the chapter engages with particularly Latter-day Saint notions of masculinity, which David Knowlton has succinctly described as follows: "Mormons value a man who is spiritual" (1992, 13). Combating evil spirits nearly always centers on the special powers, or keys, of the priesthood and how priesthood holders invoke those powers. However, as we will see, the gendered nature of the priesthood and the use priesthood powers to cast out spirits is contested.

A recent issue of the journal *Anthropological Quarterly*, edited by William Dawley and Brendan Jamal Thornton, tackles the relationship between masculinity and religion (Dawley and Thornton 2018). In the introductory essay, Dawley and Thornton observe that while much scholarship in recent decades has tackled the ways in which female gender roles are constituted in religious domains, fewer studies have looked at how male roles are constituted. Certainly, religion and gender are "co-constitutive social categories," and one of the unifying points the authors make is that "most religious concepts, practices, affects, and institutional relationships are gendered."

In some of the accounts discussed in this chapter, those who are saved from evil spirits by the efforts of the male priesthood holders are young women. When I began this project, several of the first narratives I read in the Utah State University student folklore archive described young women harassed by menacing spirits, and I expected this gendered pattern was going to be prominent: a damsel in distress rescued by a man holding the priesthood. However, as the project developed and I read more narratives and incorporated ethnographic research, I learned that men are just as frequently plagued with such negative experiences. A more common pattern that emerged is that *young* women and *young* men are delivered from spirit harassment by older, more spiritually advanced priesthood holders. Evil spirits seem to plague the young more than the old (see Stiles 2022), and it is not simply the power of the priesthood that drives spirits away, but rather the authority that comes with advanced priesthood standing.

However, the presumed maleness of priesthood action against evil spirits is a point of tension in this community. Indeed, in the understanding of some church members, certain powers of the priesthood are not limited to men. In interviews, both women and men challenged the strict association of priesthood powers with men, often by drawing on the rich history of Mormon women's spiritual abilities. Reflecting a theme that I have addressed in other chapters, tensions around spiritual powers are often articulated vis-à-vis critical conceptions of a discrepancy between "Mormon/Utah culture," the formal institution of the church, and the true ethos of the religion. Both men and women question whether the contemporary focus on men's priesthood powers has eclipsed Latter-day Saint women's historical prowess in dealing with the menacing supernatural. A rich body of scholarship describes the spiritual prowess of early Mormon women, particularly in areas of spiritual healing (Madsen 1982; Newell 1981; Stapley and Wright 2008, 2011). In his recent work, the anthropologist Jason Palmer (2022) similarly describes Peruvian Mormon women in Utah maneuvering around male-centric priesthood blessings.

In the view of some of those I interviewed, the contemporary construction of male priesthood powers is a historical manifestation that does not reflect the "true teachings" of the church but is rather simply a patriarchal form of "Mormon culture." In essence, then, some would argue that "Mormon culture" has embraced a hegemonic masculinity (Connell 1995) that does not reflect the true essence of the religion's views on gender. In Lyne's words,

"Women have the priesthood, too." Although this chapter does not aim to provide a full account of recent debates on gender and the priesthood in the church, it will hopefully shed light on Latter-day Saint understanding and practice surrounding gender, the priesthood, and spiritual authority. . .

Thornton's (2018) work with Pentecostal male converts in the Dominican Republic provides a useful framework for understanding contested ideas of gender and spiritual power comes from recent work. Drawing on the gender theorist Judith Butler's influential *Gender Trouble* (1999), Thornton shows that men's accounts of demons tempting them away from a righteous spiritual path results in what he terms "gender distress." Dominican men who become Pentecostal face a cognitive dissonance in that they are encouraged to leave behind previous formulations of a hyper-aggressive and hypersexual masculinity and embrace another form of masculinity. Thornton shows that one way this dissonance manifests is in nocturnal visits of succubae, who tempt men to engage in illicit sex.[1] Thornton writes that "implicit in these admonitions is a sweeping indictment of femininity, a forewarning of the dangers of female sexuality to men's holiness, and not-so-oblique endorsement of male-centric gender value in the defense of male autonomy" (2018, 160). Men who struggle with competing notions of masculinity and the impossibly high standard of new ideal Christian manhood, many of whom are in difficult financial circumstance, explain their challenges as temptations of Satan. This fosters new gender antagonism as men construct novel moral identities both in opposition to women and apart from them (2018, 164), and Thornton shares evocative narratives of men's spiritual triumph. He writes that *"el hombre serio*—the quintessential man of God—is simultaneously victor and victim, the height of his accomplishments are only as spectacular as the depth reached by the failures he as overcome. His spiritual triumph is matched only by the extent of his victimhood reversed" (2018, 165).

Although the Latter-day Saint case is quite different, Thornton's articulation of gender distress and the possibility of spiritual triumph helps us

---

[1] Although the accounts Thornton describes bear some resemblance to what I have found in Utah in that evil spirits tend to visit at night, I have not found overt sexualization of the encounters , although there are perhaps implicit suggestions of sexual aggression, as we'll see in a couple of examples in this chapter. As we will see in one narrative discussed below, a young woman describes a nighttime spirit attack to her sister as an attempted "rape." And we saw in Chapter 5, when Jake and his mission companions were harassed, sexual overtones were at most only gently implied—simply because it was a female spirit whispering the missionaries' Christian names at night rather than their title of "Elder."

understand the ramifications of using priesthood authority against evil spirits. As noted, there are no clearly gendered patterns of spirit attacks or harassment in this northern Utah community, despite the profound significance of gender difference in the lived experience of Latter-day Saints (Knowlton 1992; Brooks 2016). However, a gendered notion of spiritual authority comes into play when dealing with spirit attacks, and the possibility of "spiritual triumph" over Satan and evil spirits is featured in many of the accounts. As Thornton describes among Pentecostal Dominican men, Latter-day Saint victims of spirit harassment may become victorious over evil through the power of the priesthood, and thus "simultaneously victor and victim," to use Thornton's words. In Utah, we see this in the accounts of missionaries deliberately inviting Satan order to flex their priesthood powers, which we considered in the previous chapter. In this chapter, we look at the use of priesthood powers as a site of gender distress. Although the formal priesthood is held by men, and it is through the powers of the priesthood—namely blessings, casting out, healing, and cleansing—that the influence of Satan and his minions can be effectively countered, this is not strictly the domain of men.

Domains of Priesthood Expertise

As discussed in Chapter 4, the hierarchical organization of The Church of Jesus Christ of Latter-day Saints is centered on the institution of the priesthood. There is a profound structural gender divide in the church, which Knowlton describes as "a panorama of exalted masculinity in its leadership and worship" (1992, 25). The primary manifestation of this gender divide is perhaps in the formal institution of the priesthood, which is limited to men and which Knowlton observes allows men to test and display "Mormon manhood" (1992). Here, I use the term "formal" to refer to the institutionalized priesthood in the church, and to presage the direction of the last part of this chapter, in which I discuss the way that women enact the powers of the priesthood against spiritual malevolence. This chapter is not intended to provide an extended analysis of the institution of the priesthood past and present, as several other recent works do that very effectively (Davies 2010; Hammarberg 2013; Prince 2015; Stapley 2018). Rather, the chapter considers how Latter-day Saints themselves conceive of and enact the power of the priesthood in opposing evil through specific actions. Although the priesthood is a spiritual designation, priesthood power manifests through righteous action in the world. Here, we explore two particularly important areas of this righteous action—the power to heal both spiritual and physical ailments and the power to cast out harassing spirits. Both occasions call for the priesthood holder to minster to the afflicted through a priesthood blessing, which has the power to comfort, heal, and drive away evil. In a recent book on the priesthood, the historian Jonathan A. Stapley (2018) observes that the Latter-day Saint "healing liturgy" is diverse and complex, and it is thus a fruitful way to explore Mormon cosmological ideas. It is also a fruitful way to study gendered spiritual practice.

Healing and Comfort

Today, holders of the priesthood frequently use their spiritual powers to heal. In Utah's hospitals, clinics, and doctors' offices, it is not unusual for holders of the Melchizedek Priesthood among the staff or the patient's family to give blessings. My mother, a retired hospital nurse from Cache Valley, confirmed that priesthood blessings happened frequently in her experience, especially when a patient was acutely ill. My brother, a physician in Salt Lake City, said that such blessings are also regular occurrences at his hospital, and are performed by family members or by someone on the hospital staff. The hospital has not designated a priesthood holder to perform blessings; instead, if a blessing is requested, whoever is available among the priesthood holders on staff will perform it.

As numerous scholars of Mormon history have pointed out, women were very active in administering healing practices in the early years of the church, and were sometimes thought to hold this ability as a spiritual gift along with other gifts, like speaking in tongues (Godfrey 1997; Brady 1987; Newell 1981; Stapley 2018; Stapley and Wright 2011). The historians Jonathan A. Stapley and Kristine Wright (2011) recently examined ritual healing practices among nineteenth-century Mormon women Although today most healing practices are administered by male priesthood holders, who anoint and bless the sick, Stapley and Wright show that in the early years of the church, women frequently healed through the laying on of hands (2011, 5). Other rituals included washing and anointing the sick, prayer circles for healing, and women were baptized for health and healing (Stapley and Wright 2008). Women's healing powers were thought to be a result of the spiritual direction of the

Holy Ghost or, sometimes, patriarchal blessings administered by church leaders. Stapley and Wright (2008) designate this as "liturgical authority" in that it was non-ecclesiastical. Elsewhere, Stapley has argued that this was a unique domain of women's authority in the early decades of the church, and women healers were sometimes thought to rank even higher than male leaders (Stapley 2016). One notable early woman healer was one of Brigham Young's daughters, Zina Presendia Young Williams Card, who often spoke in tongues and performed blessings (Godfrey 1997; Stapley 2018).

The tradition of women's healing extended to Cache Valley. Austin and Alta Fife introduce us to the sisters Hulda Bassett and Elizabeth Bullock, who served as doctors in the town of Providence (my hometown) in the early years of its settlement (Fife and Fife 1956). The Fifes observed that the sisters used various plant-based remedies and wrote that "these divinely chosen doctors never failed to recommend the ritual of laying-on-of-hands" by the elders (1956, 258). In her well-known article, "A Gift Given, a Gift Taken" (1981), the feminist historian Linda King Newell describes occasions on which Mormon women performed healings in the valley in the late nineteenth and early twentieth centuries. For example, in 1868, the apostle Ezra T. Benson, a member of the Quorum of the Twelve, called on all women who had been "ordained" to wash and anoint the sick to use their powers to rid the valley of a spreading illness (Newell 1981, 32). Newell comments that there is no mention in the historical source of what "ordained" meant in this context, so we can only surmise that they were somehow recognized for their abilities in healing. She also describes a 1910 Cache Valley Relief Society meeting that was focused on women's healing practices. Since the earliest years of the church, the Relief Society has been the formal organization for women. At this 1910 meeting, the Relief Society President Lucy S. Cardon noted the importance of "having the Spirit of the Lord" when healing (1981, 38). The local president, Margaret Ballard, remarked that the bishop should know about their healing work, and another woman, Martha Meedam, commented at the meeting that she "had done as much anointing and blessing as anyone in the stake" (1981, 38).

A few years later, however, things changed. Newell writes that, in 1914, then-president Joseph Fielding Smith sent a letter to church leaders stating that although in some cases it made sense for women to lay hands on their children or other women, they were to be discouraged from taking on responsibilities that were deemed the purview of the priesthood. Newell writes that with this statement, the official body of the church entered a phase of clarifying priesthood powers as strictly the domain of men, and "Church leaders made it clear that women did not have priesthood powers" (1981, 39; see also Stapley and Wright 2008 for changes in healing). In her work on women's visitations by spirit children, which we discussed in Chapter 3, Margaret Brady argues that the domain of such "visions" was one of the few remaining areas of spiritual power for women. She writes "the only spiritual 'gift' still allowed Mormon women today is the ability to have visions" (1987, 468).

This limitation of priesthood powers to men did not go uncontested. Newell describes a fascinating exchange in 1935 between a Cache Valley woman, Martha Hickman, and the then Relief Society General President, Louise Yates Robison, about whether women could continue to minister to pregnant women by washing and anointing in the temple. Robison replies to Hickman that, although the washing and anointing was indeed a "beautiful ordinance," in some places it was no longer permitted by the priesthood. However, she advised that women may continue to do so quietly in places "where it is permitted." Robison writes, "It is something that should be treated very carefully, and as we have suggested, with no show or discussion made of it" (Newell 1981, 40). Newell writes that a 1946 letter from Elder Joseph Fielding Smith to Relief Society President Belle S. Spafford effectively ended even lukewarm support for women's ministrations by setting a clear preference for the ministrations of male priesthood holders. Given this, it is unsurprising that nearly all accounts of healing that I have collected are men using their priesthood powers. However, as we will see, both men and women reference women's roles in early church history as evidence of women's spiritual abilities in the "true" religion.

First, however, let us look at some accounts of healing priesthood blessings administered by men. A number of narratives in the Utah State University folklore collection describe the miraculous healing power of the priesthood blessing. In one account from 1991, a teenage boy who was preparing for his mission hit his head while swimming at a public pool and fell unconscious. He was underwater for four minutes. When he was rescued, a bystander gave him mouth-to-mouth resuscitation, but the account relates that the boy did not start breathing until his father gave him a priesthood blessing. When the young man's family took him to the hospital, the doctor said he had a "perforated ear" [sic. maybe eardrum?], which his father healed with another priesthood blessing. The writer of the account notes that the young man was able to enter the MTC on time due to the two blessings from his father (McEntire 1991). Another account tells of a missionary serving somewhere in the Pacific who was similarly restored to life after a near drowning. The writer explains that the drowning missionary's spirit left his body and then told another missionary to restore him to life through a priesthood blessing (Miller 1999). In another account, a student explains that when he was a teenager in the 1980s, he was seriously injured in a tractor accident. When he got to the hospital, X-rays showed severe physical damage. A nurse asked his father if he was going to give the boy a priesthood blessing. His father gave him the blessing, and when the doctors ordered more X-rays, they showed, "no broken ribs, no punctured lung, and the bleeding had stopped" (Ballard 1998). A similar account from 2008 describes a disabled teenager whose doctor, when reviewing new X-rays, asked his parents if they "did that thing with the men and the hands?" The mother said "Yes, a blessing," and the doctor told them that he had no more spinal cord damage (Krenicky 2009).

Another group of narratives describe "false" healings performed by non-Latter-day Saint healers and religious leaders. In most of these, the false healings are administered to young missionaries serving outside of the United States. In most, a senior priesthood holder, typically the mission president, identifies a healing as false, then reverses and remedies it through his own priesthood powers. For example, in one account, a missionary broke his leg while on a mission in Argentina, and the pastor of a what is described as a "rival" Argentine Christian church healed it for him. The writer, who heard the story while serving a mission in Argentina, notes that this story is commonly told among missionaries to warn them of other churches' claims to healing. In the narrative, because a non-member managed to heal his leg, the missionary begins to doubt his "own claim to divine authority" through the Latter-day Saint priesthood. Perplexed, he approaches his mission president, who gives him a blessing in order to restore the leg to its broken state! This caused the missionary even more distress, which exacerbated his crisis of faith, and so he approached the mission president again. "This time the mission president responded with great authority. 'I know why your leg was healed by the preacher. Even Satan has power, even the power to heal. When I gave you the blessing, it removed the satanic blessing from you. While it healed your leg, it was not from God.'" The mission president then blessed the leg again to heal it, and the writer concludes, "The missionary had the greatest awareness of the power of Satan and his ability to impersonate God in many forms" (King 2010).

A nearly identical story describes a missionary who breaks his arm while serving in Japan. In this case, the healer is described as a Buddhist or Shinto healer, not a Christian pastor. However, as in the other story, upon learning of the healing, the mission president re-breaks the arm with a priesthood blessing, then takes the missionary to a hospital to have "the arm fixed right." He tells the young man that, "he doesn't want his missionaries healed with the wrong power. He said that the missionaries [sic] arm was healed with an evil power and when cast out (with the blessing) the arm when back to being broke. This taught the missionaries to be wary of evil influence" (Harrison 1991).

A third account, which the writer heard from a friend who served a mission in Brazil, tells of a mysterious Brazilian woman healing the dislocated knee of missionary (Tolton 2009). The missionary hurt his knee while running down a dark road, and the woman appeared in order to help him. The missionary was perplexed by the woman's ability to heal, which led him to doubt his own authority as a priesthood holder. The writer states that the missionary even began to question the gendered nature of the priesthood: "The elder spent the next few days confused at what had happened, for he had been told his whole life that only men were eligible to receive such a power, which is known as the Priesthood." When the young man visited his mission president to tell him about what happened and his resulting confusion, the mission president blessed him, and the knee dislocated again. In pain, the missionary asked the older man why he did this to him, and he was told, "Don't ever doubt the power of God again!" (Tolton 2009). Tolton, also a former missionary, offers a comment on the story in which he expresses surprise that a mission president would cause pain, as he had a mission president who was "very loving." He concludes that the story was "circulated to help elders trust in God more" (Tolton 2009).

Together, these faith-promoting narratives seem intent on establishing the God-given nature of the Latter-day Saint priesthood as true religious authority that is profoundly distinct from authority in other traditions. The stories teach missionaries to be wary of non-Latter-day Saint influences under the guise of righteous healing, and they showcase that the legitimate power of healing is with the Latter-day Saint priesthood, not with other Christian pastors, not with Buddhist or Shinto healers, and not with mysterious women. Intriguingly, the righteous holder of the priesthood in these tales—in a show of remarkable power—actually *removes* the healing with his own blessing as a lesson to the young missionaries. Herein lies an important point of tension: an act of healing is highly suspect if the wrong person—meaning someone who does not hold the priesthood—performs it.

Invoking the Comfort of the Holy Spirit

Priesthood blessings are not only administered for physical healing, butmay also soothe the spirit. In 2020, Jessica, aged twenty-four, a college graduate and a recently returned missionary, told me about an experience that she had on her mission that led her to seek a priesthood blessing. Jessica served her mission in Mexico City. She loved being a missionary and loved Mexico City, and quickly became fluent in Spanish, and she was eager to tell me about her wonderful experiences. She did so, but also described a frightening encounter with an ominous presence. One afternoon, she told me, she and her companion were visiting an unfamiliar part of the city. The young women noted a fancy car outside of the house they were visiting, and a man who spoke fluent English got out of the car and approached them. Jessica said he could tell she was American, and he started berating her in English. As she listened in shock to his words, she began to sense something very threatening.

She said, "I felt like almost like a coldness. Like, just like icy cold and I was, obviously, terrified."

Jessica remembered that the whites of his eyes seemed to turn black, and she felt that he had some kind of a grip on her, although he was not physically touching her. She said it seemed like he was staring into her soul. The experience terrified her, but she eventually managed to tell him that she could not talk anymore, and she and her companion ran down the street. Jessica was so shaken by the incident that she sought the counsel of an older member of her Mexico City ward. She reached out to him and his wife, and she asked him for a priesthood blessing. He blessed her, which she explained as "invoking the comfort of the Spirit."

Jessica was clearly referring to the Holy Spirit/Holy Ghost here, and she told me that when she was in the presence of the threatening man, she felt "a total absence of the Holy Ghost . . . . the darkness totally dispelled any goodness around."

Eventually, she felt the Holy Ghost telling her to leave. In reflecting on the experience, Jessica observed that she probably could have just knelt on the ground and prayed for the Spirit herself, but that asking for the blessing was "an extra call for that comfort through a blessing."

On this project, Jessica is highly intelligent, analytical, and reflective, and she took care to carefully explain her understanding of the situation in a Latter-day Saint framework. She told me that she did not connect the darkness that she felt in Mexico City with the spirit realm that is inhabited by the benevolent pre- or post-mortal spirits that we have discussed in earlier chapters. Rather, in her view, "the darkness exists in its own realm . . . it is like a whole other thing." The encounter was perplexing, and she did not identify the threatening man as possessed, nor did she confirm the presence of an evil spirit. Rather, she explained, it was more a feeling that darkness had driven away the Holy Ghost, and she sought a priesthood blessing to restore the feeling of the Spirit within her.

The "Mormon Superpower": Casting Out Evil Spirits

In many other negative encounters, however, the victims or observers specifically identify the malevolent agent as a spirit or Satan himself, and priesthood holders frequently take the righteous action of *casting out* spirits. "Casting out" is the term most Latter-day Saints use for what other Christian churches describe as "exorcism" or "deliverance." Casting out may refer to a technical "exorcism" of a possessing spirit from a body, or it may refer to driving a menacing spirit out of a room or a home; the latter action is far more common than the former, as incidents of "possession" are unusual in the Latter-day Saint contexts. The ability to deal with evil spirits by casting out is part of the rich cultural heritage of the church as a whole and northern Utah in particular. Joseph Smith is reported to have said that evil spirits "possess a power that none but those who have the priesthood can control" (reported in *History of the Church*, 4:576). Accounts of Joseph Smith casting out demons are well known; Stephen Taysom traces four accounts of "exorcism" from Smith's time until the 1970s, beginning with Smith's casting out of a devil tormenting his friend Newell Knight in 1830 (2017, 58). Taysom observes that despite the "official" modern church remaining silent on "exorcism," [2] as he chooses to call it, "Mormons have long and continuing history of casting our evil spirits" (2017, 59). Taysom argues that by drawing on

---

[2] Noting that Catholics have tended to use the term "exorcism" and Protestants "deliverance," Taysom states that as there is no local emic Mormon term, he decides to use "exorcism" as it is more widely recognized than "dispossession" (2017, 57). However, I propose that "casting out" *is* the local emic term; Taysom also uses the term "casting out" throughout his article.

various sources in the American intellectual and religious landscape of the nineteenth and twentieth centuries, Latter-day Saints managed to construct a view of possession and exorcism that had connections to, but was distinct from, Protestant and Catholic practices and understandings of the Devil (2017, 85). Much like an anthropologist, Taysom argues that understanding Latter-day Saint religious lives requires going beyond the "official" view of the church. I certainly agree with Taysom in this regard, and doing exactly this, my research shows that possession is only small part of much wider range of Latter-day Saint understandings of the power of Satan and his minions. For Latter-day Saints in northern Utah, the power of Satan manifests much more often as harassment than overt possession.

Douglas Davies (2010) has shown that in early writings of church members, the Devil and evil spirits are depicted in opposition to the power of the priesthood. As discussed in Chapter 5, Davies argues provocatively that Jesus, Satan, and Joseph Smith make up a trinity of sorts, with Jesus as the antagonist of Satan, and Joseph Smith as inheritor of Jesus's priestly authority. In early Latter-day Saint writings on the troublesome nature of evil spirits, Davies notes that the writers tend to identify the Devil as the source of evil and describe "the devil and Jesus as combatants" (2010, 216). Taysom similarly describes the "ongoing cosmic warfare between God and the Devil" (2017, 85). My research shows that this cosmic warfare is indeed ongoing, and the opposition is alive and well in contemporary practice. Elsewhere, I have observed that there are intriguing similarities between Latter-day Saint and other American Christian understandings of evil and attendant practices of spiritual warfare and exorcism (Stiles, 2022). These parallels are particularly clear in Evangelical churches, which conceive of a persistent, menacing evil that must be resisted by Christians in ongoing warfare (DeBernardi 1999; Cuneo 2001; DeRogatis 2009; McCloud 2013, 2015; Luhrmann 2012; for similar work on spiritual warfare in Haiti, see McAlister 2012). Although there are similarities in the general ideas of cosmological warfare between good and evil, some of the particularities of this struggle are quite different in the Latter-day Saint tradition, such as the lack of a complex demonology or inheritance of demons (Stiles, 2022).

As discussed in the previous chapter, most people in Cache Valley are familiar with tales of the early days of the Logan Temple, when Satan and his minions tried to thwart the activities held within (Olsen 1978). In these tales, the temple president commanded Satan to leave through the power of the priesthood. In one account, for example, the writer reports, "President

Merrill of the Logan Temple, then proceeded to dismiss Satan and his hosts. Raising his right hand to the square and by the power of the Priesthood, he sent them away" (Christensen 1997). However, it should be noted that in many of the narratives, the president's ability to drive Satan away does not rid the community of his influence entirely. Rather, through "whisperings" and "temptations" in the community, the ritual work at the Logan Temple ceased for a time. Casting out is not absolute, and the threat of aggressive evil can always return.

In one of our conversations, Shauna told me that as a young girl, she thought the ability of the priesthood holders to "cast out" spirits was something akin to a "Mormon superpower." She explained:

> I recently listened to a podcast about teenage girls and the supernatural (such as Bloody Mary) which made me realize that Mormon teenagers of my day were not really any different than the others, besides our belief that we could command evil spirits to leave in the name of the priesthood and they would *have* to obey.... being in command of the evil spirits is kind of a Mormon superpower. Talking to my Jehovah's Witness friend kind of confirmed that it is a perceived Mormon superpower—she was more afraid of them [the evil spirits], and we felt kind of superior to them.

Many people reference and use the ability to cast out, although Shauna is the only one who referred to it as a superpower. Elder Neilson and Elder Collins, the two young missionaries, explained that the power of priesthood holders to cast out demons stems directly from Jesus's example in the gospels. Elder Neilson read Mark 5:2–13 aloud to me,[3] and then remarked upon the many other New Testament examples of Jesus casting out devils. He explained how

---

[3] "And he says: and when he was come ... this is Jesus Christ coming out of the ship ... immediately there came to him out of the tombs, a man with an unclean spirit, who had his dwelling among the tombs and no man could bind him, no, not with chains because he had often been bound with fetters and chains and the chains had been plucked asunder by him and the fetters broken in pieces, neither could any man tame him. And always by night and day he was in the mountains and crying and cutting himself with stones. But when he saw Jesus far off, he ran and worshipped him. And cried with a loud voice and said, what have I to do with thee Jesus, thou son of the most high God? I adjure thee by God that thou torment me not, for he said unto him, come out of the man, thou unclean spirit. And he asked him, what is thy name? And this is Jesus asking to the spirit, what is they name? And he answered saying, my name is legion, for we are many. And he besot him much that he would not send him away out of the country. Now there was nigh unto the mountains a great herd of swine feeding and all the devils besot him saying, send us into the swine that we may enter into them. And forthwith Jesus gave them leave and the unclean spirits went out and entered into the swine. And the herd ran violently down a steep place into the sea, there were about 2000 and they were choked in the sea" (Mark 5:2–13).

living an unrighteous life could attract the attention of evil spirits who frequently try to possess the body. However, he said, "We believe that with the priesthood, you can cast these devils out, which is what Jesus did in Mark." They confirmed that although they believed in "exorcism," they preferred to use the term "casting out." They drew connections to other Christian churches that held similar beliefs about spirits and the ability to cast them out because of the "will of God." However, like Mr. Anderson's explanation that was discussed in Chapter 4, the missionaries noted the unique nature of the priesthood in The Church of Jesus Christ of Latter-day Saints as a means of differentiating it from other Christian churches.

Elder Neilson said, "I know that God still does love all of his children. Whether they are possessed or not, he doesn't want to see them go through . . . that trial, as long as they have to. And so, other churches that are able to cast out devils, it's because of the will of God."

"And that's what it all comes down to," added Elder Collins, "if it's God's will that the Devil be cast out, or the spirit be cast out, then it's going to happen, but if it's not His will then it's not going to happen."

Elder Neilson continued, "And we believe that . . . the priesthood is the authority to act in our Heavenly Father's name. We believe that one of the priesthood functions is to cast out devils in the name of Jesus Christ."

The missionaries noted that the ability to cast out spirits was limited to holders of the Melchizedek Priesthood. In reflecting on this, Elder Collins emphasized the connection to Jesus Christ.

He said, "It is called the Melchizedek Priesthood because Melchizedek in the Old Testament was a really, really righteous man. So, it just stuck. And this priesthood is what can be used to cast out devils, to give priesthood blessings, to bless homes. This is the priesthood that Jesus Christ restored to the earth."

When I asked how frequently they were called as missionaries to give blessings, they said that people would normally call on a priesthood holder who was member of their ward, not a visiting missionary. However, they conceded that sometimes people did need their services.

Elder Neilson explained, "Every now and then we will come across it, because even though we're in Utah we're not . . . what's the word . . . we're not *exempt*. We're not immune to the effects of the adversarial Satan . . . . Bad experiences can happen in Utah, too, and missionaries and members can encounter those as well."

Now let us turn to some accounts of priesthood holders casting out devils or evil spirits. As discussed in Chapter 5, negative experiences with spirits may have some of several common elements: a sense of a malevolent presence, a visible dark cloud, a sense of immobility or paralysis, or a pressure on the chest while sleeping or awakening. The crisis is typically resolved when a priesthood holder expels the spirit or blesses the space. In a vividly descriptive account of casting out in the Utah State University student folklore collection, a young woman describes an incident from her childhood. The account is so evocative that I include it in full here:

> We used to all wake up at 6 a.m. for family prayers. And my sister was sitting on the couch shaking and both my parents were crying, and I was like "What happened?" And my mom said that in the middle of the night, my sister started screaming and well what had happened is . . . my sister down the hall started screaming, so my parents ran down the hallway and they couldn't get her door open. Like it was totally being held back, like it would open but as my dad would push it, something would push it back. And so they ran into her room and the whole time me and my brothers were asleep . . . And my dad said that as he ran into the room, he could see something, like, on top of my sister, like this black figure. And my sister was screaming hysterically, "Get off of me." And my dad ran into the room and my dad's ordained a priest in the Mormon Church [sic]. And he's like a very, very spiritual man and not that that has anything to do with anything, but in the Mormon church they teach you if you're . . . encountered by a spirit, you say "In the name of the father, the son, and the holy ghost [sic], either what do you want or I command you to leave." So my dad said "In the name of the father, the son, and the Holy Ghost, I command you to leave this house." And my mom described it like all the darkness from the corners just . . . zoomed into the middle of the room and then it shot into a closet and the door slammed. And they went over and got my sister and sat up with her all night. And she was wearing a Walkman and . . . to this day it plays totally backwards, like, from that night. My sister's point of view of it was . . . she was laying there asleep and she started having these dreams that her friends were like "Laura, come with us." And she climbed out the window and she was standing in the black fog. And she woke up and she was like . . . I could feel it on top of me, it was trying to rape me. And it totally freaked her out. The thing is—I would have heard her screaming. And my mom was like, either something really good or really bad was keeping you guys asleep. But my sister said that she could just feel like every detail, like his hands around her neck. (Ray 1998)

164   THE DEVIL SAT ON MY BED

In this narrative, the young woman's father, a priesthood holder, is able to drive out the evil spirit. The writer calls him "very spiritual," and she vividly describes the effects of casting out the spirit. It is interesting that her sister characterizes the spirit visit as attempted rape as this is not typical; indeed, this was the only instance I came across in which someone used the term "rape" to describe a spirit attack.[4]

Similar narratives abound in the student folklore collection; there are many accounts of priesthood holders blessing a space, driving out spirits, or praying with the frightened recipient of a malevolent visitor. In one narrative from 2007, a student writes that when her sister and her sister's roommate moved into a new apartment, both reported "pressurized sleep"—the sister told the writer that, "one night, I woke up with this really constricting, heavy feeling on my chest. It was like something was sitting on my chest and wouldn't leave and I couldn't breathe." The sister reported that her roommate experienced the same thing, and they were both "freaked out and so called someone.... I think it was bishop" to bless the apartment. After the bishop—by necessity a member of the priesthood—blessed the apartment, the young women did not have a further problem (Goodsell 2007). A similar account that I first discussed in Chapter 5 describes an incident at Snow College and highlights the special sensitivity associated with the priesthood powers of returned missionaries. The narrative tells of a young woman who was harassed in her dormitory by a malevolent presence while her father was "taking the teachings" of missionaries. The following year, two male returned missionaries were visiting other young women in the same dorm room. The young men said that they felt a "bad spirit" in the room and blessed the room. According to the writer, "The girls hadn't even felt anything in the room but the missionaries said they just did not feel a good spirit in the room, so it kind of worried them." Two male missionaries were able to sense a threatening presence that the girls did not feel, and decided to use their powers of the priesthood to bless the room (Fryer 1983).

Another account, also introduced in Chapter 5, tells of a young woman's frightening experience that she attributed to the presence of evil spirits. She called a male friend, a priesthood holder, who came to her house to pray with

---

[4] Of course, this does not mean that people are not interpreting attacks as attempted rapes or sexual assault; it is possible that they are just not describing them that way to me. Many of the attacks have a physical dimension, and in keeping with norms of discourse in Cache Valley and wider Utah, it is possible that out of norms of delicacy and polite discourse, terms denoting extreme violence or sexuality would not be used.

her. Concerned, the young man then called their bishop. When the bishop arrived, the writer reports that the young woman "went up to her room and let the priesthood holders take care of the situation" (Weaver 1994). Weaver notes that the men found her housemates holding a séance, and that they had hypnotized a young woman. The hypnotizer commanded her to wake up, and then she received a blessing from the priesthood holders. Weaver states that "she did not know who she was and didn't know the people there. The men were told what had happened and they immediately gave her a blessing. The girls [sic] countenance changed as soon as the men said 'Amen.' She looked around the room and began to cry" (Weaver 1994).

All these accounts describe male holders of the priesthood casting out evil. However, gendered spiritual authority is not the only significant point of hierarchy here. In many cases, older men, such as ward bishops, who hold superior priestly authority, save their younger counterparts from evil tormentors. In Chapter 5, we discussed an account of a party-loving young man who believed that he was "possessed" at a wild party. When fellow partygoers realized what was happening, someone "ran next door" to get a member of the bishopric. In the words of the writer, the bishop "came over, blessed me, and made satan [sic] leave" (Brown 1982). Another account from the 1980s describes a man afflicted by evil and rescued by a more spiritually advanced man. The writer collected the story from a female acquaintance, who said that she first heard the faith-promoting story during Family Home Evening.[5] In the tale, a seminary teacher, Brother Heap, received a call one night from the wife of a friend:

> He rushed over to the trailer where his friend lived. When he entered the trailer the lights were very dim, and he could feel the presence of an evil spirit. The wife talked to Brother Heap to explain, her husband was over in the corner, possessed by the evil spirit. Brother Heap commanded the spirit to leave in the name of Jesus Christ. When he said this the evil feeling left, and the lights came on again. (Smith 1982)

The respondent tells the writer that she will eventually share the story with her children "as an example of the power of the priesthood." In Smith's

---

[5] Family Home Evening is strongly encouraged by the church: one night per week, families or households are encouraged to stay home and spend time together. Often, this will include lessons or activities in religion. The church's main website describes it in more detail (The Church of Jesus Christ of Latter-day Saints, 2023b).

commentary on the tale, she argues that the story was surely told to highlight the "to opposition of the devil to the church, and also power of the priesthood in overcoming evil."

Back to the Mission Field

In Chapter 5, I described Jake's experience with a menacing spirit while he was serving his mission in the United Kingdom. Once he and his roommates had identified that it was a spirit who was causing the problems in the flat, not a young woman, the young men proceeded to address the problem using their priesthood powers. As Jake explained, they decided to "rededicate" the flat to cast out the menacing spirit. He described the process of dedication by commenting on the "proper" authority of the priesthood. As with Mr. Anderson, Elder Collins, and Elder Neilson, Jake focused on the authoritative powers of the Latter-day Saint priesthood as a defining characteristic of the church. Explaining the dedication, he said,

> Basically, it is just like any other prayer. We all [the four missionaries] kinda knelt down there in a circle, and it's not, you know, holy water and this that or the other. [You] just kneel down in a circle like you're gonna say a prayer. And [we] basically told whatever it was that was goin' on there to just depart. And in doing it by the authority—and that's something that is big in our church, that we feel like we have *proper* priesthood authority that was restored. It was lost when all of Christ's apostles finally died, that's where it came from, and it was lost, it was restored with what happened with Joseph Smith, and there's been an unbroken line since. So, authority is a big deal. And so the authority, not meaning "you do this" authority but, you know, authority like a policeman has to arrest you or something *that* kind of authority. So it's an unbroken line, and that's very important, and it has to be done, you know, to have that authority.

In Jake's view, priesthood authority is essentially about action. It is not about telling other people what to do, but rather having authority akin to a police officer able to make an arrest: the authority is not about *instructing* people to behave in a certain way, but to be able take *action* (like an arrest) when something goes wrong.

Jake told me that once they were all kneeling, he led the blessing, although he could not recall exactly why he was the one to lead it. He surmised that it might have been because he was the missionary who had been there the longest. The blessing was simple, and he recalled commanding the spirit to leave using words that were something like "Depart from this place, and don't trouble us anymore."

I asked if the words were formulaic, and he explained that as it was not a "rote prayer" it could be any sort of statement, but that the speaker must state verbatim that he was giving the command to depart, "by the authority of the holiness of the priesthood, and in the name of Jesus Christ."

As with most accounts of casting out, the rededication of the flat was ultimately undramatic. Jake chuckled and explained, "So we did that. And it wasn't like you know, the end of the *Raiders of the Lost Ark*, where the ghosts are flying everywhere and the windows open and the wind and you know [like] the end of *Poltergeist* and the bodies comin' up. It wasn't anything like that, it was nothin.'"

Jake's mission president had given him guidance on how to perform the blessing, and advised him to, "just ask it to depart firmly. Just whatever it is, ask it to depart and not to return again." The mission president was not surprised when Jake reached out for assistance, as similar things had been happening all over the mission area. Indeed, Jake said when he spoke to other young women and men serving in that mission, he heard similar tales. A spirit had even thrown one sister [a female missionary] out of bed onto the floor!

That was not Jake's only experience with casting out spirits. Many years later, just a few weeks before our conversation, he found himself performing a similar blessing. He told me that earlier that year, a spirit had repeatedly harassed his teenage daughter in her bedroom, and he used the power of the priesthood to cast it out. When Jake told me about his daughter's frightening experience, he emphasized that she had not heard many stories about evil spirits. Even though his wife had been similarly harassed by a spirit as young girl, it was not a topic that came up regularly in family conversations. By telling me this, Jake stressed his initial skepticism about his daughter's account and, later, what he saw as the particularly concerning nature of the spirit attack. He surmised that the episode was not something his daughter could have imagined as a consequence of extensive exposure to spirit stories.

Jake explained that when his daughter first told him about the shadowy shape in her basement bedroom, "I said, what are you talkin' about? And he [the spirit] comes into the room and out of the room, and goes through a wall, whatever. And she says when he's there she feels it, and she knows it, and she'll look and she'll sometimes see him, and it's just frightening. And you know she started to do one of those— on your phone there's an app that'll record when noise starts, and she'd leave it on when she was sleepin' to see if there was ever any noise or anything, and there never was."

When I asked how he handled the situation, he said he did "the same thing" as when he was on his mission. However, before he performed the blessing, he tried to impress upon his daughter that this was a matter of religion, and therefore very serious, and that she should not be lying about it. Jake told me that, when he was a kid, he thought that such experiences seemed to happen more to teenage girls, but he did not attribute this specifically to Mormonism. Rather, he explained that he had read something about poltergeists, and recalled thinking that poltergeists usually attached themselves to teenage girls: "Yeah, and it may have been because of that movie [*Poltergeist*] that I was readin' about those kinda [things], 'Well I wanna know more about that kinda stuff!' and I remember thinkin' that when my sister started to be a teenager. Thinkin', 'Oh crap I hope we don't get a poltergeist!'"

Jake's views on evil spirits and poltergeists have changed over the years, and due to his own experiences as a missionary, he no longer thought there was a gendered dimension to negative visitations. Indeed, Jake told me that his son had also reported strange occurrences around the same time his daughter was experiencing the frightening visits. As noted in an earlier chapter, Jake's wife theorized that the spirit was harassing their daughter because of her penchant for wild behavior (recall that she gave her parents a "rodeo"). However, Jake's teenaged son was different. Even though he was preparing to go on his mission and was being "super good," in Jake's words, he was also harassed by a malevolent spirit. When the young man reported being "pinned down" on the bed, Jake at first expressed doubt about the boy's experience. Jake himself had experienced that sensation before, which he simply attributed to sleep paralysis. "Not everything is supernatural," he told me, "I try to find the rational explanation first." However, when he suggested to his son that he might have simply experienced sleep paralysis, the young man told him that he actually had seen the spirit and nearly got his shotgun.

Jake said, "He's like, 'Yeah Dad, I totally saw that' .... And he was like, 'I just about got my shotgun.' 'Cause you know, he hunts and stuff. And I'm like,

'Well, I'm glad that you didn't.' And so then that's when we decided, yeah, we better do somethin' about this. For whatever reason, something is going on."

Because his son had actually seen the menacing spirit, Jake decided to "nip this in the bud" and cast it out. He asked his bishop to come over and assist with the casting out: "I called him over . . . . I know him, and feel comfortable enough with him to [call him to help]. And I could have done it myself. You don't have to have the bishop or anything like that."

I asked about the priesthood implications of the action and whether the casting out had to be performed by a priesthood holder. Jake confirmed that this was the case, although later he shared his more nuanced views on the subject. Jake explained that the priesthood status that he held was the same as the prophet (the president of the church), but that they had different keys because they had different responsibilities. Clearly, all priesthood holders have the ability to deal with menacing spirits, and Jake also asked his son to assist with casting out the spirit. "I actually had my son come in and do it with me, because . . . who knows if he'll ever have to deal with this, and it was the first time he'd ever done something like that."

Clearly, this was not an everyday occurrence. Although Jake had previous experience with casting out spirits, his bishop and his son had never done it before. Despite the novelty of the situation, it was met with seriousness rather than skepticism: Jake said the bishop had heard of such things happening, so he was not caught by surprise and was prepared to participate. Ultimately, the casting out was undramatic. The three men went down to his daughter's bedroom, cleared everybody else out, and then blessed the room and asked the spirit to depart.

All of this transpired just a few weeks before our conversation, and Jake told me that the blessing should have taken care of the problem. Although he was not expecting further problems, he was "hyper alert," and was concerned that his youngest child, now also a teenager, had started reporting odd happenings in her own room. Thus far, however, he had come up with rational explanations. He explained that although the original spirit should not come back, he realized that another one might show up, but that he would "take action" when that happened and try not to worry too much about it. Jake's tempered optimism about whether the spirit was truly gone reflects a common pattern: people always understand that casting out a spirit or cleansing a home with a blessing is temporary. The spiritual conflicts between good and evil that play out in earthly life are just battles—they do not end the war, which wages on.

Encounters with Possession

Accounts of possession are rare in northern Utah, although the possibility of possession is certainly recognized in the community. Taysom (2017) has recently shown that even though possession dropped out of "official" church discourse, possession and exorcisms have been a reality in Latter-day Saint lived experience since the first days of the church. He traces instances of possession and casting out from the days Joseph Smith to 1977 against the broader backdrop of American religious history, and he differentiates Latter-day Saint views on possession from both Catholic and Protestant understandings. In doing so, Taysom shows that "the belief in an incorporated yet physically powerful Devil who came with an army of disembodied spirits who had sided with him in the war in heaven became as significant Mormon view that served to set Mormons part from most manifestations of contemporary Protestant Christianity" (2017, 70). As in the early days of the church, Latter-day Saints in northern Utah today view possession as inherently negative and nefarious. It is the minions of Satan who possess mortals; possessing spirits are never the benevolent spirits of ancestors or future children. Furthermore, Latter-day Saints do not refer to inspiration or presence of the Holy Ghost (what is sometimes glossed as "getting the Spirit") as possession, as is sometimes the case for other Christians (Robbins 2017).

Although Latter-day Saints in northern Utah are conversant on the subject of possession, and many have mentioned the possibility of possession as a consequence of taking too much interest in evil, as noted earlier, very few have any experience of possession. As we saw in Chapter 5, having been denied bodies themselves, devils or evil spirits seek embodied pleasure and use human beings to this end. Elder Neilson explained possession as centering on the jealousy devils have of the human body: "The reason why devils want to possess bodies is because they don't have one and there are certain feelings and certain pleasures that you can only have with a body, and they want to experience that. So, if they have an opportunity, if they see a man who lives very unclean, sins a lot, or is inviting those devils into his life, they will try to enter."

The few accounts of possession that I will discuss in this chapter come from missionaries who witnessed possessions when serving outside of the United States. In one account collected in 1989, a young man describes seeing a young woman possessed when he was serving his mission in rural Mexico. The young man writes that he and his companion knocked on a door "to see if anyone was interested in hearing their message" (Bean 1989). A woman opened the door, and when she saw they were missionaries, she requested her help with their daughter, who was "with the devil in the back room." The woman and her husband led them to a room at the back of the house that was closed with a steel door. Through a slot in the door, the missionaries saw a young woman of about nineteen years old who, "immediately went crazy, madly screaming and jumping around." Despite their alarm, the missionaries were confident in their ability to help. They told the girl's parents that they needed to prepare, and they returned the next day to cast out the evil spirit. When they returned, they heard the girl scream at them to leave in English, using their first names; this is notable because male missionaries are normally called by the title "Elder" preceding the surname. Bean explains that they then successfully cast out the spirit. Later, however, they were surprised when the girl's parents told them that she "didn't know a word of English." Bean offers her use of English and the use of the Elders' first names as proof of the spirit's presence: the young woman did not know English, nor did she know their first names. As in Jake's account, the spirit's use of first names— not their title of "Elder"—seems to index nefarious intent. The spirits do not respect the status or priestly authority of the missionaries, yet in both cases, the missionaries successfully cast out them out.

In a similar account from 2009, a student writes about his experiences while on a mission in Brazil. The writer and his companion were teaching a woman who had been possessed a number of times. The woman's parents had asked the missionaries to help, and they went to visit the young woman, who was howling and "acting like a wolf" (DeVries 2009). DeVries reports that his companion told him that, "She was very wild that night and was jumping up and down on the bed and hanging from the ceiling and stepping all over the walls. We eventually got her to calm down and the evil spirits no longer wanted to be around her body because of how we helped her. The spirits left and she could not remember what happened to her" (DeVries 2009). DeVries notes that he also once saw the woman "go through a similar event." Although he does not tell us what the missionaries did to "calm her down," their efforts caused the spirit to leave (DeVries 2009).

Darren, Shauna's husband, told me about a similar experience he had when he was on his own mission in Brazil. He served in a region of Brazil where he said he had a great deal of exposure to Afro-Brazilian religions like Macumba, Umbanda, and Candomblé. Darren said he knew several *guias*, or Candomblé guides, and he paid numerous visits to their homes during his mission. Although the visits were ostensibly in the context of being a missionary and he was offering the usual missionary teachings to the *guias*, Darren explained the visits were actually more about "exchanging ideas," and he learned a fair amount about Candomblé practices and beliefs, including experiences of possession. He described his own encounter with a possessed woman, which he said was frightening. Although he and his companion were asked to assist, they were ultimately unable to do so. His story follows:

> We had been teaching a family . . . that had other family members involved in Macumba and Candomblé. I don't actually know which one it was, but one of those. And in teaching them, they said . . . a sister of the person we were teaching had a daughter that suffered from being possessed by evil spirits. At least that was *their* context. And . . . they're like, "Oh, so you guys are missionaries? You guys have some level of priesthood? Can you cast out spirits? Can you make this go away?" And that's how we were approached. And we're like, "Well, technically that's what we believe, yeah we could do that. Yeah we could do that." Not knowing really what we were stepping into. Um, you know, we're young, twenty-years-old, "Sure, we can do it!"

He paused to make sure I was following along, then continued:

> So, we actually were invited to go into this home where this individual was supposedly possessed or whatever. And so we go over to visit . . . . I did not know this at the time, but I've later learned that . . . Candomblé believes that you can have "morphing." Your body can be possessed and you can take on the shape of other things and people or whatever. I don't profess to know what their actual doctrines are, but we were asked to go over there and "pray over," "bless," "cast out," whatever you want to call it.

Darren is an excellent storyteller, and he described the experience in detail. He said when they arrived at the house of the afflicted daughter, he and his companion saw a girl of about fifteen years old in a wheelchair. It was clear that the young women had some kind of mental disability, he explained, and it was difficult for her to communicate. Darren said that he and his companion were expected to "pray over, bless, or cast out" the spirit. In the midst of discussing a strategy for casting out, the girl suddenly suffered some kind of physical attack. Darren said that she began to transform in front of them:

I don't know how to explain it. She falls out of her wheelchair. She may have already had physical deformities, I wasn't really totally paying attention. But what we perceived and what we saw was her kind of like, inflating. I don't know how else to explain it. This is bizzaro, but like, almost kind of like snakeish, and she's swerving, like she's wiggling around on the floor like a snake! But not just wiggling in place, but actually making forward movement. And we're like "What's going on?" Like, "Yeah, see she's possessed!" And they're [the girl's family] like, "You guys should get out of here, like everybody run, like she'll go crazy, she goes crazy!" I'm like, "What do you mean crazy?" ". . . She'll like start sticking out her tongue like a snake."[6]

Darren remembers being both stunned and perplexed. He said he was "half doubting" what he saw, and wondered if the girl was "faking it." He recalled the teenager then taking on additional shapes, and he did not know if the girl had a "mental disturbance" or a "spiritual disturbance." Darren and his companion left the room without administering any sort of treatment to the girl.

He said, "They just told us to get out. They were like, you guys should get out of here, like. We're like no we can help. And they're like, 'No, this is bad' and whatever. And so they kind of convinced us. We were kind of freaked out to be quite honest."

He paused, and then said, "We took off."

I asked, "So you didn't attempt a healing or anything?"

He replied, "We just got out of there."

I asked Darren what he and his companion would have done if they had stayed and attempted to cast out the spirit. Like Jake, he said that the procedure would have been simple, much like any other priesthood blessing.

He said, "We do very calm laying on of hands . . . so you give someone a blessing and you'll say, 'In the name of Jesus Christ, by the authority which I have,' you know, 'I bless you to do this,' or, 'I cast out this,' or, 'I whatever,' right?"

Continuing, Darren said, "I'm not really aware of many experiences where something erratic is happening and you invoke this authority or whatever in the name of God and then it just goes away."

---

[6] In both accounts from Brazil, it is notable that the young women take on animal forms: one becomes a wolf, and the other a snake. In his discussion of early exorcisms done by Latter-day Saints, Taysom (2017) observes that accounts of possessed people moving like or taking on forms of animals has been common in European and American folklore for centuries, and cites Jeffrey Burton Russell's (1984) work on Lucifer in the Middle Ages.

Darren approached his encounter with possession critically and analytically. He framed the event and his interpretation of it in terms of "Mormon culture." Specifically, he called it "not *doctrinal*, but *cultural* weirdness." He explained that because Mormons accept the reality of evil and the possibilities of courting it, for example with a Ouija board, it is relatively easy for Mormons to believe that *others* believe. "Mormons believe that *they* [the others] believe that you can [have] negative visitations, you can be possessed, you can allow yourself to be possessed; you can do all of these different things." In a sense, then, Darren argues that Latter-day Saints take seriously other ontologies and the reality of others' spiritual experience, because they echo Mormon imaginaries about evil potentialities. It is not a difficult ontological exercise: Latter-day Saint cultural frameworks that make space for nefarious intervention and possession—even if it rarely happens—open minds to the reality of possession in other contexts and gives them the confidence to attempt casting evil spirits out.

Indeed, in all these accounts of missionaries being summoned to help possessed non-members in Mexico and Brazil, the missionaries expressed confidence in their abilities to cast out spirits, even if they eventually fled the scene. This cultural receptivity to various kinds of religious experience is not a one-way street in Darren's view. He explained that Brazilians were very receptive to Latter-day Saint missionary teachings. Because of shared rich cultural imaginings of spirit worlds and religious possibilities, Darren told me that Brazilians were particularly open to baptism: "There are a lot of baptisms in Brazil."

He said, "Yeah, people are open. There's all kinds of different traditions and country culture[s] that allow people to change, and or convert one way or the other."

In his opinion, Latin America was culturally very Catholic, but with little overt focus on religious practice. He described the success of Latter-day Saint mission efforts in Brazil as the result of a "faith-driven people" with an "undirected faith" that left open possibilities for conversion.[7]

---

[7] Darren's comments reflect the growing literature on religious conversion in Latin America and the rapid growth of Pentecostal, Evangelical, and other non-Catholic forms of Christianity throughout the region (e.g., Dawley 2018; Thornton 2018).

The Limits of Priesthood Power

The priesthood is at the center of the institutional body of the church. Knowlton (1992) argues that as boys and young men are inculcated into the formal progression through its various levels, the accumulative acquisition of priestly power strongly shapes a Latter-day Saint conception of an ideal "spiritual manhood." As I have shown thus far in this chapter, priesthood holders enact this spiritual manhood in a righteous, active masculinity through giving blessings that not only heal and cure, but that are also the primary means of dealing with negative visitations and overt spiritual attacks through the process of casting out. However, this authority is not absolute. The power of the priesthood is far from infallible, and efforts to cast out devils or evil spirits do not always go as planned.

As we saw in Chapter 5, numerous faith-promoting stories tell of missionaries intentionally tempting the Devil in a show of bravado, hoping to display the powers of the priesthood in battling evil. These attempts do not typically go well, and the didactic intent of the narratives seems to show the folly inherent in a missionary's arrogance and over-confidence in the power of the priesthood. Recall that in one memorable tale, an overzealous missionary who summoned the Devil so they could have it out "once and for all" ended up soundly defeated: he was thrown onto the roof, "every bone in his body broken" (Hurst 1992). In another account, two missionaries in the MTC invited the Devil in specifically so they could cast him out. Satan accepted the invitation, but when they tried to cast him out, they failed. The MTC president then evacuated the building and told the missionaries that, "their priesthood power was not effective in casting out Satan because they had invited him in" (Erickson 1988). Erickson writes that the building was closed for a month, and the "General Authorities" (the highest-ranking members of the priesthood) had to be called in to rid the building of the evil spirits.

In interviews, people similarly commented on the limitations of priesthood power. As we saw with Jake, he hoped that casting out the spirit in his daughter's bedroom had taken care of the problem, but he knew the spirit could always come back. And according to Darren, the recipient of priesthood interventions must welcome the intervention for it to be effective—Darren made it clear that the power of priesthood was only effective if the recipient *wanted* the priesthood holders' intervention.

He explained, "You know in the Mormon traditional belief, if someone is going to use what we call 'the priesthood'—some power that you have—you'll have to want it, right? I can't come to you and say 'Oh, I declare x, y, or z!' and it's gonna work, right? You have to be permissive of whatever it is you're doing. And it's always on the positive side, right? Mormons don't really practice trying to cast spells."

Darren assured me that priesthood holders would never use their power for anything nefarious or underhanded. He explained, rather, "It's for healing, and calmness, and feeling at peace with things." In his analytical style, Darren also emphasized that healings and other interventions were essentially "faith-based" and that the procedures would not work if someone did not believe they could work.

In short, then, it is evident that the priesthood is not a foolproof superpower. Hubris can lead to downfall. Moreover, while spirits may be cast out temporarily, the power of Satan is never vanquished completely, and evil influence may return. Moreover, those receiving priestly ministration must accept the ministrations for them to be effective. And, as we will explore now, the assumption that the priestly domain of power is exclusively male does not go unchallenged.

Contesting Masculine Authority: Women's Spiritual Power

The masculine domain of priesthood power is a point of tension, and both men and women contest this exclusivity by asserting women's abilities to wage significant spiritual power. The gendered nature of the formal priesthood in The Church of Jesus Christ of Latter-day Saints has been a subject of debate for decades, and has attracted a great deal of attention in recent years with the increasing visibility of the Ordain Women movement. The movement was launched in 2013 to advocate for women's ordination to the priesthood and, as noted in an earlier chapter, it made news with excommunication of its founder Kate Kelly, who is well known for arguing that "equality is not a feeling" (Kelly 2016). According to its mission statement, Ordain Women recognizes the inherent spiritual equality of women and men in the Latter-day Saint tradition and calls on the formal body of the church to ordain women accordingly (https://ordainwomen.org). There is already an abundant and growing literature on feminist movements and gender in the church (Brooks, Hunt Steenblik, and Wheelwright 2016; Feller 2016; Kane 2018; Kinney 2017; McDannell 2018; Petrey 2020; Reiss 2019; Shepherd,

Anderson, and Shepherd 2015; Toscano 1995), and a particular recent academic interest in media and social media analyses of feminist discourses (Falk 2018; Feller 2016), and thus my modest goal here is to add a discussion of gender and spiritual power to this ongoing conversation.

As noted, the question of women and the priesthood is a point of "gender distress" in the contemporary Latter-day Saint climate, particularly for younger members. This should be considered in the broader context of gender issues in the church, as described recently by the writer Jana Reiss in her book, *The Next Mormons: How Millennials are Changing the LDS Church* (2019, 98–100). Here, I consider how articulations of spiritual power in lived practice contest the masculine nature of priestly authority. Conversations about gender and spiritual power are not only an avenue for identity formation, but also a site to contest both what are sometimes perceived as deleterious aspects of "Mormon culture" *and* the official position of the institutional Church that many see as at odds with the true nature of the religion regarding women and spiritual authority.

Raising the Hand to the Square

All the accounts described in this chapter thus far feature a male priesthood holder casting out evil spirits or the Devil; I have found only very few accounts of women doing the same. However, in interviews, many people made a point of noting that the special powers of the priesthood were not necessarily limited to men. Indeed, a common theme was that in the past, women had much more power in the church than they do today, and that it was "Mormon *culture*"—not the true essence of the religion—that had brought about incorrect notions of women's limited roles in the church and the common assumption that only male priesthood holders could exercise spiritual authority in casting out evil spirits. In a number of conversations, I was told that women were able to use priesthood powers to handle negative spirit visitations. Typically, these conversations began with a discussion of a well-known performative gesture used to cast out spirits that is known as "raising the hand to the square" (or "raising the arm to the square"). This refers to holding up the arm with the elbow at a right angle and the palm facing forward. There are numerous references to the gesture in priesthood manuals, and priesthood holders use it in contexts like baptisms.[8] When encountering

---

[8] Used in baptism guidelines as per the Priesthood Ordinances and Blessings outlined in general church handbook (The Church of Jesus Christ of Latter-day Saints, 2022). Not being Mormon, there

an evil presence, raising the hand to the square may be combined with speech acts commanding the spirit to leave in the name of Jesus Christ (Stiles and Davis 2018). For example, as we saw in the narratives surrounding the Logan Temple, the temple president drives Satan away with his arm to the square and commands him to leave in the name of Jesus Christ.

Shauna recalls practicing the action with her girlfriends when she was a child at slumber parties. "Yeah," she said, noting that in the case of a spirit attack, "obviously it was better if a priesthood holder was there, and *they* would have more power against the Devil. But, if there wasn't one, we could still try."

She laughed at this recollection and told me the girls would practice raising their hands to the square and saying, "In the name of Jesus Christ I command you to leave!"

Shauna said she remembered thinking that "If you say it just like *this*, then they *have* to obey . . . because they're also subject to God's power."

However, reflecting on the potential for failure and the ongoing nature of the struggle between good and evil, Shauna observed that, "In a lot of ways, Satan's power seemed a little more powerful." Even though she and her girlfriends were practicing the action, she noted pointedly the self-assurance that comes from being a missionary, "I can understand how only [male] missionaries would feel confident enough to mess with that [because they have the priesthood]."

Jake and I also discussed the gesture, and I asked if it was something that people generally learned at slumber parties or from formal religious training. Jake explained that the action had significant symbolic significance, and it came out of the formal training in the church, "You know, the hand to the square thing . . . [is a] symbol that means something within the Mormon religion. As far as . . . making a more solemn and formal type of thing."

---

are certain things I cannot know, such as ritual practices and symbolic meanings within the temple ceremonies. However, in addition to these cultural frameworks for using the arm to the square, it is recognized publicly by the church in public webpages which refer to the "sacred act of raising the hand to the square": Elder Loren C. Dunn explained the responsibilities that accompany the sustaining process: "When we sustain officers, we are given the opportunity of sustaining those whom the Lord has already called by revelation. . . . The Lord, then, gives us the opportunity to sustain the action of a divine calling and in effect express ourselves if for any reason we may feel otherwise. To sustain is to make the action binding on ourselves to support those people whom we have sustained. When a person goes through the sacred act of raising his arm to the square, he should remember, with soberness, that which he has done and commence to act in harmony with his sustaining vote both in public and in private" (In Conference Report, Apr. 1972, p. 19; or *Ensign*, July 1972, p. 43).

When I asked if part of his formal missionary training emphasized dealing with spirits by raising the hand to the square, Jake told me that the application of this maneuver came more out of folklore and tales about the pioneers, in which they drove evil away by raising the hand to the square, which he called a "Told-'em-to-depart-in-the-name-of-Jesus-Christ type of thing." Like Shauna, when Jake was young, he had frequently heard that if you commanded a spirit to leave in the name of Jesus Christ, then it was required to leave.

The Gospel According to Jake

It was at this juncture of our conversation that, entirely unbidden, Jake remarked that a person did *not* need to hold the priesthood to drive evil away—*anyone* could command a spirit to leave.

He explained, "Men or women can do it, and . . . yeah, you don't have to be the damsel in distress and wait for the guy to come and say, 'Hey, you can do that yourself.'"

In what he called his typical "seeing shades of grey" sort of way, he offered a highly nuanced view of gender, the priesthood, and modalities of dealing with spirit visitations. Jake explained that in situations where there were just women, and "there was no priesthood available," then it would entirely possible *and* permissible for women to exercise priesthood authority through giving blessings.

He emphasized the fraught contemporary debates about gender and the priesthood in the church, and said, "That's one of these things the church is kind of wrestlin' with right now, too."

Jake explained that things were different in the past, and there were "more situations back in the early church where the women—even though they didn't hold the priesthood—they called on it to use it . . . and [did] not have to wait for a man to come do it, they [could] do it themselves. That's kind of [been] lost over the years." Although he did not give specific examples, he was clearly referencing the important spiritual role of women in the early years of the church that we discussed earlier in this chapter (see also Madsen 1982; Newell 1981; Stapley and Wright 2011).

Jake said that, in his perspective, the church had changed over the years since the early days and had "ossified" certain things—particularly concerning gender and certain kinds of spiritual actions—that were flexible in the past. Jake made sure that I knew that this was "the Gospel according to me." He told me that in his view:

> It's kind of this patriarchal . . . hierarchy that's come along. And it's not really seen that way, although you know women *could* do that [the blessings] if they wanted to . . . . If you know what's goin' on with the Mormon church, I know you know that's kind of a big thing. You know women in the priesthood, and stuff like that, so . . . . So if there was no men priesthood holders around there, some woman that's got a non-LDS husband and you're an LDS woman, you—the LDS woman—could say a prayer and do that [the blessing].

Jake emphasized that, in his view, the true nature of the church was "informal" and the institutional attempt to make things "rigid" or "formal" ended up transforming things in ways that were not true to the original teachings of the church:

> To me, I look at it like, we're kind of an informal religion, and there's a lot of people that want to formalize it a lot. And I look at it, like, if we have this loving Heavenly Father—and this is the Gospel according to me right now—if we have a loving Heavenly Father, and something like what I just described is going on [evil spirit visitation], and the woman needs to give a blessing or do this or do that, I'm pretty sure He's not gonna be sittin' up there goin', "Nope, you didn't do it right. Screw you, you're dyin.'" You know, I think we lose a lot of common sense and compassion when we start getting too . . . what's the word . . . dogmatic? Is that the word?

Jake's comments evoke a sense of pragmatism in spiritual action: if a blessing is needed then God will have no problem with a woman giving that blessing. In the Gospel according to Jake, gender and gendered roles in spiritual action are a point of tension and gender distress. The contemporary institutional church—particularly in its drive to "formalize" gender roles in spiritual practice—is in some ways at odds with what he regards as the true, informal, pragmatic nature of the religion.

"Women Have the Priesthood, Too"

Over one of many lunches together, this time at a popular, noisy pizza place near the campus of Utah State University, Lyne and I spent a long time discussing gender and the priesthood. I had just come from the university library, where I had been reading student folklore narratives. I told Lyne about my morning in the archives, and we talked about her impressions of "Mormon culture" and religion. Lyne remarked that, in her view, some people claim to be "active" in the church but do not live the teachings in their actions. As an illustration, she told me about an adverse experience she had had in her ward in a small town in the valley. Lyne had faced several personal challenges in her life, and she reflected on how these experiences had opened her mind and taught her to think more expansively, perhaps, than those whose paths had been easier. The incident happened when she was teaching an adult gospel doctrine class. She explained:

> There's a guy in our ward who didn't really think it was appropriate that I was a single woman teaching gospel doctrine . . . . He just really didn't think that was appropriate because I'm a woman and I'm single. I didn't have a "priesthood man" behind me to tell me how to think. Oh my gosh, and I can get sassy even in church! . . . . He just did not like that [I was teaching] and I was okay that he didn't like it and I didn't feel guilty that he didn't. And he didn't like *that* either [that she didn't feel guilty] because he went to BYU and he was taught by so-and-so and when he told me that I said, "I don't care who you were taught by, that doesn't mean you know anything anymore than I do."

I had no doubts she could get sassy in church, and I smiled at thought. Lyne is highly intelligent, confident, and charismatic, and it was easy for me to imagine her putting an overly critical man in his place. She was referencing the fact that she was divorced and the head of her household. In the eyes of her critic, as a single woman, she did not have a husband as priesthood holder to give her credibility as a teacher.

We had also had lunch together a few days before this, sitting in the sunshine at a café by the Logan River. I had introduced Lyne to the term "mansplaining," although I don't recall why. The term was becoming more common in popular discourse, and Lyne was very amused by it. When she later told me about the man in her ward assuming he knew the Gospel better than she did, I said that this seemed like a good example of mansplaining.

She laughed and remarked, "There are some guys that really, truly believe that because they're men and they have the priesthood that they forget, *women have the priesthood*, too. We just have a different calling of it."

When I expressed surprise, she told me, "Yes! When go to the temple, we dress in our temple clothing, they're the robes of the Holy Priesthood. The same robes!"[9]

Lyne is certainly not alone in her views on women and the priesthood. In the 1990s, in an essay in the progressive Latter-day Saint journal *Dialogue*, the feminist literature scholar Margaret M. Toscano argued that the power of the priesthood relies not on formal ordination, but rather on gifts of the Holy Spirit. Women have been using the power of the priesthood through giving blessings, preaching and teaching as missionaries, and performing temple ordinances for other women. However, Toscano observed that many women do not recognize this as a use of the priesthood, and many do not want the priesthood. She argued that: "Instead of being an instrument for spiritual empowerment to lead each individual to God, the priesthood is too often used to compel obedience to an earthly power system which privileges some people above others. I believe that the priesthood has become the chief idol of the modern church because it is the object we are asked to give allegiance to, above Christ himself" (Toscano 1995).

Somewhat earlier, the historian Carol Cornwall Madsen wrote of the significance of women's temple work in the early church as priesthood in action: "As both initiates and officiators they knew they were participating in the essential priesthood ordinances of gospel in the same manner as their husbands, their fathers or their brothers" (1982, 45). And, most interesting for our purposes, we learn this power extended to combating the harassment of evil spirits: Lucy Meserve Smith, who was married to an early apostle of

---

[9] Lyne's rendering of the temple roles of men and women is a nuanced take on official teachings, as expressed in the following: "The man holds the Priesthood, performs the priestly duties of the Church, but his wife enjoys with him every other privilege derived from the possession of the Priesthood. This is clear, as an example, in the Temple service of the Church. The ordinances of the Temple are distinctly of Priesthood character, yet women have access to all of them, and the highest blessings of the Temple are conferred only upon a man and his wife jointly" (*Priesthood and Church Government* [1965], 83).

the church, expressed this shared priesthood in the late nineteenth century when she observed that the Holy Spirit had affirmed to her that she had the power to "rebuke" a harassing evil spirit through the shared power of the priesthood (Madsen 1982, 45).

Lyne similarly recognizes women's ability to use the priesthood, although she told me she has never personally been harassed by evil spirits. She shared with me an extensive explanation of temple ceremonies and women's roles. As a devout church member, she made it clear that she was only sharing aspects of temple practice that were appropriate for me to know as a non-member. Lyne argued that the spiritual status of women actually exceeds that of men, which was the reason for certain modes of dress in temple ceremonies:

> Well, I'm not telling you what they are [the ceremonies] but, yeah, you wear a cap and this veil part, the women when we—you can't [unclear in recording] pray, and everybody prays. One person says the prayer and everybody says—anyways, it's just a prayer saying, "Bless the missionaries, bless the prophet and bless the president and He can lead the world in the way that's positive." I mean we are always praying for positive things. But—um, the women veil their faces, and a lot of people think "Well, that's just cruel!" because that's showing that we're 'submissive.' No it isn't. The whole symbolic reason for the veiling of the face is when Moses was on Mount Sinai and went and talked to God about the Ten Commandments, right? He was touched by the Holy, by God. So he was too bright for the people to behold, right? Because he had been transfigured. So he had to veil his face because he was so Holy at that point that people couldn't lay their eyes upon him. That's why the women veil their faces because the men have to prove themselves worthy to come up to her level to see her face so in the end, we unveil our face. So people think it's us being all submissive, and it isn't, it's having the men step it up to be like the women. So people get really confused, and think we put women behind, but we just don't.

I asked her to explain more about what she meant by women already "having the priesthood," and her explanation was similar to the Gospel according to Jake. Lyne emphasized that certain matters had changed since the early days of the church and, as she indicated, not for the better as far as women's roles were concerned. Again, we see a point of gender distress for both Lyne and Jake: "Mormon culture" is at odds with the true teachings of the religion. In the early days, women regularly gave blessings, and in Lyne's view, she is able to do that for her children. She explained:

> When the pioneers came, Mary Martha Smith (is that who it was?)—she was married to Joseph Smith's brother. Joseph Smith's brother had been killed along with Joseph Smith and when she came across the plains, the oxen were having a hard time and she blessed the oxen. Well, in today's culture you would have people say, "Well, only the men can give the blessings." That's just because, culturally, that's what we do. So, no, I don't walk around and put my hands on somebody's head and give a blessing but that doesn't mean I can't do the same prayer and bless my children. I don't have to have a priesthood member in my home in order to receive those same blessings.

I nodded, and she continued:

> Even in the temple—and I'm not telling you what the ordinances are—but the women are on one side getting their ordinances and then men on the other, obviously, but the women are the ones laying their hands on their heads giving other women their blessings . . . . So when people say that when we die, you'll see us in our priesthood clothes that's what they are.

Indeed, as we have seen, the role of Latter-day Saint women in healing—particularly healing of a spiritual nature—is an important part of Latter-day Saint history and an aspect of local folklore. An intriguing narrative collected by a student in 1994, entitled "The Midwife's Blessing" (West Walker 1994), emphasizes the spiritual power women and local opposition to it. West Walker tells of her Scottish ancestors who settled in Wellsville in the mid-nineteenth century. The writer heard the story from her aunt, and it tells of a midwife who had the gift of "second sight"—she was able to receive visions of the future and used this to help people, and even save lives. Late one night, the midwife heard a cry in the darkness, and she set out to visit the second wife of a local farmer who was expecting a baby—the writer notes this happened "during the days of polygamy" (West Walker 1994). When she arrived, the town doctor was already there, inebriated and clumsily trying to save the "stuck" baby, crushing part of the baby's skull with forceps in the process. The family members attending the birth thought the baby would die, but the midwife quickly rode out to a sacred spring to fetch its special water, which she sprinkled on the baby's head while "saying some words no one could understand." West Walker continues:

> The baby recovered and when the doctor awoke [he had passed out drunk] he was furious because only men were supposed to perform blessings. But later, even the elders of the church said that in the absence of a man, it was permissible for a woman to bless. The midwife lived a long time, always going to her sacred source for healing waters. She died of old age on the first day of May in her ninety-eighth year. When she died it is said that the sacred spring she went to so often dried up. Once a year in the spring it flows on the day she died. (West Walker 1994)

I have not had any women tell me that they have cast out evil spirits, although through the shared power of the priesthood there is certainly a recognition that this is possible, and there is historical precedent, as we saw with Lucy Meserve Smith's account. Hildi Mitchell reports an account of casting out from her research in northern England. A middle-aged woman told Mitchell that her husband, a priesthood holder who had been experiencing depression, had at one point also become possessed. The woman explained to Mitchell that as "an *endowed* woman, who had entered into the priesthood covenant of *celestial marriage*, she felt that she shared in the priesthood of her husband, so she *raised her arm to the square* and commanded the spirit to leave her husband" (Mitchell 2001, 172; emphasis in original).

Mitchell relates this story in the context of her larger project on Latter-day Saint cosmology and economic change, and therefore she does not discuss extensively the intriguing gender dimension of this account, other than to note that the woman's actions were "unorthodox" and "challenging" to the priesthood (2001a, 173). Indeed, although numerous people have indicated that priesthood power may be inherently less gendered than is commonly assumed in "Mormon culture" and by the official teachings of the institutional church, I have yet to collect accounts of women casting out spirits. (Although recall Jessica's comment that she could have "prayed for the Holy Spirit" herself during her frightening encounter in Mexico City when she sought out a priesthood blessing.) Mitchell emphasizes that in these accounts (she relates two), the power of the "exorcisor" is more emphasized than that of the spirit doing the possession, and she suggest that the accounts "reaffirm the power of the place of the priesthood and the moral superiority of mortals over spirits, being, as they are, partway to godhood" (2001a, 173). Drawing an important contrast to arguments from anthropologists Aihwa Ong (1987) and Jeanne Comaroff (1985), who demonstrate how spirit possession is a form of resistance for oppressed populations in Malaysia and South Africa, respectively, Mitchell argues that in the Latter-day Saint context possession is not about giving voice to the oppressed but about upholding the moral order of Mormonism through the power of the "exorcisor," and it can then serve as lens through which other forms of "worldly activity" are understood (2001, 173).

Conclusion

When I began this research project, my first readings of narratives in the Utah State University folklore collection struck me as being gendered in a particular way, and I expected to find a pattern in which young women were harassed by evil spirits—often in a physically menacing way—and were then heroically rescued by male holders of the priesthood. This working hypothesis, although informal, was likely informed by my own experiences growing up in the community. Most of my memories of tales of evil spirits or the Devil were from young girls—my friends—telling me about devils or spirits sitting on the bed, starting at them with menacing red eyes. I was also likely interpreting this based on my knowledge of a profoundly gendered Latter-day Saint institutional structure, in which men and women are distinctly gendered beings with distinctly gendered roles in both the church and in life. A common refrain I have heard frequently is that although "men have the priesthood" and thus serve as priesthood leaders of their families, "women have motherhood," a separate but equally important role. Furthermore, Latter-day Saint theology incorporates a belief in a Heavenly Mother as a counterpart to a Heavenly Father. Indeed, in the introduction to a comprehensive collection of writings on Mormon feminism (Brooks, Hunt Steenblik, and Wheelwright 2016), the scholar Joanna Brooks points to this Heavenly Mother and the agency attributed to Eve as evidence of a progressive Latter-day Saint theology: "With its view of a female God and its celebration of Eve as an exemplar of the principle of agency for her decision to eat the fruit of the tree of knowledge, Mormon theology offers in some respects a more progressive gender theology than the more conservative forms of Judeo-Christianity" (Brooks, Hunt Steenblik, and Wheelwright 2016, 2). However, Brooks also notes the "contradictory" approach to gender in that

Heavenly Mother is rarely mentioned or recognized and there are profound differences in church gender roles (2016, 4).

As my research developed, I saw that my original hypothesis could not stand. I have found no distinctly gendered pattern of either positive or negative visitations: men and women are equally likely to experience visits from benevolent spirits, and men and women are equally likely to experience visits from harassing spirits. What is more notable is age. Evil spirits or Satan seem to target young people more often than older people. Moreover, when the power of the priesthood is used to drive away evil spirits, it is spiritual authority and religious status that ultimately determines power: in many narratives, higher-ranking older men come to the rescue of both women and younger men. Taysom (2017) made a similar observation in his discussion of a high profile exorcism in the 1970s in Washington, DC. In the story (related by church historian Leonard Arrington), a woman was possessed but the Devil would not depart at the injunction of missionaries or the stake president; it had to be cast out by the most high-ranking priesthood holder in the area, M. Russell Ballard. "At various levels of ecclesiastical administrative authority, the Devil seemed to respond differently. He apparently could ignore the missionaries completely, but he had to respond in a limited way to the adjurations of the Stake President. Only Ballard, 'the ultimate authority in the region,' however, could command Satan to leave permanently" (Taysom 2017, 82–83).

In common understanding, then, spiritual authority does not simply reflect a male–female gender binary, but also spiritual advancement within the formal structure of the priesthood. However, as we have seen, what constitutes spiritual authority is a profound point of gender tension today, and both women and men contest assumptions of the inherently gendered spiritual power of the priesthood. For many, an authoritative Latter-day Saint spirituality includes the spiritual capabilities and abilities of women, which many understand as *women's* holding of the priesthood. As Lyne observed, "women have the priesthood, too." It is not solely men who are capable of, or responsible for, preserving the moral order by actively engaging in the defeat of Satan and his minions. The accounts and views shared in this chapter present a view of gender that is in sharp contrast to what formal teachings about the priesthood—and current gender politics in the church—might suggest. They illustrate a nuanced view of the powers of the priesthood today that is more like views of the priesthood in the past in that its power are not limited to male holders of the formal, institutional priesthood.

Respondents' views seem to attribute rigid definitions of gendered ability and gendered spiritual power in the church to "cultural Mormonism," or "Mormon culture" rather than the true essence of the church. Stapley, in his work on the priesthood and Mormon cosmology, similarly contrasts the present with the past, and writes that, "This vivid contrast between Mormonisms provides one of the best opportunities to analyze the concept of authority that is so fundamental to the church" (Stapley 2018, 80). Some Latter-day Saints contend with conviction that women are able to give blessings of various kinds and should be fully able to counter the effects of negative visitations through driving a spirit away or through restoring the presence of the Holy Spirit, and they frequently draw on women's complex roles in the Mormon past to do so. Both Jake and Lyne reflect on the early years of the church and women's powers during that time. Considering the fraught nature of the debates over gender and gender roles in the church today, some people are advocating a more nuanced understanding of gender and spiritual aptitude and ability.[10] As we have done in previous chapters, it is again helpful to think of Latter-day Saint conceptions of the religion as having three dimensions: (1) the formal institution of the modern church, (2) a "cultural" Mormonism, and (3) the essence or true original meaning the faith. In the tensions surrounding gender and the powers of the priesthood, we see nuanced conceptions of how what church members consider both the formal institution and "Mormon culture" (or "Utah culture") are standing in the way of what are viewed as the true and essential teachings of the religion. Members express a nostalgia of sorts for the early church when women's spiritual authority and power was more recognized. Discussions about the means to handle spirit attacks provide fertile ground for contesting views of a righteous, spiritual masculinity in which men are the rightful actors engaging in spiritual power to defeat the powers of evil.

---

[10] It should be noted that gender imbalance is a reason that some are leaving the church. Jeannette and Shauna both ended up leaving the church, and both cited gender issues as one of the driving factors. In a 2014 talk with Jeannette, who describes herself as "very liberal," she expressed extreme anger and frustration about Kate Kelly's excommunication and concern about what was then the looming excommunication of John Dehlin, a well-known podcaster, for his stance of LGBTQIA+ rights and acceptance in the church. He was excommunicated in 2015.

7
Conclusion

As we have seen, spirit visits are common and they can happen to anyone: the righteous, the unrighteous, and those in particular need. There is ample "cultural kindling" in northern Utah that makes fertile ground for spirit encounters. Local folklore is filled with stories of uncanny encounters of all kinds, and Latter-day Saint scripture emphasizes the reality and the importance of the spirit world. However, although the teachings on the spirit world are well known, and popular folktales and legends about spirit visitations circulate widely, people do not always share their own *individual* spiritual experiences. Recent research in anthropology on spiritual experiences in other contemporary Christian contexts suggests that we might expect Latter-day Saint encounters with the spirit world to be leveraged as charisma, in Max Weber's sense (1947), and thus not only understood as a mark of righteousness and "right living," but used to assert spiritual adeptness, ability, or authority. Brendan Jamal Thornton (2016), for one, has written about the leveraging of spiritual aptitude and the related "performance of piety" among Pentecostal converts in the Dominican Republic. Naomi Haynes (2017) has similarly discussed spiritual "moving" among Pentecostal Christians on the Zambian Copperbelt, where "in moving by the Spirit prosperity follows what can broadly be termed 'charisma': facility with religious practices like prayer and singing and, in rarer cases, prophecy and healing" (2017, 12).

However, as we have seen, many Latter-day Saints in northern Utah express ambivalence about sharing spiritual experiences, even positive ones. Most of those I spoke with told me that they had never shared their experiences before or had only rarely shared them. As discussed in Chapter 3, the anthropologist Tom Mould found a similar ambivalence in his research among North Carolina Latter-day Saints, and he proposed that there are two norms in sharing personal revelation: the norm of humility and the norm of spirituality. This is quite similar to what I have observed in northern Utah.

But not all tales of spirit encounters are believed, of course. And in the context of ever-present spirit possibilities in northern Utah, there is also the possibility of using stories of spiritual experience to self-console, manipulate,

The Devil Sat on My Bed. Erin E. Stiles, Oxford University Press. © Oxford University Press 2024.
DOI: 10.1093/oso/9780197639634.003.0007

or posture. Recall John, mentioned in Chapter 3, who hinted that church members would sometimes suggest they had had a profound spiritual experience to gain status. I will relate two additional short accounts, keeping identities concealed due to their sensitive nature. In one, a man who was considering leaving the church told me that a relative was visited by the spirit of a deceased family member to urge him to return to the church. In another, a young woman who is in active in the church told me that after her partner passed away, many of his relatives told her that his spirit had visited them. Both were skeptical about whether the experiences were genuine. In the former case, the man thought his relative made up the story to try to convince him to rejoin the church. In the latter, the woman thought that her relatives were using the stories as a coping strategy. She said, "I think they just do it either to comfort themselves or make themselves feel better to convince themselves of something . . . I don't think they're trying to hurt any people or . . . anything."[1]

Latter-day Saints in northern Utah experience the realm of the spirits in a particularly Mormon way. This is one of the key arguments of this book. In conducting this research, I occasionally turned down opportunities to talk with interested people about their own experiences of spirits and spirit worlds because they did not ground them in the Latter-day Saint tradition. For example, a non-Mormon friend of my mother was intrigued by this project and was kindly willing to talk to me about her own uncanny experiences with spirits of the dead in Cache Valley. However, because she was adamant that these experiences had nothing to do with the Mormon tradition, I decided to decline (although perhaps that will be a future project). A few other people have generously shared their own experiences with me or have offered to sit down for an interview. As with my mother's friend, however, I decided that for this project, I was only focused on those who ground their understandings of spirit in a Latter-day Saint framework.

---

[1] Recent work in the anthropology of religion has taken up the question of doubt, and this would be worth exploring more extensively in a future project in this or another Latter-day Saint community. In his study of witchcraft in Papua, Indonesia, Nils Bubandt (2014) argues that witchcraft is always in doubt, and it behooves us to remember, as even Evans-Pritchard (1937) did in his study of Azande witchcraft, that there is always room for skepticism, even among believers. Naomi Haynes (2019), for example, has written about what she calls the "creativity" and "productivity" of doubt on the Zambian Copperbelt: if blessings are not manifest in material prosperity as the prosperity gospel emphasizes, then certain other blessings must be understood as what God really means. Haynes (2019) has also explored cases of what she calls unproductive doubt that do not lead to a rethinking of one's circumstances in line with one's beliefs. The expressions of doubt I describe here in the Utah case are doubts about others' experiences and it is important to note that these doubts come from both those who are active in the church and those who have left the church.

As we have seen throughout this book, this Latter-day Saint framework is evident in the way that people reference key cosmological ideas in Mormonism when discussing or interpreting their own spirit encounters and those of others. As discussed in Chapter 2, Brad, the seminary teacher, told me that the experience of the spirit world, for Mormons, is *the core of religion in practice*. Those who have received visits from the spirits of deceased or future kin understand them as confirmatory of key religious teachings. These benevolent, helpful visitors confirm the reality of the eternal family that is perhaps the core concept of Latter-day Saint teachings. As living members of the family help one another along a path to spiritual development, so do spirit members. Experiences with these spirit visitors show a clear reciprocity. Just as the spirit of a deceased grandfather encourages a living descendant to serve a mission, so does a living person assist a deceased relative by baptizing her spirit by proxy in the temple. Just as the spirit of a young woman's future child visits to assure her that she will marry and bear children, so does a living couple provide a spirit child with the mortal body that is necessary for spiritual progress and salvation.

Harassment from evil spirits is also interpreted in a Latter-day Saint framework. As we have learned, in Mormon understanding of the War in Heaven in the pre-existence, one-third of spirit beings chose not to follow Jesus but to follow Lucifer, and thus were denied the chance of ever being born in a mortal body. This desire for the mortal body and the attendant desire to tempt the living down an unrighteous path leads such spirits to harass and torment the living. As we have seen, unlike benevolent spirits who are always identifiable as individuals, malevolent spirits—never having had a body— are never identifiable by name or visage. In the Latter-day Saint framework of northern Utah, evil is not simply a gloss for a person's bad habit or vices, but a consequence of a never-ending battle with Satan, who, with his minions, is always trying to sow discord in the moral community.

But we should not make the mistake over-simplifying this as a bounded "Mormon framework." As we have seen in a number of chapters, even in Utah, people frequently identify different registers of what is truly "Mormon." Several project participants differentiated between what they view as the true meaning of the religion and what they regard as "Mormon culture" or "Utah culture" or, sometimes, the institutional body of the church. This distinction is particularly evident in questions about the powers of the priesthood and whether they are accessible only to men, or to women as well. The way in which people in Utah differentiate between "Mormon culture" or "Utah culture" and their understandings of the "true" meaning of the church has relevance far beyond understanding of people's relationship to the spirit realm and spirit power, and it speaks to key issues of concern—and polarization—among Mormons today, which are so carefully documented by Jana Reiss (2019) in her excellent recent book on millennial Mormons. The key areas of polarization she identifies include concerns about gender and gender roles in the church, LGBTQIA+ issues, the nature of authority in the church, and race and minority Mormons, among many other issues. In concluding the book, Reiss prognosticates that moving forward in the twenty-first century, ardent believers will stay in the church, but "those who don't fit in, including many young adults, will pull up stakes and leave" (2019, 234). She warns that the institutional body of the church could become an echo chamber, although she draws inspiration from Armand Mauss's book, *The Angel and the Beehive*, which stresses that the church has always moved back and forth between otherworldly and this-worldly concerns (Mauss 1994). Reiss writes, "This ever present pendulum between assimilation and retrenchment has ensure that Mormonism has successfully maintained a distinctive edge even while making theological changes that might have been unthinkable to previous generations: it eliminated polygamy in 1890, theocracy in the early twentieth century, and a racially determined priesthood temple ban in 1978" (2019, 235).

Building on this, what I would like to do here is differentiate the institution and hierarchical governing body of The Church of Jesus Christ of Latter-day Saints from the people of the church. What we see in this book is that, even among those whom Reiss might call "orthodox Mormons," such as Jake, Lyne, Jessica, and others, the membership of the church is not simply living in an echo chamber. Rather, people are drawing on their own experiences and their understandings of the early history of the church—and particularly women's roles in it—to consider their own roles and abilities in highly nuanced ways. Recall that the Gospel According to Jake, from Chapter 6, stresses that it is an "informal religion." What we might take from this is that northern Utah Mormons themselves see the institutional body of the church as related to but somewhat different from the lived experience of Mormon life, and what it should, ideally, be. An ethnographic approach to understanding religion shows us that the lived experience of the religion is not equivalent to the formal body of the church, the Sunday teachings, or what is contained in scripture. Perhaps, as Jake says, it is indeed an "informal" religion. Religious lives in northern Utah are rich, complex, and multifaceted.

Bibliography

Utah State University Student Folklore Collection

Abrams, Jim. 1980. "The Little Boy Who Fell in the Canal." USU student folklore genre collection of supernatural religious legends, 1960–2018. (FOLK COLL 8a, Group 7: SRL, Box 3: Folder 2: L.1.1.3.2.2.20). Utah State University. Special Collections and Archives Department.

Alder, Elise M. 1984. "The Voice from Above." USU student folklore genre collection of supernatural religious legends, 1960–2018. (FOLK COLL 8a, Group 7: SRL, Box 3: Folder 10: L1.1.3.6.16.12). Utah State University. Special Collections and Archives Department.

Allen, Susan. 1997. "The Logan Temple." USU student folklore genre collection of supernatural religious legends, 1960–2018. (FOLK COLL 8a, Group 7, Box 3, Folder 16: Call# L1.1.4.1.7.8). Utah State University. Special Collections and Archives Department.

Allred, Deanne. 1994. "The Voice in the Dark." USU student folklore genre collection of supernatural religious legends, 1960–2018. (FOLK COLL 8a, Group 7: SRL, Box 2: Folder 23: Call # L 1.1.2.7.4.2). Utah State University. Special Collections and Archives Department.

Bair, Allison Kinsey. 1995. "Item 2: Family Legend, Supernatural Religious." USU student folklore genre collection of supernatural religious legends, 1960–2018. (FOLK COLL 8a, Group 7: SRL, Box 2: Folder 30: Call # L1.1.2.12.3.2). Utah State University. Special Collections and Archives Department.

Ballard, 1998. "The Priesthood Blessing" USU student folklore genre collection of supernatural religious legends, 1960–2018. (FOLK COLL 8a, Group 7: SRL, Box 5: Folder 1: Call # 1.3.4.87.1). Utah State University. Special Collections and Archives Department.

Bean, Brent. 1989. "Possessed Girl." USU student folklore genre collection of supernatural religious legends, 1960–2018. (FOLK COLL 8a: Group 7, box 3, folder 21: Call # L1.1.4.5.7.2). Utah State University. Special Collections and Archives Department.

Bevan, Kailee. 2011. "With Help from the Angels." USU student folklore genre collection of supernatural religious legends, 1960–2018. (FOLK COLL 8a, Group 7: SRL, Box 3: Folder 17). Utah State University. Special Collections and Archives Department.

Boman, Jolene. 1984. "Baptism for the Dead." USU student folklore genre collection of supernatural religious legends, 1960–2018. (FOLK COLL 8a, Group 7: SRL, Box 3: Folder 10: Call # L1.1.3.6.16.13). Utah State University. Special Collections and Archives Department.

Brown, Sharon. 1982. "The Party." USU student folklore genre collection of supernatural religious legends, 1960–2018. (FOLK COLL 8a: Group 7, Box 3, Folder 22: L1.1.4.5.1.5). Utah State University. Special Collections and Archives Department.

Camp, Elizabeth. 2016a. "Priest Healing Back with an Evil Spirit." USU student folklore genre collection of supernatural religious legends, 1960–2018. (FOLK COLL 8a, Group 7: SRL, Box 3, Folder 17: FL 1.1.4.1.28.1). Utah State University. Special Collections and Archives Department.

Christensen, Ralph. 1997. "The Logan Temple." USU student folklore genre collection of supernatural religious legends, 1960–2018. (FOLK COLL 8a, Group 7: SRL, Box 3: Folder 2: L1.1.4.1.7.8). Utah State University. Special Collections and Archives Department.

Demke, Randi. 2011. "Watching over you." USU student folklore genre collection of supernatural religious legends, 1960–2018. (FOLK COLL 8a: Group 7, Box 3, Folder 22: L1.1.2.1.32.) Utah State University. Special Collections and Archives Department.

DeVries, Clair. 2009. "Demon Woman 2." USU student folklore genre collection of supernatural religious legends, 1960–2018. (FOLK COLL 8a, Group 7: SRL, Box 3, Folder 17: folder 23). Utah State University. Special Collections and Archives Department.

Erickson, Mark. 1988. "Evil Spirits Take over the Room." USU student folklore genre collection of supernatural religious legends, 1960–2018. (FOLK COLL 8a: Group 7, box 3, folder 22: L1.1.4.5.25.3). Utah State University. Special Collections and Archives Department.

Fox, Marcha. 1986. "Untitled." USU student folklore genre collection of supernatural religious legends, 1960–2018. (FOLK COLL 8a: Group 7, box 3, folder 11, Call#: L 1.1.3.7.1.7). Utah State University. Special Collections and Archives Department.

Fryer, Lynette. 1983. "Evil Spirit Contact." USU student folklore genre collection of supernatural religious legends, 1960–2018. (FOLK COLL 8a: Group 7, box 3, folder 22: L1.1.4.5.21.1). Utah State University. Special Collections and Archives Department.

Gereaux, Julia Kim. 1982. "Death at the Logan Temple." USU student folklore genre collection of supernatural religious legends, 1960–2018. (FOLK COLL 8a, Group 7, Box 3, Folder 15: L1.1.3.0.17.1). Utah State University. Special Collections and Archives Department.

Giles, Natalie. 1991. "The Ouija Board and the CTR Ring." USU student folklore genre collection of supernatural religious legends, 1960–2018. (FOLK COLL 8a: Group 7, box 6, folder 15: L1.9.0.2.5.). Utah State University. Special Collections and Archives Department.

Goodsell, Jennifer. 2007. "Pressurized Sleep." USU student folklore genre collection of supernatural religious legends, 1960–2018. (FOLK COLL 8a, Group 7, Box 3, Folder 20: L1.1.4.5.1). Utah State University. Special Collections and Archives Department.

Hall. 1994. "John." USU student folklore genre collection of supernatural religious legends, 1960–2018. (FOLK COLL 8a, Group 7, Box 4, Folder 8, 1.3.2.23.1). Utah State University. Special Collections and Archives Department.

Hardman, Valerie, 1978. "Temple Story." USU student folklore genre collection of supernatural religious legends, 1960–2018. (FOLK COLL 8a, Group 7: SRL, Box 3: Folder 2: L1.1.3.2.2.25). Utah State University. Special Collections and Archives Department.

Harrison, J. Shawn. 1991. "Healings." USU student folklore genre collection of supernatural religious legends, 1960–2018. (FOLK COLL 8a, Group 7: SRL, Box 5: Folder 1: L1.4.5.2). Utah State University. Special Collections and Archives Department.

Hatton-Ward. 1964. "No Title." USU student folklore genre collection of supernatural religious legends, 1960–2018. (FOLK COLL 8a, Group 7: SRL, Box 2: Folder 30: L1.1.2.12.3.1). Utah State University. Special Collections and Archives Department.

Hodgkinson, Jennifer. 1995. "Deceased Instructs Living Niece to Do Genealogy." USU student folklore genre collection of supernatural religious legends, 1960–2018. (FOLK COLL 8a, Group 7: SRL, Box 3, Folder 12: L1.1.3.8.7.2). Utah State University. Special Collections and Archives Department.

Hodgson, Marsha. 1997. "Strangers." USU student folklore genre collection of supernatural religious legends, 1960–2018. (FOLK COLL 8a, Group 7: SRL, Box 3: Folder 2: L1.1.3.2.1.3). Utah State University. Special Collections and Archives Department.

Holt, Sarah, 1999. "The Grouchy Neighbors." USU student folklore genre collection of supernatural religious legends, 1960–2018. (FOLK COLL 8a, Group 7, Box 2, Folder 18: L1.1.2.3.13.3). Utah State University. Special Collections and Archives Department (informant Tiffany Murray).

Hunsaker, Marian. 1983. "Temple Story." USU student folklore genre collection of supernatural religious legends, 1960–2018. (FOLK COLL 8a, Group 7, Box 3, Folder 16: L1.1.4.1.7.6). Utah State University. Special Collections and Archives Department.

Hurst, Bobbie. 1989. "The Unborn Child." USU student folklore genre collection of supernatural religious legends, 1960–2018. (FOLK COLL 8a, Group 7, Box 2, Folder 30: L1.1.2.12.3.3). Utah State University. Special Collections and Archives Department.

Hurst, Jeanne. 1964. No Title. USU student folklore genre collection of supernatural religious legends, 1960–2018. (FOLK COLL 8a, Group 7, Box 2, Folder 30: L1.5.1.2.1). Utah State University. Special Collections and Archives Department.

Hurst, Kimberly. 1992. "Satan and the Missionary." USU student folklore genre collection of supernatural religious legends, 1960–2018. (FOLK COLL 8a: Group 7, box 3, folder 22: L1.1.4.5.25.6). Utah State University. Special Collections and Archives Department.

Johnson, Darrel. 1995. "Satan's Visit to the Logan Temple." USU student folklore genre collection of supernatural religious legends, 1960–2018. (FOLK COLL 8a, Group 7, Box 3, Folder 16: L1.1.4.1.7.7). Utah State University. Special Collections and Archives Department.

Johnson, Mary. 1997. "The Patriarchal Blessing." USU student folklore genre collection of supernatural religious legends, 1960–2018. (FOLK COLL 8a, Group7, BOX 6, folder 16: L1.10.6.2). Utah State University. Special Collections and Archives Department.

Keeley, Rebecca. 1988. "Aunt Mary's Choice." USU student folklore genre collection of supernatural religious legends, 1960–2018. (FOLK COLL 8a: Group 7, box 3, folder 22: L1.1.2.4. 18. 2). Utah State University. Special Collections and Archives Department.

King, Daniel. 2010. "The Missionaries [sic] Broken Leg." USU student folklore genre collection of supernatural religious legends, 1960–2018. (FOLK COLL 8a: Group 7, box 3, folder 17: L1.1.4.1.27. 1). Utah State University. Special Collections and Archives Department.

Krenicky, Jim. 2009. "Miracles Brought on by Fate." USU student folklore genre collection of supernatural religious legends, 1960–2018. (FOLK COLL 8a, Group 7, Box 4, folder 13: L1.3.4.82). Utah State University. Special Collections and Archives Department.

Larsen, Tiffany. 2004. "Ouija Board." USU student folklore genre collection of supernatural religious legends, 1960–2018. (FOLK COLL8a, Group 7, Box 6, folder 15: L1.9.0.2.1). Utah State University. Special Collections and Archives Department.

Mackelprang, Sierra. 2018."Sleep Paralysis Demons." USU Student Folklore Fieldwork. Paper 418. Utah State University. Special Collections and Archives Department.

Maughan, C. 1990. "Supernatural Legend." USU student folklore genre collection of supernatural religious legends, 1960–2018. (FOLK COLL 8a: Group 7, box 2, folder 16: L1.1.2.2.14). Utah State University. Special Collections and Archives Department.

McEntire, Jonathan. 1991. "Bless Ben." USU student folklore genre collection of supernatural religious legends, 1960–2018. (FOLK COLL 8a: Group 7, box 4, folder 11: L1.3.4.38.2). Utah State University. Special Collections and Archives Department.

McKee, Suzette. 1988. "Angels Guard the Temple." USU student folklore genre collection of supernatural religious legends, 1960–2018. (FOLK COLL 8a: Group 7, box 3, folder 22: L1.1.4.5.31.3). Utah State University. Special Collections and Archives Department.

Miller, Mandy. 1999. "The Dead Restored to Life." USU student folklore genre collection of supernatural religious legends, 1960–2018. (FOLK COLL 8a, Group 7, Box 4, Folder 15: L1.3.6.12.1). Utah State University. Special Collections and Archives Department.

Moffit, Jen, 1996. "Lady Godiva." USU student folklore genre collection of supernatural religious legends, 1960–2018. (FOLK COLL 8a, Group 7, Box 3, Folder 11: L1.1.3.7.7.1). Utah State University. Special Collections and Archives Department.

Morris, Deborah. 1983. "Spirit World Story." USU student folklore genre collection of supernatural religious legends, 1960–2018. (FOLK COLL 8a, Group 7, Box 2, Folder 16: L1.1.2.2.13.1). Utah State University. Special Collections and Archives Department (informant myself).

Page, Kathy. 1982. "One Has Not Been Done." USU student folklore genre collection of supernatural religious legends, 1960–2018. (FOLK COLL 8a, Group 7: SRL, Box 3: Folder 10: L1.1.3.6.16.7). Utah State University. Special Collections and Archives Department.

Paulsen, Jennifer. 1997. "A Special Boy." USU student folklore genre collection of supernatural religious legends, 1960–2018. (FOLK COLL 8a, Group 7: SRL, Box 6: Folder 16: L1.10.6.5). Utah State University. Special Collections and Archives Department.

Peterson, Kirk E. 1984. "Grandma's Visitor." USU student folklore genre collection of supernatural religious legends, 1960–2018. (FOLK COLL 8a, Group 7: SRL, Box 2: Folder 25: L1.1.2.8.10.7). Utah State University. Special Collections and Archives Department.

Price, Bill. 1991. "Untitled." USU student folklore genre collection of supernatural religious legends, 1960–2018. (FOLK COLL 8a, Group 7: SLR, folder 21, L1.1.4.5.15.2). Utah State University. Special Collections and Archives Department.

Pugmire, Merrill C. 1996. "Baptism for the Dead." USU student folklore genre collection of supernatural religious legends, 1960–2018. (FOLK COLL 8a, Group 7: SRL, Box 3: Folder 10: L1.1.3.6.16.18). Utah State University. Special Collections and Archives Department.

Randall, Natalie. 2017. "Shadows." USU Student Folklore Fieldwork. Paper 64. Utah State University.

Ray, Rachel. 1998. "Unwanted Spirit." USU student folklore genre collection of supernatural religious legends, 1960–2018. (FOLK COLL 8a: Group 7, box 3, folder 22: L1.1.4.5.21.2). Utah State University. Special Collections and Archives Department.

Reese, Tina. 1991. "A Call Home." USU student folklore genre collection of supernatural religious legends, 1960–2018. (FOLK COLL 8a, Group 7, Box 2, Folder 20: L1.1.2.4.18.4). Utah State University. Special Collections and Archives Department.

Shearer, Jim. 2001. "A Dying Child and His Visit from the World of the Dead." USU student folklore genre collection of supernatural religious legends, 1960–2018. (FOLK COLL 8a: Group 7, box 3, folder 22: L1.1.2.1.8.4). Utah State University. Special Collections and Archives Department.

Shelton, Marina G. 1995 "Baptism for the Dead." USU student folklore genre collection of supernatural religious legends, 1960–2018. (FOLK COLL 8a, Group 7: SRL, Box 2: Folder 25: L1.1.2.8.10.9). Utah State University. Special Collections and Archives Department.

Simpson, Amy. 1991. "Hidden Blessings." USU student folklore genre collection of supernatural religious legends, 1960–2018. (FOLK COLL 8a, Group7, Box 6, Folder 16: L1.10.6.4). Utah State University. Special Collections and Archives Department.
Smith, Holly Sue. 1982. "Evil Spirits and Curses." USU student folklore genre collection of supernatural religious legends, 1960–2018. (FOLK COLL 8a, Group 7, Box 3, Folder 33: L1.1.4.5.26.1). Utah State University. Special Collections and Archives Department.
Smith, Terry Jean. 1992. "Young Man in White." USU student folklore genre collection of supernatural religious legends, 1960–2018. (FOLK COLL 8a, Group 7, Box 2, Folder 30: L1.1.2.12.1.3). Utah State University. Special Collections and Archives Department.
Sondrup, Sherry. 1974. "Untitled." USU student folklore genre collection of supernatural religious legends, 1960–2018. (FOLK COLL 8a, Group 7, Box 3, Folder 16: L1.1.4.1.7.2). Utah State University. Special Collections and Archives Department.
Sorensen, Bonnie. 1995. "The Unborn Children." USU student folklore genre collection of supernatural religious legends, 1960–2018. (FOLK COLL 8a, Group 7, Box 2, Folder 30: L1.1.2.12.7.2). Utah State University. Special Collections and Archives Department.
Speth, Matthew. 1997. "Warding off the Devil." USU student folklore genre collection of supernatural religious legends, 1960–2018. (FOLK COLL 8a: Group 7, box 3, folder 22: L1.1.4.5.25.2). Utah State University. Special Collections and Archives Department.
Talbot, Casey. 2001. "Whisperings." USU student folklore genre collection of supernatural religious legends, 1960–2018. (FOLK COLL 8a, Group 7: SRL, Box 2: Folder 30: L1.1.2.12.4.3). Utah State University. Special Collections and Archives Department.
Thompson, Kirk. 1985. "Unworthy Elder." USU student folklore genre collection of supernatural religious legends, 1960–2018. (FOLK COLL 8a: Group 7, box 3, folder 22: L1.1.4.5.13.1). Utah State University. Special Collections and Archives Department.
Thompson, Monica. 1996. "Family Story." USU student folklore genre collection of supernatural religious legends, 1960–2018. (FOLK COLL 8a, Group 7, Box 2, Folder 16: L1.1.2.4.1.2). Utah State University. Special Collections and Archives Department.
Tolton, Andy. 2009. "The Healed Knee." USU student folklore genre collection of supernatural religious legends, 1960–2018. (FOLK COLL 8a, Group 7, Box 5, folder 2: FLR 1.4.28). Utah State University. Special Collections and Archives Department.
Toone, JoAnne. 1994. "The Lesson of a Life Time." USU student folklore genre collection of supernatural religious legends, 1960–2018. (FOLK COLL 8a: Group 7, box 3, folder 22: L1.1.2.0.1.0.1) Utah State University. Special Collections and Archives Department.
Wakefield, Sarah. 2011. "Mary." USU student folklore genre collection of supernatural religious legends, 1960–2018. (FOLK COLL 8a, Group 7: SRL, Box 2: Folder 30: LNR 1.1.2.12.x). Utah State University. Special Collections and Archives Department.
Watts, Jennifer. 1994a. "Baptism for the Dead." USU student folklore genre collection of supernatural religious legends, 1960–2018. (FOLK COLL 8a, Group 7: SRL, Box 3: Folder 10: L1.1.3.6.16.19). Utah State University. Special Collections and Archives Department.
Watts, Jennifer. 1994b. "Memorate." USU student folklore genre collection of supernatural religious legends, 1960–2018. (FOLK COLL 8a, Group 7: SRL, Box 2: Folder 30: L1.1.2.12.8.1). Utah State University. Special Collections and Archives Department.
Weaver, Camille. 1994. "Legend." USU student folklore genre collection of supernatural religious legends, 1960–2018. (FOLK COLL 8a: Group 7, box 3, folder 22: L1.1.4.5.24.1). Utah State University. Special Collections and Archives Department.
West Walker, Rosanna. 1994. "The Midwife's Blessing." USU student folklore genre collection of supernatural religious legends, 1960–2018. (FOLK COLL 8a, Group 7: SRL, Box

2: Folder 30: LNR 1.1.2.12.x). Utah State University. Special Collections and Archives Department.

Wilson, Maria. 2011. "Car Crash Savior." USU student folklore genre collection of supernatural religious legends, 1960–2018. (FOLK COLL 8a, Group 7: SRL, Box 2: Folder 16). Utah State University. Special Collections and Archives Department.

Young, Chelise. 1994. "Legend-Memorate." USU student folklore genre collection of supernatural religious legends, 1960–2018. (FOLK COLL 8a, Group 7: SRL, Box 2: Folder 30: L1.1.2.12.3.4). Utah State University. Special Collections and Archives Department.

Published Sources

Asad, T. 1986. The idea of an anthropology of Islam. Washington, DC: Center for Contemporary Arab Studies, Georgetown University.

Asad, Talal. 2009. "The Idea of an Anthropology of Islam." *Qui Parle* 17, no. 2: 1–30. https://doi.org/10.5250/quiparle.17.2.1.

Bahloul, Joelle. 2017. "Kinship in Historical Consciousness: A French Jewish Perspective." In *New Directions in Spiritual Kinship: Sacred Ties across the Abrahamic Religions*, edited by T. Thomas, A. Malik, and R. Wellman, 109–130. New York: Palgrave Macmillan.

Bialecki, J. 2015. "The judgment of God and the non-elephantine zoo: Christian dividualism, individualism, and ethical freedom after the Mosko-Robbins debate" (available online: https://www.new-directions.sps. ed.ac.uk/occasional-paper-bialecki-the-judgment-of-god-and-the-non-elephantine-zoo).

Bialecki, J. 2022. "The Mormon Dead." In *The Dynamic Cosmos: Movement, Paradox, and Experimentation in the Anthropology of Spirit Possession*, edited by D. Espírito Santo and M. Shapiro, 133–148. New York: Bloomsbury.

Bielo, James. 2009. *Social Life of Scriptures: Cross-Cultural Perspectives on Biblicism*. Piscatawy: Rutgers University Press.

Bowen, John R. 1992. "Elaborating Scriptures: Cain and Abel in Gayo Society." *Man* 27, no. 3: 495–516. https://doi.org/10.2307/2803926.

Bowen, John R. 1993. *Muslims through Discourse: Religion and Ritual in Gayo Society*. Princeton, NJ: Princeton University Press.

Bowman, Matthew. 2011. "A Mormon Bigfoot: David Patten's Cain and the Conception of Evil in LDS Folklore." In *Between Pulpit and Pew: The Supernatural World in Mormon History and Folklore*, edited by W. Paul Reeve and M. S. van Wagenen, 17–39. Logan: Utah State University Press.

Brady, Margaret K. 1987. "Transformations of Power: Mormon Women's Visionary Narratives." *The Journal of American Folklore* 100, no. 398: 461–468. https://doi.org/10.2307/540905.

Brooke, Johne L. 1994. *The Refiner's Fire: The Making of Mormon Cosmology 1644–1844*. Cambridge: Cambridge University Press.

Brooks, Joanna. 2016. "Mormon Feminism: An Introduction." In *Mormon Feminism: Essential Writings*, edited by Joanna Brooks, Rachel Hunt Steenblik, and Hannah Wheelwright, 1–23. New York: Oxford University Press.

Brooks, Joanna, Rachel Hunt Steenblik, and Hannah Wheelwright. 2016. *Mormon Feminism: Essential Writings*. New York: Oxford University Press.

Brown, Samuel Morris, and Kate Holbrook. 2015. "Embodiment and Sexuality in Mormon Thought." In *The Oxford Handbook of Mormonism*, edited by Terryl L. Givens, and Philip L. Barlow, 292–305. Oxford: Oxford University Press.

Bubandt, Nils. 2014. *The Empty Seashell: Witchcraft and Doubt on an Indonesian Island*. 1st ed. Ithaca, NY: Cornell University Press.
Butler, Judith. 1999. *Gender Trouble: Feminism and the Subversion of Identity*. New York: Routledge.
Campbell, Hyrum A. 1948. *Providence and Her People: A History of Providence, Utah 1857-1949*. Logan, UT: The Historical Society of Providence.
Cannell, Fenella. 2005. "The Christianity of Anthropology." *Journal of the Royal Anthropological Institute* 11, no. 2: 335–356.
Cannell, Fenella. 2013a. "The Re-Enchantment of Kinship." In *Vital Relations: Modernity and the Persistent Life of Kinship*, edited by Susan McKinnon and Fenella Cannell, 228–251. Sante Fe: SAR Press.
Cannell, Fenella. 2013b. "The Blood of Abraham: Mormon Redemptive Physicality and American Idioms of Kinship: The Blood of Abraham." *Journal of the Royal Anthropological Institute* 19: S77–94. https://doi.org/10.1111/1467-9655.12017.
Cannell, Fenella. 2016. "Ghosts and Ancestors in the Modern West." In *A Companion to the Anthropology of Religion*, edited by Janice Boddy and Michael Lambek, 202–222. West Sussex: Wiley-Blackwell.
Cannell, Fenella. 2017. "'Forever Families'; Christian Individualism, Mormonism, and Collective Salvation." In *New Directions in Spiritual Kinship: Sacred Ties across the Abrahamic Religions*, edited by T. Thomas, A. Malik, and R. Wellman, 151–171. New York: Palgrave Macmillan.
Cassaniti, Julia L., and Tanya Marie Luhrmann. 2014. "The Cultural Kindling of Spiritual Experiences." *Current Anthropology* 55, no. S10: S333–S343. https://doi.org/10.1086/677881.
Caton, Stephen C. 2010. "Abu Ghraib and the Problem of Evil." In *Ordinary Ethics: Anthropology, Language and Action*, edited by Michael Lambek, 165–184. New York: Fordham University Press.
Clough, Paul, and Jon P. Mitchell. 2001. *Powers of Good and Evil: Social Transformation and Popular Belief*. New York: Berghahn Books.
Comaroff, Jean. 1985. *Body of Power, Spirit of Resistance: A History of a South African People*. Chicago: University Of Chicago Press.
Connell, R. W. 1995. *Masculinities*. Berkeley: University of Califonia Press.
Crapo, Richley H. 1987. "Grass-Roots Deviance from Official Doctrine: A Study of Latter-Day Saint (Mormon) Folk-Beliefs." *Journal for the Scientific Study of Religion* 26, no. 4: 465. https://doi.org/10.2307/1387098.
Csordas, Thomas J. 1997. *The Sacred Self: A Cultural Phenomenology of Charismatic Healing*. Berkeley: University of California Press.
Csordas, Thomas J. 2013. "Morality as a Cultural System?" *Current Anthropology* 54, no. 5: 523–546. https://doi.org/10.1086/672210.
Cuneo, Michael. 2001. *American Exorcism: Expelling Demons in the Land of Plenty*. New York: Doubleday.
Davies, Douglas J. 2000. *The Mormon Culture of Salvation: Force, Grace, and Glory*. Aldershot: Ashgate.
Davies, Douglas J. 2010. *Joseph Smith, Jesus, and Satanic Opposition: Atonement, Evil and the Mormon Vision*. London: Routledge.
Dawley, William. 2018. "From Wrestling with Monsters to Wrestling with God: Masculinities, 'Spirituality,' and the Group-ization of Religious Life in Northern Costa Rica." *Anthropological Quarterly* 91, no. 1: 79–131. https://doi.org/10.1353/anq.2018.0003.

Dawley, William, and Brendan Jamal Thornton. 2018. "New Directions in the Anthropology of Religion and Gender: Faith and Emergent Masculinities." *Anthropological Quarterly* 91, no. 1: 5–24.

DeBernardi, Jean. 1999. "Spiritual Warfare and Territorial Spirits: The Globalization and Localisation of a 'Practical Theology.'" *Religious Studies and Theology* 18, no. 2: 66–96. https://doi.org/10.1558/rsth.v18i2.66.

Denham, Aaron R. 2017. *Spirit Children: Illness, Poverty, and Infanticide in Northern Ghana*. Wisconsin: University of Wisconsin Press.

DeRogatis, A. 2009. "'Born Again Is a Sexual Term': Demons, STDs, and God's Healing Sperm." *Journal of the American Academy of Religion* 77, no. 2: 275–302. https://doi.org/10.1093/jaarel/lfp020.

Dorson, Richard. 1964. *Buying the Wind: Regional Folklore in the United States*. Chicago: University Of Chicago Press.

Eliason, Eric A. 2014. "Spirit Babies and Divine Embodiment PBEs, First Vision Accounts, Bible Scholarship, and the Experience-Centered Approach to Mormon Folklore." *BYU Studies Quarterly* 53, no. 1: 21–28.

Engelke, Matthew. 2007. *A Problem of Presence: Beyond Scripture in an African Church*. Berkeley: University Of California Press.

Evans-Pritchard, Edward E. 1937. *Witchcraft, Oracles, and Magic among the Azande*. Oxford: Clarendon Press.

Falk, Jasmin. 2018. "Framing Faith: A Media Analysis of the Ordain Women Movement within the Church of Jesus Christ of Latter-Day Saints." ProQuest Dissertations Publishing.

Feller, Gavin. 2016. "A Moderate Manifesto: Mormon Feminism, Agency, and Internet Blogging." *Journal of Media and Religion* 15, no. 3: 156–166. https://doi.org/10.1080/15348423.2016.1209393.

Fife, A. E. 1940. "The Legend of the Three Nephites among the Mormons." *The Journal of American Folklore* 53, no. 207: 1–49. https://doi.org/10.2307/535372.

Fife, Austin, and Alta Fife. 1956. *Saints of Sage and Saddle: Folklore of Mormons*. Bloomington: Indiana University Press.

Fleisher, Kass. 2004. *The Bear River Massacre and the Making of History*. Albany: State University of New York Press.

Glaskin, Kate. 2005. "Innovation and Ancestral Revelation: The Case of Dreams." *Journal of the Royal Anthropological Institute* 11: 297–324.

Godfrey, Donald G. 1997. "Zina Presendia Young Williams Card: Brigham's Daughter, Cardston's First Lady." *Journal of Mormon History* 23, no. 2: 107–127.

Hammarberg, Melvyn. 2013. *The Mormon Quest for Glory: The Religious World of the Latter-Day Saints*. Oxford: Oxford University Press.

Hand, Wayland D. 1983. "Magic and the Supernatural in Utah Folklore." *Dialogue—A Journal of Mormon Thought* 16, no. 4: 51–64.

Hartley, William J. 1996. "From Men to Boys: LDS Aaronic Priesthood Offices, 1829–1996." *Journal of Mormon History* 22: 80–136.

Haynes, Naomi. 2017. *Moving by the Spirit: Pentecostal Social Life on the Zambian Copperbelt*. Oakland: University of California Press.

Haynes, Naomi. 2019. "The Benefit of the Doubt: On the Relationship Between Doubt and Power." *Anthropological Quarterly* 92, no. 1: 35–57. https://doi.org/10.1353/anq.2019.0001.

Heaton, John W. 1993. *The Cache Valley Shoshones: Cultural Change, Subsistence, and Resistance, to 1870*. Logan: Utah State University.

Hickman, Jacob R. 2014. "Ancestral Personhood and Moral Justification." *Anthropological Theory* 14, no. 3: 317–335.

Holland, Jeffrey R. 2008. "The Ministry of Angels." Presented at the General Conference.

Hubert, Henri, and Marcel Mauss. 1981. *Sacrifice: Its Nature and Functions*. Chicago: University of Chicago Press.

Hufford, David. 1982. *The Terror That Comes in the Night: An Experience-Centered Study of Supernatural Assault Traditions*. Philadelphia: University of Pennsylvania Press.

Itzhak, Nofit. 2021. "A Sacred Social: Christian Relationalism and the Re-enchantment of the World." *Journal of the Royal Anthropological Institute* 27, no. 2: 265–284. https://doi.org/10.1111/1467-9655.13494.

Kane, Nazneen. 2018. "'Priestesses unto the Most High God': Gender, Agency, and the Politics of LDS Women's Temple Rites." *Sociological Focus* 51, no. 2: 97–110.

Kelly, Kate. 2016. "Equality Is Not a Feeling." In *Mormon Feminism: Essential Writings*, 265–267. Oxford University Press.

Kinney, Tiffany Dawn. 2017. "Cultivating Legitimacy in a Religious Context: A Pan-Historical Analysis of Mormon Feminism." ProQuest Dissertations Publishing.

Knowlton, David. 1992. "On Mormon Masculinity." *Sunstone* (August): 19–31.

Kramer, Bradley H. 2014. "Keeping the sacred: structured silence in the enactment of priesthood authority, gendered worship, and sacramental kinship in Mormonism." Ph.D. dissertation, University of Michigan.

Kwon, Heonik. 2016. "The Social and Political Theory of the Soul." In *A Companion to the Anthropology of Religion*, edited by Janice Boddy and Michael Lambek, 189–201. West Sussex UK: Wiley-Blackwell.

Lambek, Michael. 2010. "How to Make Up One's Mind: Reason, Passion, and Ethics in Spirit Possession." *University of Toronto Quarterly* 79, no. 2: 720–741.

Lee, Hector. 1949. *The Three Nephites: The Substance and Significance of the Legend in Folklore*. Albuquerque: University of New Mexico Press.

Lester, Rebecca J. 2005. *Jesus in Our Wombs: Embodying Modernity in a Mexican Convent*. Berkeley: University of California Press.

Luhrmann, T. M. 2012. *When God Talks Back: Understanding the American Evangelical Relationship with God*. Westminster: Knopf Doubleday Publishing Group.

Madsen, Carol Cornwall. 1982. "Mormon Women and the Struggle for Definition." *Dialogue: A Journal of Mormon Thought* 14, no. 3: 40–47.

Mahmood, Saba. 2011. *Politics of Piety: The Islamic Revival and the Feminist Subject*. Princeton: Princeton University Press.

Mauss, Armand L. 1994. *The Angel and the Beehive: The Mormon Struggle with Assimilation*. Chicago: University of Illinois Press.

McAlister, Elizabeth. 2012. "From Slave Revolt to a Blood Pact with Satan: The Evangelical Rewriting of Haitian History." *Studies in Religion/Sciences Religieuses* 41, no. 2: 187–215.

McCloud, Sean. 2013. "Mapping the Spatial Limbos of Spiritual Warfare: Haunted Houses, Defiled Land and the Horrors of History." *Material Religion* 9, no. 2: 166–185. https://doi.org/10.2752/175183413X13703410896690.

McCloud, Sean. 2015. *American Possessions: Fighting Demons in the Contemporary United States*. New York: Oxford University Press.

McDannell, Colleen. 2018. *Sister Saints: Mormon Women since the End of Polygamy*. New York: Oxford University Press.

McKay, David O. 1961. "Every Member a Missionary." *Improvement Era*, 710–711.

McLachlan, James. 2015. "The Problem of Evil in Mormon Thought." In *The Oxford Handbook of Mormonism*, edited by Terryl L. Givens, and Philip L. Barlow, 276–392. Oxford: Oxford University Press.

Meyer, Birgit. 1999. *Translating the Devil: Religion and Modernity among the Ewe in Ghana*. Edinburgh: Edinburgh University Press.

Meyer, Birgit. 2006. "Religious Revelation, Secrecy and the Limits of Visual Representation." *Anthropological Theory* 6, no. 4: 431–453.

Mitchell, Hildi. 2001a. "Good, Evil, and Godhood: Mormon Morality in the Material World." In *Powers of Good and Evil: Social Transformation and Popular Belief*, edited by Paul Clough and Jon P. Mitchell, 161–184. New York: Berghahn Books.

Mittermaier, Amira. 2012. "Dreams from Elsewhere: Muslim Subjectivities beyond the Trope of Self-Cultivation." *Journal of the Royal Anthropological Institute* 18, no. 2: 247–265.

Mould, Tom. 2011. *Still, the Small Voice: Narrative, Personal Revelation, and the Mormon Folk Tradition*. Logan: Utah State University Press. https://muse.jhu.edu/book/10566.

Newell, Linda King. 1981. "A Gift Given, a Gift Taken: Washing, Anointing, and Blessing the Sick Among Mormon Women." *Sunstone* 6, no. 6: 30–43.

O'Dea, Thomas. 1957. *The Mormons*. Chicago: University of Chicago Press.

O'Donnell, S. Jonathan. 2021. *Passing Orders: Demonology and Sovereignty in American Spiritual Warfare*. New York: Fordham University Press.

Olsen, Nolan P. 1978. *Logan Temple: The First 100 Years*. Providence, UT.

Ong, Aihwa. 1987. *Spirits of Resistance and Capitalist Discipline*. Albany: State University of New York Press.

Padro, Manuel W. 2020. "Redemption: The Treasure Quest and the Wandering Soul." *The John Whitmer Historical Association Journal* 40, no. 2: 40–81.

Palmer, Jason. 2022. "La Familia versus The Family: Matriarchal Patriarchies in Peruvian Mormonism." *Journal of the Mormon Social Science Association* 1, no. 1: 123–151.

Park, Benjamin E. 2010. "'A Uniformity So Complete': Early Mormon Angelology." *Intermountain West Journal of Religious Studies* 2, no. 1: 2-37. https://digitalcommons.usu.edu/imwjournal/vol2/iss1/2.

Parkin, David J. 1985. *The Anthropology of Evil*. New York: Blackwell.

Perreault, Gregory P., Margaret Duffy, and Ariel Morrison. 2017. "Making a Mormon?: Peacemaking in U.S. Press Coverage of the Mormon Baptism for the Dead." *Journal of Media and Religion* 16, no. 4: 141–152. https://doi.org/10.1080/15348423.2017.1401410.

Petrey, Taylor. 2020. *Tabernacles of Clay: Sexuality and Gender in Modern Mormonism*. Chapel Hill: University of North Carolina Press.

Pina-Cabral, João. 2019. "My Mother or Father: Person, Metaperson, and Transcendence in Ethnographic Theory." *Journal of the Royal Anthropological Institute* 25, no. 2: 303–323. https://doi.org/10.1111/1467-9655.13027.

Pocock, David F. 1985. "Unruly Evil." In *The Anthropology of Evil*, 42–56. B. Blackwell.

Prince, Gregory A. 2015. "Mormon Priesthood and Organization." In *The Oxford Handbook of Mormonism*, edited by Terryl L. Givens, and Philip L. Barlow, 167–181. Oxford: Oxford University Press.

Reeve, W. Paul. 2011. "'As Ugly as Evil' and 'As Wicked as Hell': Gadianton Robbers and the Legend Process among the Mormons." In *Between Pulpit and Pew: The Supernatural World in Mormon History and Folklore*, edited by W. Paul Reeve and M. S. van Wagenen, 1–16. Logan: Utah State University Press.

Reeve, W. Paul, and Johnson. 2010. "Mormonism and Men." In *Mormonism: A Historical Encyclopedia*, 298–305. Santa Barbara, CA: ABC-Clio.

Reeve, W. Paul, and Michael Scott van Wagenen. 2011. "Between Pulpit and Pew: Where History and Lore Intersect." In *Between Pulpit and Pew: The Supernatural World in Mormon History and Folklore*, edited by W. Paul Reeve and M. S. van Wagenen, 1–16. Logan: Utah State University Press.

Reiss, Jana. 2019. *The Next Mormons: How Millennials Are Changing the LDS Church*. Oxford: Oxford University Press.

Ricks, Joel Edward. 1953. "The Beginnings of Settlement in Cache Valley." Faculty Research Lecture, no. 12. Logan: The Faculty Association of Utah State Agricultural College.

Robbins, Joel. 2004. *Becoming Sinners: Christianity and Moral Torment in a Papua New Guinea Society*. Berkeley: University of California Press.

Robbins, Joel. 2017. "Keeping God's Distance: Sacrifice, Possession, and the Problem of Religious Mediation: Sacrifice, Possession, and Religious Mediation." *American Ethnologist* 44, no. 3: 464–475. https://doi.org/10.1111/amet.12522.

Sahlins, Marshall. 2013. *What Kinship Is—And Is Not*. Chicago: University of Chicago Press.

Sanders, Todd. 2008. "Buses in Bongoland: Seductive Analytics and the Occult." *Anthropological Theory* 8, no. 2: 107–132. https://doi.org/10.1177/1463499608090787.

Scherz, China. 2018. "Enduring the Awkward Embrace: Ontology and Ethical Work in a Ugandan Convent: Enduring the Awkward Embrace." *American Anthropologist* 120, no. 1: 102–112. https://doi.org/10.1111/aman.12968.

Seeman, Don. 2017. "Kinship as Ethical Relation: A Critique of the Spiritual Kinship Paradigm." In *New Directions in Spiritual Kinship: Sacred Ties across the Abrahamic Religions*, edited by T. Thomas, A. Malik, and R. Wellman, 85–108. New York: Palgrave Macmillan.

Shepherd, Gordon, Lavina Anderson, and Gary Shepherd, eds. 2015. *Voices for Equality: Ordain Women and Resurgent Mormon Feminism*. Sandy, UT: Greg Kofford Books.

Shipps, Jan. 1985. *Mormonism: A New Religious Tradition*. University of Illinois Press.

Stapley, Jonathan A. 2016. "Women and Mormon Authority." In *Women and Mormonism: Historical and Contemporary Perspectives*, edited by Kate Holbrook and Matthew Bowman. Salt Lake City: University of Utah Press.

Stapley, Jonathan A. 2018. *The Power of Godliness: Mormon Liturgy and Cosmology*. Oxford: Oxford University Press.

Stapley, Jonathan A., and Kristine Wright. 2008. "'They Shall Be Made Whole': A History of Baptism for Health." *Journal of Mormon History* 34, no. 4: 69–112.

Stapley, Jonathan A., and Kristine Wright. 2011. "Female Ritual Healing in Mormonism." *Journal of Mormon History* 37, no. 1: 1–85.

Stasch, Rupert. 2009. *Society of Others: Kinship and Mourning in a West Papuan Place*. Berkeley: University of California Press.

Steadman, Lyle B., Craig T. Palmer, and Christopher Tilley. 1996. "The Universality of Ancestor Worship." *Ethnology* 35, no. 1: 53–76.

Stiles, Erin. 2014. "Imagining Mormon Culture." *Proceedings of the Southwestern Anthropological Association* 8: 10–14.

Stiles, Erin. 2022. "The Evil Spirits Are Always Trying to Bring You Down: Righteousness and Spirit Harassment among Latter-Day Saints in Northern Utah." *Journal of the American Academy of Religion* 90, no. 3: 695–712.

Stiles, Erin. 2023. "They Have Shown Me What I Need to Know: Spirits, the Eternal Family, and Collective Ethical Responsibility in Utah Mormonism." *JRAI Journal of the Royal Anthropological Institute.* https://doi.org/10.1111/1467-9655.13954.

Stiles, Erin, and Katryn Davis. 2018. "Mediating Encounters with the Spirit World: Spirits and Spiritual Worth in a Utah Mormon Community." *Proceedings of the Southwestern Anthropological Association* 12: 36–40.

Taussig, Michael T. 1980. *The Devil and Commodity Fetishism in South America.* Chapel Hill: University of North Carolina Press.

Taysom, Stephen. 2017. "'Satan Mourns Naked upon the Earth': Locating Mormon Possession and Exorcism Rituals in the American Religious Landscape, 1830–1977." *Religion and American Culture: A Journal of Interpretation* 27, no. 1: 57–94. https://doi.org/10.1525/rac.2017.27.1.57.

The Church of Jesus Christ of Latter-day Saints. 1974. What is Temple Endowment? https://www.churchofjesuschrist.org/study/new-era/1974/10/q-and-a-questions-and-answers/what-is-a-temple-endowment?lang=eng.

The Church of Jesus Christ of Latter-day Saints. 1987. Priesthood Blessings. https://www.churchofjesuschrist.org/study/ensign/1987/05/priesthood-blessings?lang=eng.

The Church of Jesus Christ of Latter-day Saints. 2012. Priesthood Keys. https://www.churchofjesuschrist.org/study/new-era/2012/05/priesthood-keys?lang=eng.

The Church of Jesus Christ of Latter-day Saints. 2022. Performing Priesthood Performances and Blessings. In *General Handbook: Serving in The Church of Jesus Christ of Latter-day Saints.* https://www.churchofjesuschrist.org/study/manual/general-handbook/18-priesthood-ordinances-and-blessings?lang=eng.

The Church of Jesus Christ of Latter-day Saints. 2023a. Elder. https://www.churchofjesuschrist.org/study/manual/gospel-topics/elder?lang=eng.

The Church of Jesus Christ of Latter-day Saints. 2023b. Why We Hold Family Home Evening. https://www.churchofjesuschrist.org/topics/family-home-evening/purpose?lang=eng.

Thomas, Todne, Asiya Malik, and Rose Wellman, eds. 2017. *New Directions in Spiritual Kinship: Sacred Ties across the Abrahamic Religions.* New York: Palgrave Macmillan.

Thornton, Brendan Jamal. 2016. *Negotiating Respect: Pentecostalism, Masculinity, and the Politics of Spiritual Authority in the Dominican Republic.* 1st ed. Florida: University Press of Florida.

Thornton, Brendan Jamal. 2018. "Victims of Illicit Desire: Pentecostal Men of God and the Specter of Sexual Temptation." *Anthropological Quarterly* 91, no. 1: 133–171. https://doi.org/10.1353/anq.2018.0004.

Toscano, Margaret Merrill. 1995. "If Mormon Women Have Had the Priesthood since 1843, Why Aren't They Using It?" *Dialogue—A Journal of Mormon Thought* 27, no. 2: 219–226.

Weber, Max. 1946. *From Max Weber: Essays in Sociology*, ed. H. H. Gerth and C Wright Mills. New York: Oxford University Press.

Weber, Max. 1947. *The Theory of Social and Economic Organization.* New York: The Free Press.

Wellman, Rose. 2017. "Substance, Spirit, and Sociality among Shi'i Muslims in Iran." In *New Directions in Spiritual Kinship: Sacred Ties across the Abrahamic Religions*, edited by T. Thomas, A. Malik, and R. Wellman, 171–94. New York: Palgrave Macmillan.

White, Hylton. 2013. "Spirit and Society: In Defence of a Critical Anthropology of Religious Life." *Anthropology Southern Africa*, 36, no. 3–4: 139–145. https://doi.org/10.1080/23323256.2013.11500054.

Wilson, William A. 1989. "The Study of Mormon Folklore: An Uncertain Mirror for Truth." *Dialogue: A Journal of Mormon Thought* 22, no. 4: 95–110.

Wilson, William A. 1995. "Mormon Narratives: The Lore of Faith." *Western Folklore* 54, no. 4: 303. https://doi.org/10.2307/1500309.

Index

For the benefit of digital users, indexed terms that span two pages (e.g., 52–53) may, on occasion, appear on only one of those pages.

adoption, 70–71
afterlife, 13, 25, 26, 31, 45, 52, 60, 63, 67, 70–71
agency, 15–16, 29, 30, 38–39, 53, 65, 66–67, 121–23, 147–48, 186–87
ancestors, 7–8, 14, 21, 41, 71, 81–82, 87, 89, 95–96, 104, 106, 115–16, 127, 170
ancestor worship, 81–82
angelic ministration, 20–21, 23–24, 55, 78
angelology, 20–21, 125
angels, 20–24, 31–32, 34–35, 41–43, 54, 102, 140
arm to the square. *See* hand to the square
Asad, Talal, 8
authority
    priesthood authority, 94, 151–52, 166, 179
    spiritual authority, 15–16, 77–78, 141, 150–52, 165, 177–78, 187–88
Azande, 80, 190n.1

Bahloul, Joelle, 83–84
Ballard, M. Russell, 187
Ballard, Margaret, 154
baptism, of children, 40
    baptism as an ordinance, 87, 93, 94, 95
    baptism for the dead (proxy baptism), 85–117
Bear River Massacre, 4–5
Benson, Ezra T., 154
Bialecki, Jon, 82–83
Bielo, James, 18
bishop, 19n.1, 79, 95, 145–46, 164, 165
blessings
    patriarchal blessing, 137–38, 153–54
    priesthood blessing, 95, 144, 150, 152–53, 155–57, 158

body, importance of, 14, 23, 25–26, 28, 29–30, 32, 33, 62, 67, 69–70, 71, 81–82, 119–20, 122, 125–30
Book of Mormon, 2–3, 14–15, 20, 21–22, 36, 38, 66, 109, 111, 122, 126
Bowen, John R., 8, 18
Brady, Margaret, 7, 76, 77–78, 154–55
Brazil, 83–84, 157, 171–72, 174
Brigham Young, 4–5, 146–47, 153–54
Brooks, Joanna, 151–52, 186–87
Butler, Judith, 16, 151

Cache Valley, 1, 4, 5–6, 9–10, 31, 41–42, 119, 136, 154–55, 160–61
Cain, 2–3, 109, 147–48
calling, 128n.5, 140, 182
Cannell, Fenella, 14–15, 52–53, 63, 70–71, 82–84, 93–94, 112–13
Cardon, Lucy S., 154
Cassaniti, Julia, 6–8, 58–59
casting out, 15–16, 128, 141, 151–52, 159–70, 172, 175, 177–78, 185–86
Caton, Stephen, 120–21
Celestial Kingdom, 85, 88
charisma, 77–79, 189
Charismatic Catholics, 119–20, 121
children. *See* spirit children
conversion, 60, 82, 125–26, 134–35, 142, 174
Crapo, Richley, 7
Csordas, Thomas, 119–21, 137–38
cultural kindling, 4–8, 137, 189
culture
    cultural Mormonism/Mormon culture, 9, 10–11, 15–16, 33–34, 88–89, 119, 150–51, 174, 177, 181, 183–84, 185–86, 188, 191–92
    Utah culture, 10–12, 26–27, 150, 188, 191–92

Davies, Douglas, 40–41, 88–89, 104, 114, 122, 152–53, 160
death, 27, 31, 45, 46, 54, 55, 56, 65–66, 85–86, 88–89, 105–6
  near-death experiences 110
DeBernardi, Jean, 120–21
devil. *See* Lucifer; Satan
discernment of spirits, 31–32, 34
distance (as in, from God), 113–15
Doctrine and Covenants, 22, 27–28, 31–32, 34, 47–48, 49, 87–88
Dominican Republic, 16, 77–78, 125–26, 151, 189
doubt, 80, 112, 156
Dunstan, Adam, 116

economy of heaven, 24, 54–55, 112
Eliason, Eric, 7, 77
enchantment/disenchantment, 8–9, 12, 77
eternal family, 13, 22, 24, 25–26, 29, 49–50, 52–54, 61, 67, 80–82, 83–84, 112–14, 191
Ethics, 120–21
  ethical action, 13
  ethical responsibility among kin 13–14, 52–53, 63, 67, 69–70, 82–83, 95–96
evangelical churches, 119–21, 160
Evans-Pritchard, E. E. 80, 190n.1
evil
  anthropology of 120–21
  as a cosmological force, 121, 147–38
  evil and moral boundaries, 121–22, 124
  as inversion of ideal order, 134–35
  in Mormon studies, 122
exorcism, 159–60, 161–62, 170, 187. *See also* casting out

feminism, 186–87
feminist activism, 16, 176–77
feminist scholarship, 154, 176–77, 182
Fife, Alta, 1, 7, 8, 28, 85–86, 136, 154
Fife, Austin, 1, 7, 8, 28, 85–86, 136, 154
Fortes, Meyer, 115–16

Gadianton Robbers, 2–3, 109
gender
  gender antagonism, 151
  gender distress, 15–16, 151–52, 177, 180, 183–84, 187

gender inequity in the church, 12, 152–53
gender politics, 187
gender roles, 149–50, 180, 191–92
gendered spiritual power, practice, authority, 149, 151–52, 153–54, 165, 176–77, 179–80, 188
genealogy, 18, 64, 82–83, 85–86, 89–85, 96, 104–5
ghosts, 25
grace, 40–41, 88–89

hand to the square, 118, 136, 160–61, 177–79, 185
Hand, Wayland, 7, 9–10
handshake method, 31–32, 33–35
Haynes, Naomi, 77–78, 189
healing, 61–62, 151–52, 153–58, 176, 184–85, 189
  false healing 156–58
  spiritual healing, 150, 184–85
  women in healing, 184–85
Heaton, John W. 4–5
heaven, 22–23, 24, 25–26, 28, 40, 54, 69, 75, 107, 112, 138. *See also* Celestial Kingdom
  kingdoms of heaven, 110
Heavenly Father, 25, 45, 48, 51, 79, 88, 162, 180, 186–87
Heavenly Mother, 186–87
Hickman, Jacob, 81–82, 115–16
Hickman, Martha, 155
Hmong ancestral personhood, 81–82, 115
Holland, Jeffrey, 23–24, 54
Holy Ghost/Holy Spirit 48, 54, 133, 158–59
  getting the Spirit, 129–30, 170
  inspiration or prompting of, 19, 20–21, 78–79, 102, 103
Hubris. *See* pride
Reiss, Jana, 177, 192
Hufford, David, 7, 9–10, 119

Islam, 8

Jack Mormon, 1, 10n.6
Jesus Christ, 14–15, 46–48, 67, 109–10, 122, 127, 134, 146, 160
  casting out spirts, 161–62, 173, 177–78, 179

and the priesthood 92
war in Heaven and, 25–26, 28, 29, 191
Johnson, Jeffrey, 94–95

Kelly, Kate, 16, 176–77
keys
   to discerning spirits, 32, 33
   priesthood, 94–95, 149, 169
kinship, 14, 52–53, 63, 70–71, 82–83, 115–16
   spiritual kinship, 83–84, 93–94
Knowlton, David, 125–26, 149, 152–53, 175

lay theology, 68
laying on of hands (healing rite), 48, 95, 153–54, 173
Lee, Hector, 7, 8–9
Logan, Utah, 4, 5, 9–10, 132
Logan Temple, 9–10, 85–86, 92–93, 104, 136–37, 142, 160–61, 177–78
Lucifer, 28, 29, 49–50, 122, 136, 144. *See also* Satan
Luhrmann, Tanya, 6–8, 58–59, 137, 142

Madsen, Carol Cornwall, 182–83
marriage, 79, 93–94, 139, 146–47
   temple marriage 24, 83–84
masculinity, 15–16, 125–26, 149–51, 152–53, 175, 188
Mauss, Armand 7–8, 191–92
McCloud, Sean, 119–20
McLachlan, James, 82, 122–23
Meedam, Martha, 154
Mexico, 170–71, 174
Mexico City, 158, 159, 186–87
Meyer, Birgit, 113–14, 120
Midwife, 184–85
Missionary Training Center (MTC), 57, 79, 110, 112, 140–42, 155–56, 175
missions, mission work, 57, 127, 139, 142, 146–47
   casting out or inviting evil spirits, 151–52, 166, 170–74, 175, 187
   missionaries, 15, 45–46, 53, 57, 60, 82, 118–19, 164, 178, 182
   returned missionaries, 129, 164
   spirit harassment of, 118–19, 139–47
   tales about false healing, 156–58

Mitchell, Hildi, 38, 122–23, 125, 134–35, 184
Mitchell, Jon P., 124
Mittermaier, Amira, 81, 83, 86–87
morality, 37–38, 120–22, 128, 147–48
Mormon culture. *See* culture
Mould, Tom, 2–3, 7, 78–79, 146, 189
Muslims, 8, 18, 81, 86–87

Newell, Linda King, 154–55, 159–60
New Testament, 14–15, 21, 23, 26, 28, 47, 161–62

Old Hag stories, 9, 119
Ordain Women movement, 16, 176–77
ordinances, 47, 48, 53–54, 85–86, 87, 88, 89, 92–95, 101, 116, 182–83, 184
   proxy/posthumous ordinances, 87, 93, 101–2, 103, 105–6

Padro, Manuel 115n.11
Palmer, Jason, 150
Paradise, 46–48. *See also* afterlife
Park, Benjamin, 20–21, 34–35, 125
Parkin, David, 120–21, 137–38
patriarchal blessings. *See* blessings
Pearl of Great Price, 22, 26, 28
Pentecostalism, 16, 77–78, 113–14, 125–26, 151–52, 174, 189
personhood, 12–13, 81–82, 83–84, 115–16
Pina-Cabral, João de, 2, 83–84
pioneers, 41–42, 179, 184
Plan of Salvation, 12–13, 20–28, 38, 53–54, 81, 87–88, 114
Pocock, David, 134–35
prayer, 9, 44, 75, 103, 129–30, 142, 153–54, 166, 180, 183, 184
pre-existence, 12–13, 18, 25, 26, 28, 30, 38–39, 49–50, 54, 69, 70–71, 81, 84, 121–22, 126, 191
   planning in the, 52–53, 62, 63, 65–68, 73, 135, 141
   righteous action in the, 137, 138
pregnancy, pregnant women, 42, 59–60, 74, 77–78, 155
premortality. *See* pre-existence
Price, Clark Kelley, 42
pride, among missionaries, 141, 142, 175, 176

priesthood
  Aaronic Priesthood, 94–95
  Melchizedek Priesthood, 93, 94–95, 96, 114, 153
  organization and duties of, 1–2, 93, 94–95, 116, 152–58
  priesthood authority (*see* authority)
  priesthood blessing (*see* blessings)
  priesthood keys (*see* keys)
  priesthood power, 136–38, 141, 149–88
  women and the priesthood, 16, 181
Protestantism, 88–89, 122, 159–60, 170
Providence, Utah, 4–5, 9–10, 154

Reeve, W. Paul, 7–8, 94–95
Relief Society, 154, 155
resurrected beings, 21, 23, 32, 33
resurrection, 23, 46
right action, 13, 36, 38, 39–40
righteousness, 4, 13, 15, 35–36, 37–38, 39–40, 41, 78, 112–13, 116, 138
  edge of, 126, 142
  exceptional, 120, 133–34, 142, 144–45
  path of, 41, 52, 63, 84, 122–23, 124, 129–30, 137, 139
  unrighteous, lack of righteousness 98, 120, 127–28, 134, 146–47
ritual, 14, 41, 47, 60, 85–87, 89, 92–93, 94–96, 106, 112–13, 115–16
Robbins, Joel, 53, 82, 113–15, 170

sacrament meeting, 57, 78, 99
Sahlins, Marshall, 14, 52, 82–83
Sanders, Todd, 120–21
Scherz, China, 83
sealing, in the temple, 31, 87, 93–94, 101
Seeman, Don, 82–83
seminary, 19–20, 19n.1
sexuality, 151
Shoshone, 4–5

skepticism, 77–78, 80, 167, 169. *See also* doubt
Smith, Joseph, 8, 22, 32, 34, 94, 109, 110–12, 122, 125, 127, 134, 146, 159–60, 166, 184
Smith, Joseph Fielding, 47–48, 88, 154–55
Smith, Lucy Meserve, 182–83, 185
Spafford, Belle S., 155
spirit children, 13–14, 28, 51–52, 68–78, 81, 83, 84, 86–87, 154–55
spirit prison, 45, 46–49, 89
spiritual, as in "to be spiritual" 17, 39
spiritual progress, 3–4, 12, 13, 26, 27–28, 38–39, 46–50, 52, 67, 77–79, 81–84, 87, 112–13, 125, 191
spiritual warfare, 137–38, 160
Stapley, Jonathan A., 150, 153–54, 188

Taussing, Michael, 120
Taysom, Stephen, 94–95, 122, 125, 159–60, 170, 187
Thornton, Brendan Jamal, 16, 77–78, 125–26, 149–50, 151–52, 189
Three Nephites, 2–3, 109
Toscano, Margaret, 182

United Kingdom, 38, 45–46, 57, 82–83, 166
Utah culture. *See* culture

Van Wagenen, Michael Scott, 7–8

war in Heaven, 25–26, 28–31, 49–50, 118–19, 137–38, 170
Weber, Max, 8–9, 189
Wellman, Rose, 82–83
Wellsville, Utah, 4–5, 68–69, 184–85
Wilson, William A., 7, 8–9, 99, 119
witchcraft, 80, 120–21, 134–35, 190n.1
witches, 9–10, 10n.6
Woodruff, Wilford, 28, 29
Wright, Kristine, 153–55